Rethinking Information Systems in Organizations

In *Rethinking Information Systems in Organizations* John Paul Kawalek challenges the current orthodoxy of information systems and proposes new alternatives. Bold and ambitious, this book tackles the thorny issues of integration of disciplines, crossover of functions, and negotiation of epistemological divides in IS. Historically, the IS discipline has struggled to embrace and integrate technical as well as organizational knowledge, skills and methods. Kawalek argues that there are now a new set of imperatives that will irrecoverably change IS, affecting the way many organizations deploy and access their information and technology. This book defines how the traditional practices of information systems are required to integrate into a process of organizational problem solving.

An essential read for students of business information systems, organizational theory and research methods, Kawalek's work also provides core methodological principles on organizational change and problem solving, and presents an effective rationale for their use in information systems contexts.

John Paul Kawalek has a background in IT and management consulting. He lectures in systems theory, change management and management consultancy at the University of Sheffield, UK, and is also an associate professor at the Grenoble Graduate School of Business, France.

Rethinking Information Systems in Organizations

Integrating Organizational Problem Solving

John Paul Kawalek

Routledge
Taylor & Francis Group

NEW YORK AND LONDON

First published 2008
by Routledge
711 Third Avenue, New York, NY 10017

Simultaneously published in the UK
by Routledge
2 Park Square, Milton Park, Abingdon, Oxon, OX14 4RN

Routledge is an imprint of the Taylor & Francis Group, an informa business

Transferred to Digital Printing 2008

© 2008 John Paul Kawalek

Typeset in Baskerville by
HWA Text and Data Management, Tunbridge Wells

Library of Congress Cataloging in Publication Data
Kawalek, John Paul.
Rethinking information systems in organizations : integrating organizational problem solving /
John Paul Kawalek.
    p.   cm.
    Includes bibliographical references.
    1. Management information systems. 2. Information technology–Management. I. Title.
HD30.213.K39 2008
658.4'038011–dc22   2007028923

ISBN10: 0–415–40304–9 (hbk)
ISBN10: 0–415–40305–7 (pbk)
ISBN10: 0–203–93605–1 (ebk)

ISBN13: 978–0–415–40304–7 (hbk)
ISBN13: 978–0–415–40305–4 (pbk)
ISBN13: 978–0–203–93605–4 (ebk)

To the loving memory of my parents,
Maureen Lillia Kawalek, and Tadeusz Kawalek.
Also to the fond memory of Chris Heneghan,
Tommy Burke and Steve Pullen.

Contents

Illustrations

Figures

Tables

Preface

This book is about the field of practice called 'information systems' or 'IS' for short. The reason for writing such a book is that this field has been going through radical change in recent years, because of the changes in the capability, reach and impact of information and communications technology ('IT' for short).[1] This book is written because the field of practice in information systems is again on the cusp of a new set of changes that concern the way many organizations will deploy and access their information and technology. The book is written also because certain aspects of the *discipline*[2] of IS, seems unable to keep up with the requirements of practice and of practitioners. This has resulted in a gulf between the discipline and that of practice. This gulf is sometimes expressed as a difference between 'theory' and 'practice'.

One of the latest 'revolutions' in the field of practice concerns the continued emergence of web-based hosting services, which can provide user organizations with hugely powerful, robust, highly secure, reliable IT applications. This means that organizations are often able to access hugely powerful technology, quickly, easily and cheaply. This has been termed the 'ZZZ principle' (see for example Bizwizzz, 2007). It is a trend that is already under way and, during the next decade or more, it is forecast to increase in speed with some quite significant implications. For example, it means that organizations are increasingly able to access the most up-to-date technologies via hosted services, sometimes with nothing more than a web browser. In some circumstances, they are often no longer required to buy expensive (server-side) hardware, software etc. Often, they do not need to have dedicated staff to maintain servers, or to develop software applications. It means that very powerful technology is increasingly available to the smallest of organizations. As a result, there is a prediction that in the future, much of the knowledge and expertise that is currently required to maintain sophisticated technological applications will no longer be required to be held *in-house*. Yet the sophistication of the technology implies that it will *impact* to an even greater extent on organizations and their processes. It also means that the focus of attention is shifting for many user organizations, from development and maintenance of IT applications, to the development of organizations, e.g. from *software development* to *organization development*. For most organizations, the skills and knowledge of the latter are becoming more important than maintaining the skills and knowledge of the former. The power and accessibility of the technology is becoming greater, giving greater opportunities for organization development and, at the same time, the technological challenges involved in achieving organization development are expected to reduce. The field of practice is changing, and the discipline that underpins the practice of IS is required to change with it.

Having been lead consultant in 40 or so IS or related projects, and having been involved in some other way in countless others, I have come to the conclusion that the *discipline* of IS is sometimes rather misdirected, old-fashioned and problematic; it is not preparing individuals sufficiently for practice. It is easy to pinpoint certain failings in practice, in which practitioners of IS are ill-prepared. For example, the rocketing budgets for information systems in many organizations, and the failings in the realization of benefits. In such instances, the failings might be considered to be much more deep rooted than simply 'failures of practice'. Indeed, the problems in practice might be considered the symptom, not the problem. There are more fundamental problems that are associated with the *discipline* of information systems. Could it be that the theory, the research, the learning activities and the 'science' that underpins practice do not provide sufficient guidance to practitioners? If so, does this mean that it is, in some manner of speaking, a *cause* of the problems in practice? Perhaps it is also the way the discipline is presented and taught to students, and the current gulf between the 'theory' of the discipline, and of 'practice'? If so, these are the more fundamental problems: might it be that the concerns in practice are the outcome of a failing *discipline*?

If we take this line of reasoning, we might be able to ask some more rhetorical questions of the information systems discipline as we know it today. For example:

- Are universities providing a sufficiently strong body of knowledge to help guide practitioners?
- Is research coming out from our universities sometimes overly inane, misguided and/or just simply cannot be used in practice?
- Are students coming out from our universities often ill-prepared for practice?
- Could it be that 'leaders' of the *discipline* have no experience of practice?

Asking such questions might lead to certain painful conclusions, not least the long-standing gulf between the theory and practice. The same sort of questions can be directed towards the *knowledge use* end of the discipline. For example:

- Do practitioners lack an understanding of basic research and inquiring skills? For instance, do consulting companies produce policies, documents, reports, recommendations etc., without the depth of understanding of the epistemological issues, and unsure of the flaws, reasoning and the 'science' upon which conclusions are based?

We could also ask similar rhetorical questions about the structure of the professional bodies, whose *raison d'être* is to promote standards of practice. For example:

- Are the professional standards of practice ignored, or are they not sufficiently robust to guide action?
- Have the professional bodies developed for themselves a clarity of understanding of the nature of modern day IS practice, and the underpinning disciplinary requirements?

We might also ask awkward rhetorical questions that skirt around the consequences of a rather weak discipline, or weak professional standards. For example:

• Are the chief executive officers (CEOs) and leaders of organizations generally aghast at the soaring costs of information technology and associated service investments, and at the lack of benefits realization to their organization?

In questioning the discipline in such a way, might it be concluded that there might be room for improvement? In all societies, humans rely on the effectiveness of their organizations. In modern day societies, they often rely on the effectiveness of their technology to service the needs and to improve organizations. Our organizations and businesses, our governmental institutions, our non-governmental organizations (NGOs), our hospitals, police forces, our banks, our manufacturers *et al.*, they continually demand more, and they continually demand more from the practitioners and from the discipline of IS. They require technical skills of course. But they require much more than technical skills. They require people who can transform and improve the performance of organizations by harnessing the power of information and communications technologies. They require people who can think clearly and question how technology can change organizational processes. They require people with the skills of managing change in organizational processes and their integration. They require people who can identify problems and opportunities, and resolve them. They require greater precision in the management of complex projects. They require people who can link changes in the tasks, activities and methods of organizational processes to wider interventions, e.g. to change behaviour, attitudes, norms, assumptions, human resource policy etc.

Currently, we have a situation where the computing and communications technologies are increasingly powerful. They are increasingly cheap and increasingly standardized. But as their power expands, so does their impact on work organizations, and their potential to help them to 'improve'. The problem for the early twenty-first century seems to be the *harnessing* of these powerful new technologies, to make them serve human organizational needs, and bringing about change in work practices, approaches and tasks, which make use of them for organizational 'improvement' (see also Brooks 1975, 1987; Wastell 1996; Fitzgerald 2000). It appears that the discipline of IS is rather schizophrenically torn between, on the one hand, technology development methods (database development, programming, development techniques) and, on the other, tentatively incorporating *selected* organizational issues and concerns (e.g. security, project management, end-user computing, social impacts). Sometimes, information systems includes such areas such as the social impacts of information, or of technology, or the 'competitive advantage' that may or may not accrue from technology… etc. It is a situation that is inadequate for a discipline that is meant to be leading organizations into the twenty-first century, because it provides little guidance on *the process and practice of changing and 'improving' organizations*. Currently, there is interest, but little practical guidance, in integrating 'organizational problem solving'[3] during a given process of information systems practice. This might be considered a pity, because it is inhibiting the development practitioners in their role as 'organizational problem solvers'; it also fails the development of the discipline that has the potential to become a key discipline (or even the de facto discipline) of organizational problem solving, able to integrate application development into a process of organization development.

The integration of application development and organization development is quite a gulf, and it is not easy to bridge because it crosses some very deep-rooted divides. For example, it might be rather dangerous to take 'engineering methods' for developing technology and assume that the same basic approach can be applied to 'engineering' organizations. Traversing the two domains is not a simple task because of the need to move between quite different disciplines, with their own (different) traditions and assumptions. It is for this reason that the book outlines a particular approach to organization development, centred on a set of inquiring activities that may help to bring about more effective action and change in complex organizational contexts. The book outlines an approach that integrates the human process issues, the inquiry, the learning, the action etc., assuming that organizations are not necessarily very rational contexts in which IS is practised.

This book does not claim that the current methods, theory or knowledge of the discipline is irrelevant. However, it *does* argue that current methods, theory and knowledge is generally not integrated with organizational problem-solving methods, and as such are limited in their ability to bring 'improvement' to organizations. This book is not meant to be a substitute for existing methods, theory or knowledge. Rather, it is a reinterpretation to a certain extent, and a rethink, of the *process* of information systems practice, in which existing methods, theory and knowledge is required to be integrated, used and generated. The central contribution and argument in this book is that information systems needs a new wrapping of sorts; it considers IS practice to be linked into and integrated with 'organizational problem solving'. This is based on the fundamental assumption that the *raison d'être* of IS is to develop organizations. Thus, at the heart of the book, is a set of methodological principles and guidance for thinking about, and undertaking, the 'organization problem-solving' part of information systems practice.

As will be seen, the discourse will outline a set of principles and methods that will argue for a new way of thinking in the field of practice and in certain aspects of the foundations of the discipline. It is an argument that outlines information systems practice to be underpinned by an integrated set of inquiring activities, which, together, can help to guide a process of *organizational problem solving*. It is therefore a view of the discipline of information systems that is concerned with organizational improvement. This 'improvement' is assumed to be commonly enabled by the use of (or the 'better' use of) information and communications technologies to bring about organizational change and 'improvement'.[4] Briefly, the argument presented is that in the process of organizational problem solving, the IS practitioner must be guided by a set of inquiring activities about the nature of the problem(s), the nature of the potential changes that could be made, and the nature of a particular change process. These inquiring activities are themselves underpinned by a basic set of principles, which are outlined in the discourse in the book. This book aims to outline such a set of inquiring activities to help to inform the practice and process of information systems work in organizations. It presents the theoretical basis of this (in Parts II and III), and provides an example case study (in Part IV). As will be seen, the book provides an 'end-to-end' process of organizational problem solving that reflects IS practice in general terms, in practical everyday organizational contexts.

This book will challenge the reader. There are some intellectual challenges in the discourse. In part, it is a highly abstract text, which has highly pragmatic implications and consequences. It is not designed to be a guide for the undertaking of information systems in a mechanical or prescriptive sense (there are already many of these types of books). Rather, it is designed to be an *intellectual discourse* that will challenge many assumptions about both the discipline and the field of practice.

To some, this book will be controversial. It will have its critics. Some readers may not see the relevance of viewing the information systems discipline as essentially one that integrates into a process of 'organizational problem solving'; some will not see the importance and relevance of inquiry in undertaking the process of information systems practice. Some will say, 'This is not what I do', or 'This is not what I teach', or 'This is not the way I see information systems'. Some will ask questions such as 'Where is the hardware, software, information, networks, information technology security...' or other aspects of 'as-given' knowledge in the discipline of information systems. The intention of the book is not to lay out familiar territory, but to integrate the familiar territory into a new framework and a new process, a process of organizational problem solving into which existing knowledge, methods etc., are increasingly required to integrate. It is a 'rethinking' of the nature of the discipline, its focus, its *raison d'être* and the orientation of the purposeful use of existing knowledge of the discipline.

The first Part of the book is an analysis of the discipline as we know it today, and argues that there are good reasons for thinking differently about the discipline and the guidance that it gives to practice. Parts II, III and IV are focused on 'organisational problem solving' or ('OPS' for short). The book outlines a range of considerations and perspectives on the process of OPS, based on the assumption and argument that IS is in essence an organisational problem solving discipline and activity. That is to say, neither information nor technology is the most fundamental goal of information systems. Rather, the most fundamental goal is organisational problem solving, and information and technology is a key modern day enabler and opportunity. Thus, Part II provides a discussion about some basic principles and methodological arguments about the nature of organisational problem solving. Part III outlines a set of core inquiring activities that might be expected to be found in the process of any OPS type activity, and Part IV provides a case which provides insights into certain aspects of process in practice. The book is a methodological level discourse on the process of organisational problem solving in the undertaking of IS in the complex and often contradictory context of human organisations.

The book will inevitably have its limitations. Naturally, any genuine critique will always demand an intellectual engagement with the arguments contained between the covers of the text. An intellectual engagement will of course require that the critic will have read the text, engaged in the arguments, understood them (to a large extent), and arrived at certain conclusions. It would be good if there was a *good* intellectual debate, and this may of course help to provide the new disciplinary focus in the future and, subsequently, to guide a new breed of practitioners; perhaps, currently, they are young students, who will one day lead organizations in harnessing and making effective the powerful technologies that are increasingly accessible. Perhaps they will lead organizations into the effective use of this new power, and will be able to find human benefit in doing so. In that sense, any writer would welcome critique or criticism, if it were to help in the longer term. As such, the text is purposefully designed to prompt a certain level of controversy, debate and intellectual discussion.

Acknowledgements

Humankind has, as one of its defining characteristics, the ability to engage in an intellectual manner about everyday experience. No matter what status is given to an individual by society, regardless of wealth or education, no matter what rewards are imbued on individuals, there is often a thirst for deepening understanding. I have been fortunate to have been surrounded by some special people with such a thirst, who have contributed directly or indirectly to this work. My thanks go to Nimal Jayaratna, Phil Johnson, Don White, Ray Hackney, Stuart Maguire, Roland Kaye, Peter Bednar, Mark Keen, Richard Jackson and Chris Wroe. In particular, I would like to acknowledge the work that I did with Nimal. We developed a number of unpublished papers, which provided a basis for a lot of the thinking, and some sections of this book. My thanks are also due to Professor Hans-Erik Nissen, who provided me with great feedback and pointers in the development of some key aspects of my work.

I would like to thank my students who have played a significant role in the refinement of the ideas that are presented between the covers of this text. There is of course no better way to learn than to teach. Some of my students have become personal friends, and continue to engage in the development of ideas that relate theory to practice in some way. I am lucky enough to keep in touch with many. Because they are former students, I have a very special relationship with them because they have a deep understanding of the principles and ideas that are articulated in this text. I appreciate the insights that they have given me, simply by engaging at an intellectual level regarding the difficulties they face, both during the learning process or subsequently in their own practice.

I would also like to thank the reviewers of the earlier versions of the text, who freely gave their time and insights because of the belief in intellectual endeavour. These people do not charge for their time, or for their intellectual insight. These people are often humbly going about their business – a business that is driven by the intellectual challenges and the need to use our intellectual capabilities for the betterment of humankind. I would also like to thank the individuals in the commercial, government and not-for-profit organizations with whom I have worked over the years. In particular, my thanks are due to colleagues based in the US, for developing the contractual side of the commercial consulting and IS problem-solving work. They share the vision of integrating thinking processes into practice. My thanks also go to Sheffield University in the UK, and to its Management School.

Finally, and most importantly, my thanks to Claire, Anna, Shaun and Jessica for their forbearance!

Part I

The discipline of information systems

This part discusses some of the current challenges of the discipline. First, it presents an interpretation of the history and emergence to date of the discipline of IS, and how it evolved as a response to meet the needs of practice. In order to do so, this part will outline a potted history and context of the discipline, and its past and future *raison d'être*. We will discuss the development of the discipline, and its current problems and challenges.

Second, this part questions how far it could be said that the modern discipline, as we know it today, can be considered a 'success' or otherwise. We will discuss this in terms of some of the problems and challenges in curricula design and the problems in the research activities of the discipline.

Although there have been huge successes in the field of practice, these have largely been achieved in large organizations, with significant budgets. The challenge in today's context is to replicate these successes in smaller organizations, particularly in contexts where resources are not available for bespoke application development and complex software builds.

This discussion aims to provide the basis and rationale for the conceptual rethink of some of the core principles and elements of method to be discussed in Parts II, III and IV.

Part I

The discipline of information systems

1 Emergence

Abstract

This chapter outlines a potted history of the discipline of information systems. The reason for doing so is that an historical account can provide insight into the present and future. This account of the history of the discipline of information systems is intended to help explain and contextualize the current challenges of the discipline, in terms of (i) the nature and *raison d'être* of the discipline, (ii) how the discipline has emerged to date, (iii) the nature of the discipline as it currently serves the field of practice, and (iv) the future of the field of practice, and the way the discipline will be required to change in serving practice.

Introduction

In order that a thorough analysis of the information systems discipline can take place, it is necessary to explore some of its most basic definitions, assumptions and why it has evolved in the first place. Inevitably, this requires a 'potted history' of sorts; also inevitably, such a 'potted history' is an imperfect human interpretation, but serves as a basis for exploring the most fundamental aspects the information systems discipline. It is imperfect, because of the significant ambiguity in the discipline and in the field of practice, which require making some significant generalizations. Exploring some of these ambiguities is certainly not a simple exercise because it involves an interpretation of sorts about some of the most fundamental constructs that are used within the discipline and in the field of practice, over a period of time.

For example, the term 'information' itself is ambiguous. Liebenau and Backhouse (1990) quote a number of different definitions of 'information', each of which reflects the interests, assumptions and assertions of their creators. For example, early 'information systems' work did not differentiate between data and information. The interest for Shannon and Weaver (1964) was in the coding and communication of 'information'. They used the word 'information' to mean an 'artefact' that can be represented and communicated, and therefore take on physical characteristics. Generally speaking, within the field of information systems, data is commonly considered to be a record of events, activities, observations etc., while information is considered to be the relevance and use of that data in a given context. For instance Wilson (1984) discusses the human *meaning attribution* that converts data into information. Thus, commonly, data is considered an artefact, and information is purposefully constructed via human interpretation of the data. As such, the verb 'to inform' indicates a process that is intricately tied to human cognition (via a process of human interpretation), and can have both an implicit and explicit purpose e.g. to enable informed decision making to take place, to stop decisions being made, to obfuscate, to confuse, or to constructively 'inform' etc. A further important implication is that the meaning attribution of 'information' for one person is likely to be different for another user in some circumstances; but this does not mean that there are other circumstances where there may be a degree of 'shared meaning' attribution to the same data (see also Winograd and Flores 1986).

Since the process of converting data into information is full of implicit and explicit human purpose and cognitions, tied to the political, power and ambiguities of practice, information systems, as a discipline and as a field of practice, must be concerned with that process (e.g. the purposefulness inherent in the conversion of data into information). Millions of data can be recorded on physical media (paper, computers, books, internet, in the Library of Congress, information systems textbooks). Conversion of data into a meaningful and usable form may very well involve considerable processing and, in the field of information systems, terms such as 'information processing' or 'data processing' are used to describe that activity. Nonetheless, it should not be assumed that 'information' is a *human* act (i.e. by attaching meaning to data), and that 'data' is in some way devoid of human purpose. Data cannot be considered devoid of humanly constructed *purpose*. For example, data is not 'God-given' (at least in most circumstances!). It is humanly constructed, collected (or not collected) for specific human purpose; it is stored in a particular way, based on an assumption about its utility for human use and the process of 'meaning construction'. In that sense, data itself is not 'objective' as might sometimes be assumed.

History

In organizations, information is generally seen as being central to the job tasks, politics and culture of everyday human activity, and of organizational processes. As such, both data and information are always highly integrated with the activities that they serve (e.g. for decision making, coordination of actions, power games, to justifying actions). Information and its use is an intrinsic part of organizational activities. It makes no sense in the field of practice, and in the discipline, to consider information to (i) completely separate the information processing activities from a given organizational process, or to, (ii) consider that data is in some way 'independent' or 'objective' – it is purposely humanly constructed, as is the information processing that is served by it. The organizational process, the information and the data are all inextricably linked together, although in some situations it is possible to *conceptually* separate them.

In craft production, it is quite impossible to separate the information processing from the human actions that are involved. That is to say, the information that is used to perform the task cannot be separated from the task itself. The information to undertake the task are deeply embedded in the task, and implicitly absorbed within the activity. An outsider who might want to acquire a given set of craft skills will typically work as an apprentice for a period of time. In these contexts, there is often little need of a separate 'information processing' activity because the information processing is often completely integrated with the task, and mostly carried out in the mind.

In other organizational processes, however, it can be more meaningful to *conceptually* (and temporarily) separate the 'information processing' oriented activities from the 'physical' oriented activities that use it. The conceptual separation enabled the creation of *separate* data processing tasks, e.g. in the process of bookkeeping there is a data processing component. The bringing together of similar data processing activities led to the creation of specialized roles such as accountants, statisticians and clerks. The industrial revolution sharpened the divisions between those who were engaged in data processing activities and those who were engaged in the execution of tasks, based on the information, i.e. white and blue collar workers (see Braverman 1974; Scarborough and Corbett 1992). The emergence of the white collar worker was, in a sense, a movement from physical activities to those that focus on recording and processing data. It is in this separation of the physical actions and activities in human organizations from the information processing activities that provided the *raison d'être* of the information systems discipline.

The arrival of computers marked the beginning of the automation of data processing activities. The perception of the computer as a calculating machine resulted in computing technology being allocated a home in the accounts departments of commercial organizations. In universities the same basic reasoning helped them to locate their computers in mathematics or applied mathematics departments. However, the power of computers to operate with program instructions enabled a new discipline to emerge from the mathematics departments, in the form of computer science. The ability to handle non-financial activities helped data processing to emerge as a 'sub-department' within the accounts departments in many organizations, e.g. to handle stock control, order processing etc. The primary role of computers within organizations was to handle large volumes of data, storage of that data, and the output, but with simple processing requirements; whereas computers used in the applied mathematics or computer science departments typically handled fewer data inputs and outputs, but vast amounts of processing and computations.

It was the extension of the use of the computers by mainframe and minicomputer manufacturers (IBM, Honeywell, Hewlett Packard, ICL, DEC) into diverse business domains, especially into non-financial activities (e.g. manufacturing, logistics, workflow), which enabled the data processing functions in accounting departments to grow and break away to form departments of their own. These created demand for a large number of specialists with knowledge of computers (e.g. with programming skills in languages such as COBOL), combined with knowledge of organizational functions. These were a new breed of individuals who had specific technical skills but who could operate in organizational contexts.

These changes also led to the popularity and use of the term 'information technology'. In essence the terms 'information technology' and 'computer technology' usually refer to the same technology. However, the term 'information technology' is used to emphasize the use of computers for information processing, storage and presentation to satisfy perceived needs for converting data into usable and purposeful information, given particular sets of perceived organizational and human needs. The term 'computer technology', on the other hand, is used to emphasize the experimentation and exploration of the computational power of the technology with a very different purpose. Its purpose is focused on the capabilities of the technology, its architecture etc., without consideration of the *specific* needs of a given human

In commercial organizations	First computers were most commonly located in accounts departments. Generally, there was a large volume of data which required relatively simple processing tasks, e.g payroll. A typical early language used was Cobol
In universities	First computers were typically located in mathematics departments. Volumes of data were often quite small, but required large processing capacities, i.e. 'number crunching' applications such as multiple regression and linear programming. Typical early languages were Fortran and Algol, and a little later Pascal

Figure 1.1 Early adoption of computers

organizational context. Broadly speaking, in the former, information technology is considered only to be a means to an end whilst in the latter, computer technology is often considered to be an end in itself (see Jayaratna 1994). This dichotomy continues to exist in both academic institutions and in non-academic institutions. Although there remains much overlap and many fuzzy lines, 'computer science' has emerged to reflect the advancement of the technology as a primary objective whereas 'information systems' is largely concerned with the *application* of that technology by humans in human organizations, for information processing purposes.

University contexts

The pressure to produce graduates to meet the new demands of commercial applications of computers led to the formation of information systems groups within computer science departments, or of separate information systems departments in universities. Where there was strong resistance in the computer science departments to the introduction of knowledge areas on computer applications in organizations, business schools responded by opening their own information systems or management information systems departments. It might be argued that the birth of information systems as a discipline can be attributed to the failure of computer science to deal with emerging *organizational problems*. The scientific paradigms, with which computers were associated, were not appropriate for solving many of the emerging organizational problems. The 'engineering' principles that are involved in building computers, did not easily port to the building of organizations. Commonly, early computer scientists treated COBOL and associated business-related activities with contempt and predicted the death of COBOL (for over three decades!). In situations in which information systems remained a part of computer science departments, academics who were teaching information systems topics (or 'management information systems') sometimes found themselves alienated by their colleagues because of their closeness to organizational, business or commercial applications. Equally, academics who worked in information systems departments in business schools sometimes found themselves alienated by their colleagues because of their closeness to the technology!

It remains a characteristic of the discipline that there has been a classical dichotomy and ambivalence depending on the location of the information systems department.

The failure to grasp these issues has led to fragmentation and ambivalences in the discipline, reflected in hugely variable methods, approaches, ideas, principles etc. (see the continuing quantitative/qualitative debates referenced in the literature, e.g. Kaplan and Duchon 1988; Lee 1991, 1999; Fitzgerald and Howcroft 1998). On the one hand, there are approaches that advocate the 'natural sciences' with roots in computer science; on the other, there is a common tendency in business and management disciplines towards the 'social sciences'. Commonly, those within science faculties in universities are dominated by technology-driven approaches while the IS departments in business or management schools treat technology as an issue of little significance, or even as a mysterious 'black box'. Unfortunately, these debates have not yet matured into a coherent set of principles, which is required of an interdisciplinary discipline (e.g. to help to integrate practice with research and curricula design). Unsurprisingly, neither position can be considered 'right' or 'wrong' and, also unsurprisingly, commonly neither are sufficiently close to practice to judge. Information systems has been on the cusp of this ambivalence for some time. Indeed some of these integration problems may help to explain the failings in the discipline, as will be discussed in the following chapter.

As might be observed, the *raison d'être* for information systems did not grow out of social science or humanities or liberal arts or culture or library science or management or accounting or economics, although these fields can claim the ownership of specific information-related topics. Nor did it grow out of computer science, mathematics or operations research. The *raison d'être* of information systems has its roots in solving organizational 'problems' in practice; it continues to be oriented towards the *application of technology in organizations*. It is interdisciplinary in nature, in the sense that it draws its methods, knowledge and theories from other disciplines *during the process of solving organizational 'problems'*. The integration occurs in the activity of the solving of 'problems', underpinned by *methodology for 'problem solving'* (which will be discussed in Parts II and III of this book). The entire history and *raison d'être* of the discipline of information systems remains driven by the emerging development and application of information technology to the 'improvement' of organizations and the resolution of organizational 'problems'.

'Systems analysis'

Given that the original nature of information systems was practical and application driven, it is not surprising that the literature and theory were historically dominated by development concepts and models. In its early development, the field did not have development methods of its own and hence borrowed them. One substantial influence in this regard was from 'work study' and organization and method practices (see, for example NCC, 1972, 1978). The idea behind these was to study work practices, using very specific techniques (e.g. data flow diagrams, entity relationship modelling, structured programming, entity life histories etc.). In 'work study' approaches, the methods were typically focused on the automation of manual practices in organizations, with improvements in efficiency, rather than helping to realize the potential of the technology for changing the work practices or organizations (see Zuboff 1988, 1994). They were generally influenced by scientific management and, generally speaking, tended towards a set of ontological assumptions that were fundamentally positivist in their approach to changing work practices and organizations. Although such texts may have claimed to embrace systems ideas, their use of such ideas was very limited. For example:

- The use of systems theory as a conceptual device for understanding and organizing complexity was largely ignored.
- The notion of modelling systems as *concepts*, as opposed to 'real world' activities, was not generally understood or considered important.
- The use of systems as method to guide inquiry was not fully developed.
- The potential use of systems ideas as a core component for *organizational problem solving* was not generally recognized.

The 'work study' type texts have nonetheless been used in the field of practice, and influenced the discipline, in a number of ways. For instance, it was the *selected* use of systems ideas that gave rise to new techniques such as 'Rand Corporation Systems Analysis' (see Checkland 1981 for its inadequacies) or 'BISAD' (Business Information Systems Analysis and Design) – a precursor to structured analysis and design techniques (De Marco 1978; Gane and Sarson 1978; Yourdon 1989). This is also the reason why information systems practitioners are called 'systems people'! However, systems theory and 'information systems' remain significantly different, despite the fact that 'information systems' have borrowed and used some 'systems' ideas. A number of authors and practitioners have suggested methods that were based on 'systems ideas' and have continued to suggest changes in methods, e.g. task and data separation in 'structured methods' (De Marco 1978; Gane and Sarson 1978; Yourdon 1989), to task and data integration in 'object oriented' methods (e.g. Coad and Yourdon 1991; Booch 1999). However, these approaches have failed to realize the full power of systems theory applied to the problem-solving process in organizations, and to integrate *organizational problem solving* with information processing and information technology. Thus they have remained focused on technology development. Even today, systems theory often has a place in information systems teaching, but it is usually given minimal attention.

Traditionally, one of the 'as-given' assumptions has commonly been that the field of practice, and the discipline, is concerned with 'information processing', with a largely secondary focus on instigating and managing change in organizations. For example, Keen (1980) saw information systems as the 'study of effective design, delivery, and usage of information systems in organizations and society' (Keen 1980: 10). In this definition, Keen implies that the notion that the discipline of information systems is concerned with the processing of (computer-based) information. This type of definition is quite 'classic' in the literature, e.g. information systems is 'a computer based organizational information system which provides information support for management activities and functions' (Ives *et al.* 1980: 910). The essence of both of these definitions makes the assumption that an 'information system' is computer based, and the function of information systems is in the processing of data. The quotations from Keen and Ives are relatively old, talking as they did in the 1980s, and it is rather different over a quarter of a century later. However, these definitions remain very common, e.g. an information system is an 'organized combination of people, hardware, software, communications networks and data resources that collects, transforms and disseminates information in an organization' (O'Brien 1999: 9). Sometimes these and other definitions result in a tendency to define information systems as 'information technology management', which focuses on the generic role of processing and distribution of data or information functions. This way of viewing information systems is very much a product of an historic era in which 'data processing' was a key function in organizations. Whilst this is still true to a certain extent, it is a limited view of the function and application of modern day technology. For example, should a virtual shopping mall be considered a 'data processing' function? The answer of course is that to some extent it can be, but certainly not in the way 'data processing' was perceived a quarter of a century ago. Conceiving the information systems discipline in this way would be to deny that there has been a huge leap in the capabilities of the various technologies to provide new opportunities to organizations. The background task remains 'processing data', with a vast array of organization development opportunities. Given changes in technology, the processing of data is increasingly 'as given' and standardized into software shells, non-bespoke applications, often hosted by third-party application service providers. The processing of the data is increasingly easy and accessible to user organizations. What is not easy is achieving the organization development and benefit realization. Thus 'systems analysis' itself is required to change as its goal is shifting from producing 'data processing' applications to organizational problem solving. It is no longer as relevant as it used to be to consider 'systems analysis' to be focused on technology development, or on the computerization of manual tasks. It is this shift that will become increasingly important to the discipline in order to harness the new range of capabilities of technology, e.g. to change organizational processes, improving their performance,[1] creating new sales channels, improving competitiveness etc.

Systems theory has had a very profound and central role in organizational problem solving (see, for example Churchman 1968, 1971, 1979; Ackoff 1978; Beer 1979; Checkland 1981, 1990; Jayaratna 1994). As such, it may have a very important role in the future of the information systems discipline, and in guiding practice. However, rather than using systems theory as a way to help the design of traditional 'data processing' functions and applications, its relevance in the future of the information systems discipline is in the design of organizational processes. It is this re-evaluation of the role of systems theory within the discipline that is of central concern within this book, and which is outlined in Parts II, III and IV.

Since the discipline of information systems has already embraced certain aspects of systems theory, it is perhaps a small step in theory, but could be a quantum leap for the discipline and for practice. If the discipline were to integrate the problem-solving process in organizations, underpinned by systems ideas, there will be a natural process by which information systems can mature as discipline and as a field of practice, towards one of *organizational problem solving*. As discussed, this shift is required because of the power and new opportunity that the technology gives to change and improve organizations. If information systems can harness the power inherent in systems theory, it will have the potential become a central driver of change in organizational improvement in practice. It will mean that information systems may become a key discipline in shaping the futures of organizations. Not by prescribing solutions (e.g. by the prescriptive application of specific technologies or 'work study' methods), but by being focused on organization development and 'improvement', *in which technology* may *have a central enabling role*. It is in this shift in focus which is (i) the central argument that is presented in this book and, more specifically, (ii) the rethinking of the role of systems theory in the continued development of the information systems discipline.

Interdisciplinarity in research

At this point in time, the information systems discipline displays characteristics of a 'pre-paradigm' stage, i.e. there are early, but random, attempts to impose a consensus on the paradigm of science in the field (see Kuhn 1962). Its immaturity is demonstrated by a lack of a 'cumulative tradition' (see Benbasat and Zmud 1999), whereby researchers from different disciplines, and backgrounds, can study the same or similar phenomena, using their own particular research paradigms or approaches. For example, 'strategic' policy making for information systems investments can be studied by specialists from information technology, economics, sociology and organization development etc. Each research grouping will usually bring with them their own particular 'interpretation' of the issues, and also their own methods, ontological assumptions and epistemological preferences etc. This is perhaps unsurprising when we analyze its relatively short history, and the way technology has changed rapidly, beyond all expectations. It brings with it challenges of changing the methods and dominant orthodoxies in the discipline. Whilst information systems might be considered in a 'pre-paradigm' stage, it needs to find a way to integrate the inputs from other disciplines: crudely speaking, it is currently multidisciplinary, but needs to be interdisciplinary. To become interdisciplinary means that it requires a coherent integration of the subject knowledge and relevant skills from other disciplines, but in the context of information systems *practice* (i.e. the development of human organizations using information and technology).

If it were hypothetically possible to suddenly 'impose' interdisciplinarity onto the discipline, then any contribution to knowledge in the field, from any other reference disciplines, must demonstrate clear relevance, connections and benefits to the performance of information systems practice, i.e. in undertaking the 'improvement' in organizations in practice. This does not mean that 'blue skies' research is irrelevant. However, it would be assumed that it is concerned in some manner of speaking with information systems practice and would at some stage, and in some way, integrate with the thinking about the field of practice. For example, its *raison d'être* must relate to the concerns of practitioners or the problems of practice; or its empirical component will be drawn from practice. Currently, we have a situation where research is commonly disconnected from practice.

Yet this need for 'interdisciplinarity' in information systems is, in a way, its own Achilles heel. For example:

*   The integration of knowledge and skills in undertaking the process of applying technology and information in order to improve human organizations requires a deep understanding and discovery of interconnectivity of relevant knowledge. However, in a pragmatic environment, most people find it difficult to deal with interdisciplinary topics as they are used to operating within traditional, well-established boundary sets, i.e. their 'inputs' to the discipline are considered and undertaken from the confines of their 'home' discipline.
*   The key generators of knowledge in modern day societies are their universities. However, as will be explored further in Chapter 2, universities are increasingly under pressure to produce research output, and interdisciplinary work is much more difficult to get published than work that confirms to the 'iron-cage' of the traditions and demarcation lines of feeder disciplines.

• The tradition in research is to promote the narrow, specialist research, which can easily lose sight of the 'whole' process of 'problem solving'. This is an observation that prompted Churchman (1979) to describe disciplinary science to be an 'enemy' of the systems approach, which is integrative in its nature. We will explore this in Part II.

It is the lack of commitment to a common philosophy of interdisciplinarity of knowledge that is contributing to a certain fragmentation within the discipline of information systems. Since, in a practical field such as information systems, the *raison d'être* of research is to lead the thinking processes that can assist practitioners improve or develop innovative solutions to practitioner problems, it stands to reason that the value of research can be judged by its ability to inform, question and change the action of practitioners in achieving improvements or innovations in practice. In order to ensure relevance to practice, researchers would normally be required to demonstrate their knowledge in the functions of practice, otherwise they will not be able to appreciate the nature and extent of the problems of the practitioner. Furthermore, in order to appreciate the complexities and demands of practice, researchers would be required to engage in the everyday practical issues, ambiguities, anxieties, frustrations and challenges. If researchers do not possess the knowledge of practice, there will be little motivation for them to be involved in producing research that can help to overcome the problems and concerns of the practitioners. As such, their research can only ever be an exercise in developing their awareness, rather than changing the nature of practice, which is somewhat inadequate for a practical discipline such as information systems, with its particular history and a *raison d'être*.

Current trends

In some disciplines, intervention in a change situation by a researcher is considered to be a hindrance to the discovery of knowledge, and therefore positively discouraged. As information systems is a practical discipline, research that has purposeful intervention as a way of discovering relevant and useful knowledge is preferable to research that produces rigorous research, but which avoids the undertaking or evaluation of intervention. Perhaps it might be argued that the discipline of information systems requires rigour *and* relevance. Researchers who do not engage sufficiently with practice in order to discover and/or improve practice are not contributors to the advancement of the field. Conducting research that produces little knowledge of practical relevance is not only wasteful of resources, but also does not add to the self-development of the researcher.

The discipline of information systems has had a significant growth in the last twenty years or so. This has resulted in opening up opportunities for researchers from other disciplines, as well as new researchers, to move into academic roles in (broadly) the information systems domain. In the same period, there has been changes in the academic context in which individuals work, resulting in heightened pressure on academic research outputs (e.g. to acquire tenure status or promotions). The tenure appointments are based primarily on research output in the form of journal publications. The combination of rapid expansion in the discipline, and the changes in the way academics are judged, has had the result that there has been a shift in the focus of the research within the discipline. For instance, there has been considerable pressure from these researchers for journal editors to accommodate their research output for publication, which invariably meant the acceptance from a variety of disciplinary backgrounds (e.g. sociology, psychology, computer science, mathematics, engineering, management etc.). This has resulted in much research that purports to be information systems research, but is sometimes of an 'observational' kind, rather than a 'problem-solving' kind. For example, a survey-based research report from interviews with a number of CEOs, or a literature review of other research reports etc. Such research tends to take very little time compared with the development and engagement in the problem solving of the CEO's concerns! That is to say, during the time it takes to conduct one research project of a problem-solving kind and obtain results with sufficient conceptual and empirical rigour, it is possible to 'turn around' several interview-based research reports and several literature reviews!

From this, it is quite easy to see a potentially dangerous motive and trend in the assumptions about the research methods used, and the nature of knowledge in the discipline. This can help explain the current anxieties being expressed within the discipline (e.g. Benbasat and Zmud 1999; Hirschheim and Klein 2003). The attraction of academics and researchers from diverse academic backgrounds can be a considerable strength to a multidisciplinary research field. However, the richness provided by the diversity can be muted when it is not matched by coherence or a shared understanding of the nature of the subject or the needs of practice. The diversity of research, and the accommodation of a variety of reference disciplines, was largely welcomed by many of the leaders in the discipline over twenty years ago (see Mumford *et al.* 1984). The issues facing the discipline today, however, are significantly different from those faced by the discipline twenty or so years ago. The research field today accommodates a wide range of philosophies and theories, each appearing to compete to establish itself as the relevant philosophy and theory for generating new knowledge, many of which are rooted in reference disciplines. However, they do not necessarily demonstrate their relevance to the practice of *organizational problem solving*. More importantly, none of the philosophies that are offered from the reference disciplines have been able to provide the integrating focus, and often are insufficient to provide the practical relevance, which helps to explain the reasons for the expressed anxieties surrounding relevancy that have appeared recently in a number of academic journals (e.g. Benbasat and Zmud 1999, 2003; Davenport and Markus 1999; Lyytinen 1999; Markus 1999; Watson *et al.* 1999; Baskerville and Myers 2002; Paul 2002; Hirschheim and Klein 2003).

It seems that during the last twenty years or so, the field of practice has been undergoing considerable changes, and yet the research in the field has had very little impact on practice. Since much research has focused on *observing* phenomena and not focused on *problem solving*, the research findings are also not focused on assisting practice. As a result, the primary beneficiaries of the research might be best considered to be the researchers themselves, who carry out the research (e.g. yet another publication to add to the list to obtain tenure or promotion) and provide ground material for other researchers who seek critical evaluation of practice-disconnected data. It is not that the philosophies in question are irrelevant. They have been well established and have strong reputation in other academic areas (e.g. social science, humanities, mathematics, computer science). However, there are dangers if researchers are not drawing their conclusions from practice and from practical concerns. Nor are they concerned about their own motives in undertaking the research in the first place. It is a situation that means that researchers might be considered to be attempting to make the relevance of their thinking to information systems practice in a theoretical sense, but without grounding them in practice. Sometimes, this is because they have no grounding in practice and are driven by career-related criteria.

The philosophies from reference disciplines, non-exposure of the researchers to practice, and tenure and career demands have had a profound effect on the selection of research methods and to the knowledge contributions in the field of information systems. Research methods such as surveys, structured interviews, semi-structured interviews, unstructured interviews, grounded theory, ethnographical studies and narratives have replaced traditional development, implementation, experimental and action research methods. The 'observational' research methods can make a significant contribution to the subject of information systems, but since the researchers remain within the safety of their areas of competence, the outcomes of the research has little impact on the way practice can be improved. Surveys, interviews, observations consider information systems practice as external 'phenomena' to be studied, rather than as a practice to be engaged in, changed and improved. It is noticeable how many research reports provide 'motherhood statements' (e.g. 'You need to evaluate IT benefits', 'You must align IT strategy with business strategy', 'You should include the users in development projects'!!). Such 'recommendations' are common-sense knowledge to practitioners. What the practitioners need desperately is knowledge and guidance on how to perform those activities that can help to realize benefits from information, changes to organizational processes and technology and, unfortunately, most university-based researchers do not possess sufficient knowledge of the pragmatics of information systems, or are lacking in practical knowledge or experience, to provide useful insights.

The increased use of observation-based research methods has also had significant impact in the training of future researchers, i.e. in research methods. The teaching sessions on research methods encourage the prospective researchers to compare and contrast a number of research methods, each with particular philosophical foundations (e.g. 'positivist', 'interpretive', 'critical'). The selection, justification and application by the researcher of research methods can develop useful critical skills in the conduct of research. However, this preparation is inadequate for action- or development-based research, in which there is the necessity to include, for example (i) the rationale for change, (ii) the steps, activities and actions that are required to make change happen, (iii) the critical examination of the problem-solving process, during the problem-solving process itself, and (iv) the evaluation of the 'self' in intervention situations etc. In the 'observation of phenomena'-type research, the researcher learns by observing, but loses out on the learning that can only be gained from the 'doing', or the 'experience' of practice. As a result, they develop skills in reporting (!) but not skills in, or experience of, organizational change, managing complex projects, problem solving, improvement methods, intervention etc. This makes researchers ill-prepared for undertaking useful practice or practical information systems research activity.

The researchers' experience, knowledge and skills also have had significant impact on the nature and content of the educational programmes. Instead of the development of students skills in organizational change and improvement, the curriculum has shifted to cover discussions of case study reports, quotations, interviews, surveys and success/ failure stories, e.g. how specific companies gained 'competitive advantage' by the application of information technology (e.g. the familiar case studies such as American Airlines' SABRE application, Amazon.com or Dell.com). While such discussions and observations can heighten awareness for students, they cannot develop craft knowledge and the design-type thinking that is useful for their future practice. Without the application to practice, there can only be discourses on reported phenomena, and not about the use of concepts, notions, models, frameworks and methodology for changing organizations in practice. Cynical observers may conclude that teaching students to critique reported phenomena is cheaper and logistically easier than enabling students to draw knowledge from their experience of practice.

The lack of an organization problem-solving focus is also due to the lack of practical experience of the new researchers in the field. For example, whilst they may have good experience of the technology from a user perspective, their understanding of how the technology works, how components can be put together and how the technology can support organizational processes is often limited. Sometimes there is a dangerously condescending view that assumes IT as simply 'product knowledge' that is in some way commercial, or ephemeral, and therefore has little relevance. Although the trend in the information systems field seems sometimes to decrease the technical content, students (as potential practitioners) still require considerable knowledge of the technology in order to apply it to change organizations. Without this level of understanding, it is difficult to make any realistic decisions on which technology to adopt, in which way it is to integrate and what levels of skills would be required to benefit from the investments in the technology.

This drift of emphasis from the 'doing' to a 'discussion on the doing' is, in some cases, taking the subject of information systems from being a practical discipline to that of a subject of discourse, where practice becomes the phenomena to be studied and debated (e.g. 'studies on information'). The evidence of this drift can be found in many 'information related' courses. In this way the discipline has begun to ill-prepare its graduates for undertaking practice in organizations.

Time for change?

The potted history presented in this chapter may be considered to have certain important implications. For example:

- Those associated with the development of the discipline are required to concern themselves with the 'problems' of practice primarily, and not solely, about theoretical constructs of reference disciplines.
- Research funders are required to reconsider their policy priorities, in order to encourage 'interventionist'-type research methods, i.e. action research, participative design, experimental and development projects, knowledge transfer.
- Researchers may need to clarify how generalizable knowledge should be generated from 'interventionist' research methods (i.e. researchers must avoid generating functional knowledge that relates only to the specifics of a given 'problem' in a given case, which commonly results from 'interventionist' methods).

- Curricular designers may give priority to subject teaching where students involve themselves with skill development relevant to practice, and develop abstract thinking skills which are integrated into, or derived from, the experience of practice.
- The research and curricula activities must be related to the function of organizational problem solving as a core objective, and solving problems of information or of the enabling technologies cannot be separated from the other 'organizational problem-solving' activities and associated methods.
- The curriculum is required to include and integrate a strong emphasis on skill development, inquiring methods and problem solving, with much less emphasis (as is currently) on software development methods.
- Government and policy makers are required to change the criteria for evaluation of what constitutes 'quality' in a practical discipline such as IS. The implicit criteria and process which is associated with, for example, the Research Assessment Exercise in the UK requires re-examination.
- Government and policy makers are required to consider their public-funded IS projects, to integrate a new breed of researchers and organize projects in such a way that the rigours of scientific inquiry can be brought to bear on the investments.
- etc.

We will be exploring such assertions during the course of the book. There are many implications for policy and priorities in these and other conclusions. Fundamentally, perhaps, there is a need for the discipline to undertake a rethink, in order to reinvent itself to help to lead practice. A new set of principles is required to help guide practice and to guide how knowledge is generated from practice. This is a significant challenge for a discipline that has been subject to significant and speedy growth, and one that has the consequent loss of cogency and interdisciplinarity, and one which is lacking in a 'cumulative tradition'.

2   Failings

Abstract

Information systems as a discipline can be considered to have certain failings that impact on practice. This chapter explores some of the failings, discussed in three different related areas: failure in practice, failure in the curricula design and failure in certain aspects of the research activities in the field.

Introduction

The potted history in the previous chapter has given a context from which cynical observers of the information systems discipline may conclude that it is a discipline and a field of practice that is in crisis. Could it be that information systems *as a discipline* is full of bankrupt, old-fashioned ideas – and that the failings result in (i) failings in practice, and (ii) a gulf between theory and practice? Perhaps these are over-cynical assertions?

Defenders of the discipline may consider it much too cynical. After all, they might say, 'look at the evidence look, for example, how the internet has changed, and continues to change, the way people work. Look at the explosive growth in Enterprise Resource Planning (ERP) applications and the way organizations are integrating them to improve value chain integration. Look at the growth in e-business, or services in the health sector, ('e-health'), or in the government sector ('e-government'), the new integrated and 'joined up' opportunities that the technology enables. Look at the integrated criminal justice applications that are being developed in the police and judicial services; look at the way learning technologies are being applied ('e-learning') or the impact technology is having on the way international business is conducted; look at how it is making the world a smaller place; look at how the technology is impacting our everyday lives'. The defenders may say, 'look at the evidence, look at the tremendous impact that the technology is having. How could you possibly argue that information systems is in crisis?'

But the cynics might paint a very alternative picture.

Most practitioners ignore the research of the discipline; they ignore the methods proposed within the discipline and tend to 'just do it'. Whilst there are volumes written on information systems methods, practitioners ignore them. It is a phenomenon that might be explained in a number of ways but, whatever the explanation, it remains both a characteristic and a 'problem' within the discipline. At the same time, huge resources are being consumed in organizations by their 'information systems', and those charged with sizable budgets are often left anxious, lacking guidance from a robust 'body of knowledge'. Senior managers of many organizations are frustrated at how much resource is being consumed by their information systems departments, and are commonly frustrated at how little they seem to 'benefit' from them. Sometimes they are shocked by project overruns, budgets that get out of control, projects that go awry. Project managers are left at the cusp of, on the one hand, dealing with organizational processes, politics, ambiguities and contradictions and, on the other hand, dealing with a set of hugely powerful technologies, which are developing so fast, it is difficult to keep abreast of the changes in their capabilities, possibilities and their application. There is much anxiety amongst project managers as a result of the lack of 'guiding methods', resulting in intense pressure. When new technologies come along, there is often a gut feel that they will, in the long term, be beneficial. So a justification is made. The technology is implemented. Users often either (i) do not use it, or (ii) use it only a bit, or (iii) are misguided in their use of it. There is little in the way of managing change, huge ambiguity about its organizational benefit and significant ambivalence in general attitudes towards it. The information technology industry has become very powerful, selling 'solutions' to organizations; they are of course the 'solution providers' but tend to ignore the nature of the 'problem' that they are supposedly providing a solution for! Slick sales people, sometimes (perhaps erroneously) termed 'consultants' of some sort, leave internal managers with big promises, which are often relayed to their own bosses; promises that are superficial, tied into personal ambitions and goals (e.g. career progression). There is little precision or knowledge about how the benefits promised are to be realized. The information technology industry seems to need to move from one fad to another, and to continually recreate new promises. Our cynics might point out the number of 'millennium bug' consultants who were operating up until the 31 December 1999, and then point to the rather similar number of 'e-business' consultants who were peddling their services after 1 January 2000, only to suffer (or cause?) the dot com crash. They may point to other more recent 'fads' that have been used by the information systems industry, e.g. narrowly interpreted views of 'business process re-engineering', 'knowledge management', 'e-learning', and policy initiatives around which there are fad-like responses, e.g. 'e-government', 'e-health'. They may point out the project failings that have occurred, which have used the terms without a deep understanding of their implications and meaning. They may also claim that, at the very same time, researchers in the discipline are undertaking research that is neither scientifically valid for a *practical discipline*, nor relevant. The cynics may argue that there is no 'science' in information systems. They leave the thorny problems of practice to practitioners, preferring to develop discourses or surveys that can provide publishable papers swiftly. Researchers can come from other disciplines such as computer science, mathematics, sociology, psychology etc., and use the science of their reference discipline without consideration of the unique characteristics of the 'science' that underpins the practice of information systems.

The cynics might also develop their picture by simply comparing information systems with other practical disciplines. For example, they might say, 'If you were a patient in a hospital, would you be happy if "medical theory" guided "medical practice" to the same extent as "information systems theory" guides "information systems practice"? If you were walking into an aircraft, would you be happy if "aviation science" informed the pilot of the plane as little as the discipline of information systems informs its own practitioners?'

Our rhetorical cynics might acknowledge some of the success stories. They might acknowledge that the technology is more powerful than ever before, it is more technically stable than ever before and the software is easier to develop and apply. However, our rhetorical cynics might argue that the success of the technology *is in despite of the discipline*. Not because of it. The successes are derived from the discipline of computer science, not the successes in the discipline of information systems. They might point out that the power of the technology is simultaneously creating opportunities and impacts, but benefits realization is as difficult as it ever has been. For this reason, they might argue, the discipline must integrate better with organizational problem-solving methods.

Failings in practice

There has been much written about failure of (i) information technology, (ii) projects involving information technology, and (iii) the discipline of information systems that claims to inform the practice of, and the issues involved in, (i) and (ii).[1] In the very early nineties, research was produced that suggested that there has been significant wastage and expenditure on information technology in organizations (Hochstrasser and Griffiths 1991; Hochstrasser 1994; Willcocks 1994; Willcocks and Margetts 1994). Since these studies, there have been successive studies done which point to evidence of failure. For example, in 1995, there was a well-cited report that drew on the great and the good of the discipline. This was the report of the OASIG, a special interest group in the UK concerned with the organizational aspects of information technology (see OASIG 1995). The study took a sample of forty-five 'experts' employed primarily by universities or consultancies, with an average of 20 years personal experience (representing a cumulative knowledge base of over 900 years!). They drew on a sample of experience from about 14,000 organizations, in both public and private sectors. Thirty-one of these interviewees (69 per cent) included consultancy work as a major component of their work, and twenty-seven (60 per cent) included research; many included both. Their professional areas of expertise covered primarily the domains of management, business and social science, although a small number had a background in engineering. Data was collected by interviewing researchers and consultants, using semi-structured interviews. Each interview lasted, on average, around 1.5 to 2 hours, though some lasted considerably longer. This was a significant undertaking, and there were some significant findings:

- 20–30 per cent success rates for IT projects.
- At best, 7 out of 10 projects fail in some respect.

A sample of forty-five might not be altogether conclusive. However, this was not the only report of its type with these sorts of conclusions. For example, the CHAOS Report was also published in 1995 (CHAOS 1995). This was a report from the Standish Group in the US. The respondents to the Standish Group survey were IT executive managers. The sample included managers from large, medium and small companies across major industry sectors: banking, securities, manufacturing, retail, wholesale, heath care, insurance, services and local, state and federal organizations.

The total sample size was 365 respondents. Each on average had been involved in nearly twenty-five projects, and thus the group represented 8,380 applications of technology or projects. In addition, The Standish Group conducted focus groups and personal interviews to provide qualitative context for the survey results. The Standish Group research gave some shocking results:

- 31.1 per cent of projects were cancelled before they were completed.
- 52.7 per cent of projects cost over 189 per cent of their original estimates.

The real cost, however, was not only in the projects themselves but in the lost opportunities in investments elsewhere, which significantly increased the cost of failure.

Extrapolating their findings, and based on this research, The Standish Group estimated that in 1995:

- American companies and government agencies would spend $81 billion on cancelled software projects.
- Additionally, there would be another $59 billion for IT projects that will be completed, but will exceed their original time estimates.
- They estimated that almost 80,000 projects were cancelled in 1995.

The projects that The Standish group were involved in analyzing were not only the high-risk, complex projects, using the latest (untried and untested) software, hardware and communications technologies, but the study included projects that were simple and routine, e.g. an accounting package, order entry applications, booking applications. The Standish group estimated that:

- Only 6.2 per cent of software projects were completed on time and on budget.
- In larger organizations only 9 per cent of projects were completed on time and on budget.

Even when projects *are* completed, many are not the same as their original specification; they tend to be much simpler in practice. For example, projects completed by the largest American companies have only approximately 42 per cent of the originally proposed features and functions. In small organizations, 78.4 per cent of their software projects will get deployed with 74.2 per cent of their original features and functions.

Now, a decade or so later, what has been learned from these reports?

The OASIG 1995 and Chaos (1995) reports represented a significant landmark because, prior to that time, the dominant assumption was that the potential of information technology justified the investment in it! For example, it had been assumed that the technology had so much potential that all that was needed was some clever technicians to implement it and the benefits would accrue. OASIG (1995) and Chaos (1995), and the earlier research, contradicted this perspective, and there followed a widespread realization that things were not as easy as assumed! It seemed that a new research agenda was required. But these reports were followed by other research. For example, a few years later, a report published by Robbins-Gioia LLC (2001) made a study on the perception by enterprises of their implementation of an ERP application. In this work, there were 232 survey respondents, located in many organizations (e.g. government, communications, financial, utilities and health care). At the time, 36 per cent of the companies surveyed had, or were in the process of, implementing an ERP application. The conclusions were that:

- 51 per cent viewed their ERP implementation as unsuccessful; and
- 46 per cent of the participants did not feel their organization understood how to use the technology to improve the way they conduct business.

In the same year, the Conference Board Survey (2001) concluded that of the 117 companies that had implemented ERP applications:

- 40 per cent of the projects failed to achieve their business objectives within one year of going live.
- The companies that did achieve 'benefits' said that achievement took at least six months longer than expected.
- Implementation costs were found to average 25 per cent over budget.
- Support costs were underestimated for the year following implementation by an average of 20 per cent.

Since these findings, there has been no let-up in the reports of information technology failure or concerns for return on investment. For example, Glass (1998), Alt and Fleisch (2000), Dehning and Richardson (2001), Lemon *et al.* (2002), Barker and Frolick (2003), Littlejohns *et al.* (2003), Ash *et al.* (2004),Shoniregun (2004), Drummond (2005), Garg *et al.* (2005), Koppel *et al.* (2005), Lam and Chua (2005), Pan (2005), Scott *et al.* (2005), Wears *et al.* (2005), Chaudhry *et al.* (2006): the list of references could almost be endless.

The explanations and policy recommendations are also endless. Unfortunately, and sadly, the recommendations largely come in the form of *motherhood statements* dressed up as 'findings', e.g.

- 'the commitment of senior management can be a critical factor in securing a successful outcome'
- 'The end users must be identified before the project commences so that their needs are taken into account fully during design and development'
- 'The scale and complexity of projects is a major influence on whether they succeed or fail'
- 'the successful implementation of IT systems calls for imagination and well-conceived risk management, as well as sound project management methodologies'
- 'any lack of clarity, or debatable interpretation in a contract can lead to expensive misunderstandings that might have to be resolved in the courts'
- 'Training must address the needs of users, and of those operating and maintaining the system'
- 'In addition to planning and managing projects positively, Departments should therefore have contingency plans in place to maintain adequate levels of service in the event of project failures'
- 'It is essential that organizations learn lessons from the projects undertaken'

(Public Accounts Committee report 2000)

Such 'findings' and conclusions are quite typical, and generally simply state the obvious. They are rarely based on a sufficiently detailed analysis of the failings of the practice *as it relates to the discipline*. They do not provide insight into the shortfalls in knowledge and methods of practitioners,[2] nor do they analyze the context of failings or provide an in-depth account about what to do about the situation. They do not provide new methods or changes to existing procedures. They often have very little to say, and might be considered wasteful of resources and energy.

If our exploration were to make us wake up to the failings in the practice of information systems, we may want to make some further observations about the current state of the discipline, framed around some further simple questions. For instance, how is the knowledge of the discipline being used and applied? Or, how is new knowledge in the discipline created and is this creation process sufficient?

We might observe that, like most disciplines, information systems has its own university-based researchers, whose explicit purpose is to develop new knowledge, new innovations and new ideas, and to demonstrate their usability in practice. Although such words might express an explicitly stated purpose, we might question whether that is in fact what happens in practice. Is there more ambiguity in researchers' practice, in reality? For example, do academics in the discipline determine and define their research activities, with too little consideration or clarity about the human social need for the research in the first place? Do they construct and conduct their research with sufficient clarity of the needs of practice and of practitioners? Do they have sufficient understanding of practice to be able to make judgements about the relevance of their research? Are the processes of research sufficient, in order to bring both rigour and relevance to the new knowledge that is being created? Or even, are the choices about research questions and methods being made based on the publication needs of the researchers themselves, without consideration for the 'problem-solving' requirements of research activities of a practical discipline? Are research findings based on the experience of solving problems of practice or solving the more immediate researcher problems of enhancing their publication record?

Unfortunately, most of the studies on information systems failure, including those quoted above, are largely surveys of sorts. They have not really abstracted answers to some of the more important questions, such as the questions about how knowledge is produced in the discipline. They also have tended to miss the importance of:

- pinpointing the cause of failure with reasonable accuracy, and depth of analysis; and therefore
- what can be done, or what to do about the failure.

These two are completely interrelated: without identifying the cause, it is very difficult to be precise about what to do about it. In the literature, where there are some analyses on the fundamental causes, they are often focused on the project failing in some manner of speaking, using highly theoretical constructs (see, for example Sarker *et al.* 2006), or sometimes with an empirical orientation (e.g. Markus *et al.* 2000). However, most of such analyses are not searching for answers to the causes of failure rooted in the *discipline* of information systems: their focus is on the project failings, which of course can be itself rooted in (i) the knowledge and skills of the project managers, involved in some way in information systems practice, (ii) the limitations of the fundamental constructs and assumptions used by those involved in information systems practice, and (iii) the failings of research in the discipline, in order to help guide those in practice. In other words, whilst there is little doubt that there are lessons to be learned from the failure of information systems in practice, the inquiry is not far-reaching enough, because it fails to link the identified failings to the failings of the discipline.

Failings in the curricula

From these discussions, we might start to question how information systems is currently being defined and how it is being taught in our universities. Some of the problems in teaching an IS syllabus has been the subject of some concern:

> The MIS Class is in trouble, nationally. Students hate the course; faculty avoid teaching it. Evaluations are poor. And students gain little sense of the fascinating opportunities in IT/IS. Consequently, without the hype and hyperbole of the dot com frenzy, IS major enrolments have plummeted
>
> (Kroenke 2005)

Analyzing the failings in the syllabus may provide certain insights into the reasons for information systems failure in practice. It may also help to provide insight into the link between the failings in the syllabus and the way the discipline is defined, configured and portrayed. There is perhaps no better starting point than to evaluate the texts that are currently the market leaders, based on the assumption that if these texts are selling well, they reflect what is being taught in most universities. We will analyze some of the content and pedagogic assumptions of the following: Bocij *et al.* (1999, 2006); Gupta (2000); Turban *et al.* (2001); Alter (2002); Curtis and Cobham (2002); Jessup and Valicich (2003); Stair and Reynolds (2003); Gordon and Gordon (2004); Oz (2004); Chaffey and Wood (2005); Wainright *et al.* (2005); Laudon and Laudon (2006); Kroenke (2007); Rainer *et al.* (2007).

If each of these texts are brought out and sat on a desk alongside each other, the immediate observation is that they are all very substantial. They are huge encyclopedic-type books, full of facts, data and cases. As such, each one of them represents a huge resource for students; each of them has a huge learning potential in them.

The encyclopedic-type approach to these texts may also suggest that there is an ambiguity or a lack of precision about (i) what is required to be learned, and/or (ii) the learning process and the pedagogic principles that underpin that process. If this is a reasonable observation, then it might be easy to also assert that whilst these texts are sizable, they are not as precise and succinct *as a learning tool* as they could be. Naturally, questions arise regarding the pedagogic usefulness of such a huge collection of data, and whether it could be organized in a way that could enhance the learning, rather than be presented as such a huge collection. The Library of Congress is a great collection of data, but using it as a learning resource requires a specific type of human interaction with it!

Dinosaurs

On opening the content page of each of the texts, a modern-day practitioner might be tempted to conclude that they are rather like dinosaurs in more ways than their size. For example, they generally have a structure that details various aspects of hardware, software and the software development lifecycle. Each devotes sizable sections to the feasibility stages of software development, systems analysis, systems design, implementation and post-implementation review. There are sections on data communications, networks and e-business. Some have some small sections on systems, but largely these are at the front of the text, and largely misrepresent systems theory and its role in information systems (as will be discussed in Part II of this text). Much of the content of these texts remains important and can be considered 'as given' and necessary knowledge. However, some of it appears increasingly dated for contemporary practice in the field.

For instance, the heavy emphasis and usage of the software development life cycle (SDLC) in many of these texts might be considered somewhat surprising when reading about it in the early parts of the twenty-first century. In order to explore the relevance of the SDLC we might explore the reason why it was constructed in the first place. During the 1970s and the early part of the 1980s, it was realized that:

- Software development was much too expensive to 'get wrong', and thus a good feasibility analysis and a good analysis of the business processes were essential prior to the development of software.
- There was an 'application backlog'. There was more demand for new software than there were developers to develop it. Better techniques and processes were required in order to improve the productivity of developers.

Thus in the 1970s and 1980s, the software development life cycle was a useful construct in order to gain some control over the *software development* process. It was adapted and adopted in a variety of forms; it involves stages of development, and is found in most information technology methods (e.g. in 'Structured Systems Analysis and Design Methodology' or SSADM). The basic principles of a staged set of activities to depict the stages and steps that occur during development, implementation and, subsequently, until the application 'dies', is common in information systems texts. It has also been called other things, such as the 'waterfall', i.e. that one activity follows another, as if in a waterfall. In the 1970s and 1980s, since the application of computers was dependent on programmers and programming-type interfaces, both user organizations and specialist software developers found relevance in the software development life cycle in its various forms.

However, nowadays the technology has changed to such an extent that the software development life cycle is only *somewhat* relevant; it is no longer of central concern in the discipline of IS. For instance, generally, in most IT projects in user organizations (i.e. those that are not specialist developers), there is relatively little software development undertaken in its purist form. This is because software is bought from a software developer; thus 'software development' in user organizations tends to consist of minor modifications to the software application, normally at the operational control level (e.g. a range of software parameters and how it is run via configuration, batch, or Operational Control Languages etc.). This generally does not involve any alteration to source code of the application itself. Even in situations where some aspects of code are developed or modified it is usually done in fourth generation languages, or applications that make the 'programming' swift and simple. For example, in a recent project, a web-based collaborative software application was built from start to finish in three days, from the assembly of pre-coded objects. Thus it is the software developer who *may* be rather more concerned with the software development life cycle, not the end user organization. The SDLC is likely to become increasingly irrelevant as organizations outsource their application provision to hosting services. This of course is a generalization, and historically data processing departments of user organizations have developed their own software. But, generally speaking, during the last twenty years, the trend has been away from user organizations developing their own bespoke software. Rather, their concern is to *apply* existing (off-the-shelf) software in an attempt to improve business processes. Even in situations where they are developing their own bespoke applications, they are not concerned with developing software in third generation languages. Where user organizations have retained the software development function, they generally are required to use speedy software development methods, in which there is much more prototyping, building applications from pre-coded objects, and an iterative process akin to trial and error. Increasingly, they will be using a 'Universal Data Model' ('UDM') (see Silverston 1997, 2001a, 2001b). In practice, and increasingly in the future, user organizations will no longer consider the building of applications based on unique data models. They will be applying technology that uses them. The *application* of the UDM to help develop organizations has not yet been integrated into the best-selling information systems texts.

Modern organizations are much more dynamic than is suggested in the software development life cycle: changes in circumstances, situations, politics, priorities mean that development of software projects is equally ephemeral. Software updates, changes to the specifications, enhancements to software, use of rapid development tools, the UDM etc. means that these texts that continue to discuss development of software in terms of a rather limited set of stages are increasingly outdated. This is not to say that the software development life cycle is *completely* irrelevant to students. But it is no longer sufficient as a central plank in the teaching of information systems. It may be that it is taught and critiqued as a modern-day set of guiding principles. But a critique is sadly missing from the texts. There is no critique that is based on the trends, the modern and future contexts of technology deployment in organizations. There is no consideration of the trend towards hosted applications, and the software development life cycle is presented as a set of facts. Further, the texts that use the SDLC as a central structure for part, or even all their discourse, tend to give the impression that the activities in practice are planned, rational and ordered. Given the dynamics of organizations, this gives a very unrealistic view of practice, which is rather more complex and messy.

Organization versus technology

Since some of the texts on information systems tend to have a greater emphasis on the IT development methods and techniques, they might be considered slightly more 'methods'- focused than others. However, they limit this 'methods focus' to the area of IT development. Topic areas such as 'the software development life cycle', 'hardware', 'software', 'networks', 'security' etc., are undeniably *essential knowledge* in the field.

However, the information systems texts do not provide the wider organizational context in which this knowledge is expected to be used. Such topic areas are not contextualized in terms of:

- organizations or intervention in organizations, or
- the issues and complexities of change management, or
- the analysis of 'business processes',[3] or
- making sense of the human messiness of running complex projects, or
- dealing with the politics, power dimensions, social defences, or
- etc.

The texts certainly do not embed the issues of information systems in managerial methodologies for organizational change and improvement. They do not include any meaningful discussion about *organizational problem solving*, which is considered to be key to the purposeful objectives of information systems practice. It is a major omission, and is essential for information systems professionals in the twenty-first century. This lack of organizational problem solving means that the subject matter is presented as if the domain of information systems is simply a 'collection of facts' about technology, methods and techniques for the development of technology, rather than a field of practice underpinned by methodology that has the goal of changing and 'improving' organizations. The field of IS is presented as a 'diluted computer science' discipline. The texts do not provide a focus that is pragmatic, exciting, entrepreneurial and focused on problem solving, reflective of the skills that are required of our twenty-first century graduates. There is very little evidence that in any of the content these texts encourage critical reflexive thinking and focus on organizational process improvement as an end goal. They do not give the impression that they are enthusing our young practitioners and leaders of tomorrow.

Having made the points about the factual and encyclopaedic approach taken in these texts, and the technical development orientation, even some of the very important aspects of technology opportunities are dealt with in a rather scant way. For example, there is relatively little on the organizational opportunities of certain new technologies, e.g. ERP applications, the use in organizations of mobile or grid or GPRS (General Packet Radio Service) technologies etc. For example, discussing ERP as a general concept does very little except to introduce the terminology. There tends to be insufficient detail to enable students to engage in practice at a technical level, other than in a very general way, and since there is little in the way of modelling organizational processes, it is hard to see how they can be used in a constructive manner to evaluate how the technology can be integrated into those processes. There is relatively weak introduction to project management and, where this is included, discussions centre round explanations of Program Evaluation and Review Technique (PERT) diagrams, Gantt charts or critical path analysis (CPA). They do little to help student to apply such techniques, nor is there much in the way of critique of such techniques to enable students to appreciate the limitations of the techniques in the context of the complexities involved in real organizations, e.g. managing projects in complex human situations, particularly where there is diversity in goals and purpose. Project management is treated as a rational, technical exercise, which involves the application of techniques, but not treated as a problematic social process.

Ontology and pedagogy

The market-leading texts in information systems have included 'e-business'; internet business models generally feature highly. There are normally a number of typical business models with examples. Useful as this is, there remain gaps in the way this knowledge is used in practice. For example, how does a student go about 'translating' the abstract concept into practical action: (i) to consider the pros and cons, and the political contexts of decision making in practice, and (ii) translating these rather strategic questions into practical projects and actions? A description of internet business models is of course only a start.

This highlights an ontological ambiguity in the texts. Internet business models and other models are treated in the texts 'as the real world', but not as a way of learning and considering the alternative courses of action about the real world organizations. This is in part symptomatic of the way the discipline is presented to students.

This is not something that is common in the information systems domain alone. For instance, compare two history books: the first written as a personal account by somebody who was there at a moment in time, who suffered the everyday problems of the period; the second may talk of the same events, but be written by an observer of the historical 'facts'. This latter type of book is often a cold, rational and analytical discussion. The former will typically include much more in the way of emotional accounts of events, frustrations, anxieties, feelings. The same is true of information systems texts. They tend to be written in the style of the second. They are written in a highly 'objective' style, and it perhaps indicates that the writers generally assume a 'logical-empiricist' ontological position (see Radnitzsky 1970). As such, the 'facts' are treated as being independent of the observer (the observer is the writer or the reader of the text in this case). The implication of this is that these texts make better reference books than they do 'a guide to practice' or even 'a good read', or 'a good education' because there is no process by which the objective facts are in some way internalized and critiqued in a subjective manner, i.e. an account of the use of the 'facts' in a given context. Thus, at best, they may be recounted in an examination, but cannot be internalized in such a way that it can guide future actions in practice. This is of course not necessarily always and altogether a 'bad thing', but it does have some important implications, e.g.:

(i) They need quite a lot of supplementary work done when using these texts, and quite a substantial amount of 'softening' and 'explanation' and 'relating it to practice using examples'.

(ii) There is a significant amount of work required on the part of the student in terms of applying the concepts, facts and knowledge in guiding their own actions in practice.

(iii) There needs to be group work that is sufficiently challenging in order to relate the dry concepts, facts and knowledge and make them become 'useful', 'applicable', 'practical' etc.

In some ways, there is a danger that the curricula designs in information systems are a bit like learning to play the violin as a set of conceptual or theoretical constructs, but without the presence of a violin!

The texts have some excellent mini-case examples, and some very useful questions and exercises. Unfortunately, most of the case studies tend to be rather sanitized views, and do not reveal the messiness, complexities and political context in which the technology operates. There is no sense of the serendipity that characterizes human organizations in practice. For example, the case studies (e.g. American Airlines, Amazon etc), are presented in such a way that they give the impression that the successes of the cases were planned, the technology applied, the strategic advantage gained etc., but without the complex, messy politics, other project failings, the difficulties in changing the methods of work, the associated human resource issues, dealing with unionized workforces, ethical concerns etc. The case studies appear as if they are justifying the use of technology, rather than analyzing the practice of organizational change that is associated with the technology. They present the case studies as if the organizations concerned are rational and the people in them are subservient to the 'rationality' of the implementation of the technology. Further in the texts, the cases seem to suggest that the development of information technology is an end objective. Yet, perhaps better would be to consider the improvement of organizational processes (or organizational 'systems') as the end objective, where the technology is a facilitator. The technology is not a goal, as it were. The texts might be starting in the wrong place. They start with technology, not with human organizations. They start with tasks such as 'improving information', but ignore the detail of the human organizational process that requires 'improved information'.

In most of these texts, there are 'learning objectives' inserted at the beginning of each chapter, or sometimes 'after reading this chapter, you will be able to answer the following questions'. Sometimes these feel like they have been inserted as an after-thought, rather than having driven the writing of the chapter; sometimes also they are not learning outcomes at all. For instance, is 'Discuss the use of CASE tools' a learning objective, or simply a content point? Since in most of these texts there are a great many questions being asked, it is rather unrealistic to expect students to undertake all of the questions and exercises. Perhaps more targeted questions may help achieve the learning objectives. Without wishing to be overly pedantic, there may be room for greater precision about how the texts are to be used in a process of learning, the characteristics and assumptions of a learning process, and the role of the specific learning activities in achieving the objectives. The learning objectives appear to have been imposed on an encyclopedia.

Rigour

Generally the texts lack a focus on the functions of organization, e.g. manufacturing, sales and marketing, logistics, accounting and finance. Where they do appear in the texts, generally the organizational modelling is too weak, and it becomes a rather bland discussion about the typical actions and objectives of each of the core functions. The core functions are taken 'as given' rather than being considered to be problematic, changeable, complex, context-specific etc. Indeed, because the functions are 'as given', there is very little done to encourage students to consider that they should be, or will need to be, or the requirement of, 'making inquiry into them'. Yet, no one organization is the same as another; no operations section will be the same as another.

All these books introduce information systems by defining certain things. For instance, they generally define 'data', 'information', 'systems', and 'information systems'. There is a slightly more thorough set of definitions in some, partly by virtue of the fact that they avoid discussing 'information systems' before the definitions whereas, in others, the definitions are less clear, and are undertaken as a way of defining the functions of information systems. There are some obvious observations about this:

- None of these texts discuss 'systems theory' thoroughly and in an integrated way. This is surprising in a sense because these texts are concerned with organization, and systems theory is unique in its contribution in helping to inquire into organizational processes (and hence the contribution that information technology can make to those processes). However, in the texts, 'systems theory' may be introduced, or alluded to, but little more. It is as if 'systems' has been lost in the term 'information systems'! Yet, historically systems theory has had an important role in information systems, and may be considered by some to be a core intellectual foundation for information systems.
- In the texts, the word 'systems' is often used to mean 'information and communications technology applications'. Yet, 'systems' has a particular meaning in both scientific terms and with reference to organizational systems, and the texts use 'systems' without reference to this wider meaning. In a sense, the word is muddied and used in a rather confusing way. For example, the texts may use the term 'systems development', which actually means 'IT application development'; the 'software development life cycle' is sometimes referred to as the 'systems development life cycle', but without precision about or reference to the meaning of 'systems' (see also Jayaratna 1994).
- Some of the texts introduce the notion of knowledge to help explain the difference between data and information. This gives a very limited view of knowledge because what they call 'knowledge' is simply 'human meaning attachment to data'. There is no discourse on the process of learning and engaging with data, nor is there any discussion on the epistemological issues involved in knowledge construction.
- The texts are not clear on the difference between 'information technology' and 'information systems' other than suggesting that the former is focused on hardware and software. For example, they tend to be unclear on the *functions* of information systems, on the discipline of information systems and where the technology fits within these.

Whilst this critique is based on a set of introductory texts, and as such has its limitations, perhaps, nonetheless, is there room for considering information systems to be a discipline, and an area of practice, which is focused on policy development, organizational improvement and organizational change, whilst acknowledging the complexity and the political diversity of organizational situations and the role technology plays within it? Perhaps this is a vision that considers technology to be the enabler of improved organizational processes and practices, not the end-goal? This is a vision that encourages the internalization of knowledge because it is deeply integrated with, and predicated on, action and *organizational problem solving*.

Failings in research processes

In addition to failings in the practice of information systems and failings in the teaching of information systems, it is also possible to consider certain failings in the research processes in the discipline (see also Hirschheim and Klein 2003). In recent years there has been a significant amount of interest, focus, effort and development on the assessment of research output and quality in the university sector. The desire to demonstrate greater accountability for public expenditure has driven governments to attempt to assess research output and quality of the universities e.g. the Research Assessment Exercise ('RAE') in the UK. As a result, the output and quality pressures are applied on university departments and individuals. Assessments are used as indicators of research productivity and quality for funding purposes, e.g. 'three/four star status etc.' in the UK university sector. The pressures for accountability, potential for grant income and the need to achieve or maintain reputation have driven universities to develop internal policies and procedures aimed at increasing research income and output. In addition to this, within the academic communities, there are also political pressures on favoured ideological positions that determine the construction and constitution of 'valid' knowledge; this is not just a question of epistemology. It has social impacts on research communities. For example, it can determine what papers will be accepted or rejected, or who will be accepted into key positions, e.g. referee and editorial positions. As such, it is the social process that can help to influence decisions about the constitution of 'good science' or 'bad science' in a given discipline. Since research output is measured in terms of journal and refereed conference publications, and student completion of research degrees, there is considerable pressure on maximizing these outcomes, and also predicting the changes that may or may not be being considered by those undertaking the evaluations (e.g. RAE panels), which are sometimes assumed to ensure quality and intellectual contribution to the fields of knowledge. However, the new contextual pressures on individuals, departments and institutions have resulted in evaluation activities that sometimes lead to conclusions about 'successes' in terms of the number of publications, student completions, amount of grant income and tenure achievements, but they cannot measure the quality of the research processes or of their output, both of which are essential for the future of a given discipline (including information systems). The challenging task of ensuring research quality that has to be performed by *researchers themselves*, acting in different roles such as:

- members of research grant review panels
- members of grant committees
- referees on behalf of journals and conferences
- examiners of doctoral theses etc.

This has some important implications. For instance, it means that the judgement of 'quality' is largely determined by the social processes that are involved in undertaking these activities. Quality is not in the number of publications nor where they are published, as is sometimes assumed. Unfortunately, the social processes of these activities are not subjected to evaluation, but it is easy to see why activities such as these, over a period of time, can reflect a rather homogenized set of social values and beliefs. In these new contexts, it would be rare indeed, for instance, for a refereed journal to value the inputs of a practitioner-based referee, rather than an academic. There is a social process that determines who is 'in' and who is 'out', what is 'good' and what is 'bad', based on a set of implicit or explicit beliefs about the objectives of the process and assumptions about the way it is judged. Central to this is a belief in the constitution of the objectives of research activities.

Objectives

It is reasonable to assume that central to any research effort is a desire to:

(A) discover new knowledge about existing phenomena
(B) verify, validate or falsify known knowledge (via, for instance, the process of repeatability, refutation and validation) and/or
(C) discover new knowledge, unknown phenomena and new concepts, models, theory, methods, techniques and methodology by explorative studies.

These are the general aims of academic research (sometimes explicit and stated) and thus they can provide a certain insight and guidance for the development of any inquiring process, whether it involves explicit 'intervention' (e.g. action research, product development, prototype experiments), or attempts to avoid 'intervention' (e.g. surveys, interviews, observation) or simply discourses (critical debate, theoretical analysis). That is not to say that these are the *purposeful goals of researchers in practice* because there may be other, hidden purposeful goals within the process of research. Rather, these are the explicit and stated goals of a *process* of research and inquiry in academic contexts. In practice, practitioners have their own requirements for inquiry. For example, in information systems practice the objective is to change organizational processes. Thus the *primary goal* might be considered to be to:

(D) develop an inquiring process, in order to justify action to 'improve' an organizational situation.

The inquiry in (D) is not the same as the inquiry that would be generated in meeting the objectives of (A), (B) and (C). There are of course certain ideas about how they might be combined. For example, there has been much recent interest in 'mode 2' research, cited in the management literature. If research was considered *only* the inquiry as in (D) then it would probably be accused of being nothing but consultancy. Perhaps in a practical discipline, there is room to integrate them? For example, (A), (B) and (C) might be concerned with evaluating the nature, operationalization, effectiveness and outcomes of the inquiry undertaken in (D).

For example, if a particular type of technology was to be applied in a particular way, it would involve an inquiry into the potential it may make to improve an organizational process, a set of activities, tasks, actions etc. It would involve the inquiry into those processes, activities and tasks, and the skills and knowledge that are required for their undertaking; it may involve inquiry into the way the tasks and activities are coordinated, and the way they are measured, monitored and controlled. It may involve the inquiry into how processes, activities, tasks can 'add value' in realizing certain humanly constructed objectives; it involves inquiring into the investments, risks, opportunity costs; it involves inquiry into the technical architectures, the information technologies, their architectures, the suppliers, the various platforms on which they might operate; it involves inquiry into the most appropriate project methods and structures in order to achieve the goals of effective application of the technologies in complex projects; it involves inquiry into how best to control the project, the skills involved, the constitution of teams, roles, responsibilities. It is an inquiry that involves consideration of both intended and unintended outcomes in practice etc. These types of areas inquiry are more than just (D). Although quite abstract, it is reasonable that these areas of inquiry can combine (D) with objectives (A), (B) and (C), and is appropriate for a practical area of inquiry and research.

It is reasonable to take from this discussion that 'research' objectives (A), (B) and (C) and the 'practice' objective, (D), both require inquiry. The objectives may be different, but inquiry activity is required to be designed and actioned, and there are both 'good' and 'bad' inquiring activities underpinned by the study of knowledge construction (epistemology) in both contexts, and in undertaking the different inquiring objectives. In a practical domain such as information systems, it is not unreasonable to consider that in undertaking (D), then (A), (B) and (C) might be a potential outcome. That is to say, the generalizable knowledge of the discipline can be constructed from the engagement with, and from the undertaking of, problem solving in practice. This assumes that the theoretical constructs can be explored *during the process of undertaking practice*. In this case, research findings are abstracted from the activities of practice. Research is more likely to be focused on the efficacy of the inquiring activities undertaken in the process of practice, and how it does or does not inform action.

This is not necessarily a view shared by academics engaged in the social processes, who are members of research grant review panels, members of grant committees, referees on behalf of journals and conferences, and as examiners of doctoral theses etc. It is much more likely that their social world sees the objectives as (A), (B) and (C), where insights into (D) may or may not occur, but whether it does or not, is fairly irrelevant. Is this an adequate situation in a practical discipline such as information systems? Is it an adequate situation in other, related disciplines (e.g. management)? If academics in the discipline of information systems are not engaged in practice, and their objectives are narrowly focused on (A), (B) and (C), and are not driven from (D), then the process of research will have particular characteristics imbued into it, which may not be helpful to practice. This may be helpful to explain the current chasm between 'theory' and 'practice' in the domain of information systems, and the concerns that research in the field remains rigorous but irrelevant (see, for example Benbasat and Zmud 1999).

Paradigms

Given the relative ease of identifying certain forms of words to express the common desires of all researchers in any research activity, and in any discipline, as expressed in (A), (B) and (C), it is remarkable how much variance there can be in the processes in practice. Perhaps the most obvious explanation is in the rather uncertain nature of the constitution of knowledge itself (see, for example Polanyi 1961, 1964), and the complexities that are associated with its generation (i.e. 'research processes', 'epistemology'). It seems that the easily stated desires of a research process, and the complexity, messiness and uncertainty about the nature of one of its outputs (that of 'knowledge'), provide a situation in which there is significant variation and ambiguity in the undertaking of the activity itself. Whilst there are not many arguments as to what constitute knowledge in the inquiring activities involved in practice ((D)), in the academic world, researchers have come to rely on particular philosophical traditions and their paradigms as the basis for deciding on the validity and the justification of knowledge and the processes responsible for its generation.

One of the most dominant paradigms and traditions is that of 'positivism', or 'positivistic science' (Comte 1851). Comte took the principles of 'natural sciences' and applied them to social contexts; generally speaking, the process of inquiry, using positivist principles, is largely applying the principles of 'deductive' scientific methods – establishing hypothesis and conducting experiments involving controlled and uncontrolled variables. This method can then be used to identify the characteristics or behaviour and cause and effect patterns of the phenomena under study to prove or disprove the hypothesis. In positivist 'science' the person doing the experiment (researcher) is normally considered to be disconnected from the ultimate findings (see also Kolakowski 1972). Although in most cases the scientists are engaged in experiments, the knowledge generated of the phenomena must be independent of the observer (the 'scientist') in order to be considered to be valid knowledge. Once the findings are established they are offered to the scientific community for repeatability and refutation. In 'positive' inquiry, it is the repeatability of the experiment and the ability of the findings to withstand refutation that gives the knowledge validity within a given scientific community. Mathematics is often used as a way of expressing this validity of the process of research (i.e. mathematical proof) to arrive at the conclusions in the results.

In an alternative research paradigm, there are different assumptions about the construction of knowledge, and these influence and affect the processes in practice. For example, in social research the need is to investigate and understand research processes in terms of the 'interpreted constructions' of (i) the researchers themselves, and (ii) others' perceptions of the phenomena that is the subject of research activities (see, for example, Schutz 1962, 1964, 1966; Pettit 1969; Roche 1973; Gorman, 1977; Luckman 1978). In social research, both the process of research and its findings may be expressed in terms of the historical, linguistic, cultural constructs that can be used by the subjects of the research (participants), and the researcher and their community (see Denzin and Lincoln 1994).

For readers who are familiar with the 'schools of meta-science', it will be obvious that the above discussion is a generalization, and there are of course a number of derivations and variations in 'positivist' and social research, in terms of both the logic used (e.g. deductive, inductive) and in the conduct of various activities (stages, steps etc.) during the process of research (far better would be to use Radnitzky 1970).

In recent years, possibly the most commonly cited 'paradigms' have been based around the work of Burrell and Morgan (1979) in which research types are 'grouped' based on assumptions made about the nature of the world, and the knowledge construction process. This grouping commonly uses the labels 'positivist' or 'interpretative' or 'critical' but the central underpinning arguments that divide the communities have remained the same for some time. For instance, in the natural sciences, the validity of knowledge is established by the consistent behaviour of the objects in experiments independent of the scientist engaged in the findings, while in social sciences the observer/experimenter is central to the establishment of knowledge (see, for example, Burrell and Morgan 1979; Hassard 1990; Willmott, 1990, 1993a, 1993b; Jackson and Carter 1991, 1993; Guba and Lincoln 1994; Johnson and Duberley 2000). There are of course other variations of the themes, e.g. critical theory, reflexivity and postmodernism (see, for example, Power and Laughlin 1992; Hassard 1994; Lash 1994; Alvesson and Wilmott 1996; Alvesson and Deetz 2000; Alversson and Skoldberg 2000), many of which are based around particular 'schools' of thought derived from particularly influential thinkers (e.g. Garfinkel 1967; Glaser and Strauss 1967; Habermas 1972, 1974; Strauss and Corbin 1990). It is a situation where the paradigms are also used to assess the validity of the findings (see, for example, Hopper and Powell 1985; Chua, 1986; Gowler and Legge 1986; Hassard 1991), and thus those entrusted with evaluating research (e.g. examiners, referees and review panel members) may themselves subscribe to a particular research 'paradigm' and determine the status of future researchers and influence the direction of the discipline (e.g. see Hirschheim 1985; Hirschheim and Klein 1989; Chen and Hirschheim 2004). Suffice to say for our discussions, 'science' is not absolute, and there are various 'schools' or 'paradigms' that can help to assess the validity and truth of knowledge, within a given 'scientific' community. As such, the 'natural' and 'social' sciences have established positions on the nature of knowledge and drawn certain demarcation lines and rules by which the findings are established and recognized as contributions to knowledge.

Since information systems is a relatively new area of study and of research, it has not yet established a satisfactory dominant 'paradigm' to underpin its science, which guides the researcher in their research practice (see also Baskerville and Myers 2002; Livari *et al.* 2004). For example, and generally speaking, researchers in information systems will often have a background in computer science, and thus will bring with them their dominant paradigm from their home discipline. Since computer science is based on the long traditions of the natural sciences (e.g. engineering, computation, mathematics), it tends to be dominated by 'positivistic' principles. As such, researchers who come into the field of information systems will naturally apply their 'natural science'-based inquiring activities in their research, oriented to the objectives of (A), (B) and (C).

Researchers from other disciplines will also bring their own paradigmatic assumptions from their 'home' discipline. From this it is easily concluded that the process of research practice is defined by the characteristics of the paradigm from which the researcher comes. Today we find ourselves in a situation where the methods, processes and activities of information systems researchers will commonly be located in, or associated with, a set of 'acceptable' paradigms, and research will be judged as valid or invalid where the criteria of judgement is also based on the same paradigm set (e.g. 'positivist', 'interpretive', 'critical', 'postmodern'). In itself, it may not be perceived to be problematic because it can bring richness and diversity to research. The academic argument can indeed enrich the field of practice. But there are also potential dangers in this situation. For example:

- It might promote a situation where social 'cliques' emerge who undertake research and undertake the evaluation of it for each other, but are unwilling (or unable) to engage in the possibilities of moving outside the comforts of a particular paradigm.

- There is significant disjointedness in research in practice where, for example, an ontological or epistemological 'position' (and thus to a large extent a 'method') is sometimes naively assumed *before* the research questions are formulated (!).
- It could be a situation where researchers can sometimes be focused on conforming to the expected ontological and epistemological issues of their chosen paradigm, stance, position or clique, but lose sight of certain core elements of process that would be expected of any research in practice.
- It might be that researchers and evaluators of research (assessors, examiners, referees), are unable to critique their own 'paradigm' from a deep understanding of the alternatives, and thereby are unable to provide a rationale for undertaking a particular piece of research in practice in a given paradigm.

In attempting to help novice researchers to consider a range of alternative 'positions' involving epistemological and ontological choices, there has been considerable attention and interest in publications that can help outline such choices (see for instance Easterby-Smith *et al.* 1991; Gill and Johnson 1991; Blaikie 1993; Hussey and Hussey 1997; Saunders *et al.* 1997; Johnson and Dubberley 2000). These present generic epistemological abstractions that transcend any single discipline (e.g. Blaikie 1993 discusses six classical philosophical positions and four reasoning strategies). Such discussion can assist potential researchers to structure their thinking to the tasks they have to follow. However, the danger remains that the researcher may assume that these humanly constructed abstractions are mutually exclusive (i.e. that a researcher, or a particular research process, must belong to one paradigm or another, or is unable to move between them). Further, these texts quite rightly highlight the differences between the ontological or epistemological 'positions' but again these human constructions might be interpreted as 'reality', rather than an heuristic to help refine the research process in the discovery of new knowledge in practice. Possibly much more problematic, though, is the 'as-given' assumptions in these texts that such inquiry is to fulfil the objectives of (A), (B) and (C), but not (D)! It is as if (i) inquiry for the objective (D) does not need to consider its own epistemological assumptions, and that epistemology is only for 'researchers', and (ii) there is no consideration of a research process that puts (D) first, with the requirement of simultaneously aiming towards the objectives (A), (B) and (C).

Within the disciplines themselves, there is wide disagreement and anxiety about the nature of research activities, and the role of the paradigms (see, for example, the 'incommensurability' debate in Reed 1985; Willmott 1990, 1993a, 1993b; Jackson and Carter 1991, 1993). Further, recent discussions on the nature of 'mode 2' research within the field of management (see, for example, Gopinath and Hoffman 1995; Tranfield and Starkey 1998; Fujigaki and Leydesdorff 2000; March 2000; Reed 2000; Abrahamson and Eisenman 2001; Hodgkinson 2001; Starkey and Madan 2001), and the discussions within the information systems discipline about the tensions of balancing 'relevance' and 'rigour' (see, for example, Benbasat and Zmud 1999, Davenport and Markus 1999, Lyytinen 1999). These suggest that academics are anxious about the nature of research, the role it plays in their discipline, the trends in the research practices, and in particular the lack of consensus about certain process issues (see also Wasser 1990; Geisler 1995; Van Aken 2001; Bolton and Stolcis 2003; Ylijoki 2003). It can also be a very confusing situation for the novice researcher, in particular, where the uncertainties can result as tightly defining criteria of the constitution of 'quality' of research output, in preference to focusing on the research processes. For instance Altheide and Johnson (1994: 489) offer criteria for judging ethnographic research, which is different to that of Hammersley (1992: 64), both of which are tightly focused on the research output (e.g. the thesis), rather than process (i.e. criteria applied to the output is assumed to indicate an appropriate process, rather than to think carefully about both process and output).

Rethinking

Many of the concerns about research practice in practical disciplines such as information systems can be rooted in the ambiguities and disagreements about the nature of knowledge, and it might be that some of the confusion arises from a rather narrowly focused set of ontological and epistemological assumptions driving the designs of research and the actions of the researcher in practice. These issues need rethinking. Rather than the process being designed in a 'paradigm', the epistemological and ontological assumptions that are being made can be explored during the process (i.e. to avoid being 'locked into' a paradigm). Thus the process and its characteristics, and the concepts and constructs used in guiding the thinking about the process, are important considerations *during the process*. This implies that researchers in the field of information systems must be able to critique their own paradigm, and justify the rationale for their choices (paradigmatic, ontological, methodological etc.). Most of all, they must be able to clarify their own objectives (A), (B), (C) and (D), the order of priority of the objectives, and how they are integrated as detailed above.

Researchers in information systems require a much clearer definition of their own use of research paradigms in fulfilling all objectives of knowledge development (A), (B), (C) and (D). Indeed, it may be considered that it is humanly possible to integrate (D) with (A), (B) and (C). Researchers of the discipline *are required to* consider alternative ways of undertaking research: it is unsustainable in the discipline of information systems that researchers can continue to be 'locked into' the paradigms of their home discipline. Information systems is required to develop a much greater sense of its own identity, which can construct its own paradigm of research, which integrates (D) with (A), (B) and (C). Indeed, it is unsustainable that research can be undertaken with very little recourse to action in information systems practice – there must be room for a justifiable research method, and an underpinning 'paradigm' that is both rigorous and relevant, which can integrate practice into the process of inquiry, for practice, and also make generalizable abstractions.

Part II

Principles of organizational problem solving

How can practitioners 'prepare their thinking' for practice, given the ambivalences that characterize the discipline? In this part we will explore some of the most fundamental ontological and methodological ideas that may help to provide an intellectual basis for the future practice of information systems. This is based on the argument that the discipline is required to incorporate organizational problem-solving methods and principles. It is also based on the assumption that the *raison d'être* of information systems as a field of practice, and as a discipline, is to attempt to 'improve' organizations in some way. Thus current methods and knowledge in information systems will be integrated into organization development methods.

This part outlines some of the essential theoretical characteristics of 'organizational problem solving'. Information systems practitioners might be able to see that there are some rather distinct differences between 'engineering' technology applications and 'engineering' in organizations! Indeed, in the field of practice, and in the discipline, the former must be integrated into the latter because, as discussed in Chapters 1 and 2, information systems is at the cusp of both. The integration of both is essential if the discipline is to become interdisciplinary in nature (i.e. it integrates knowledge from other disciplines together, around some core principles).

In this part, we will outline some of the most basic principles and assumptions of the process, in preparation for the discussion on the specifics of inquiry to be discussed in Part III, and the operationalization of them in the case material in Part IV.

3 Ontology

Abstract

It seems reasonable to assume that those undertaking the role of 'information systems practitioner' will have prepared their thinking processes sufficiently. But how could they, given the current ambivalence and ambiguity about what constitutes 'information systems practice' as discussed in the previous chapters? This chapter concerns itself with some of the most fundamental challenges in undertaking information systems practice.

Introduction

What constitutes suitable 'preparation' for undertaking an 'information systems role' might be considered to be one of the most important and key challenges to the discipline of information systems. It is a challenge to designers of degree programmes, courses of study, courseware, books and papers. Perhaps, more importantly, it is a key challenge to those who are undertaking or preparing themselves for a role within the field of practice. It might be considered to be a particularly difficult challenge because, unless we have knowledge about the nature of information systems work in practice, it is not possible to define the attributes necessary for the undertaking of such work, and the preparations that are necessary.

If engagement in the question about 'how best to prepare' is *not* undertaken, it would be easy for others to argue that there is some sort of abrogation of a certain responsibility for learning about how to manage, develop and improve the thinking. Sometimes, practitioners find it difficult to know how to prepare. This is perhaps hardly surprising given the current ambiguity in the *discipline*, as discussed in Part I of this book. For instance:

- There is ambivalence in the core purpose of the discipline; it is torn between technology development and organization development.
- There is very little consensus about the nature of information systems practice (e.g. what it means in everyday terms).
- The impact that reference disciplines have, which sometimes can serve to undermine the integration into the core subject knowledge required for information systems practice.

As a consequence, 'abrogation' is something that is common in practice. Questions might be raised about the degree to which we (i.e. the human race) are happy to live with poor preparation, and the consequent mistakes being made, and organizations that are underperforming as a result. As outlined in Part I, the ambiguity about the nature of the discipline, its practice and research, results in a situation where those who undertake the task commonly feel that they lack guidance and/or that the guidance given is considered to be irrelevant. This is sometimes expressed as a difference in 'theory' and 'practice'.

In this chapter we will explore some of the most fundamental aspects of thinking upon which an integrative discipline must be based.

Muddles

If we were to think about the nature of the contexts in which information systems work is practised (i.e. in organizations), it would probably be safe to assume that normally these contexts are rather messy, complex or muddly. That is to say, information systems work requires those who are undertaking it to consider many interconnected issues and elements in 'problematic situations'. For example, IS work often involves dealing with people and their behaviour, different interest groups, the nature and structure of processes, hidden goals and control structures, complexity in roles, perspectives, power structures etc. Information systems practitioners need to deal with (often complex) organizational processes, simultaneously considering strategic issues, investment priorities and managing complex projects, as well as dealing with operational issues and changes in organizational processes. IS work involves dealing with situations that are characterized by a multiplicity of interwoven issues (people, tasks, processes, technologies, power groupings, explicit and implicit controls and performance indicators, and global market changes, involving many different perspectives and interests, crossing functional boundaries ('marketing', 'finance', 'human resources' etc)). It would be foolish to assert that *all* situations are characterized as complex, but it is also reasonable that, since information systems is practised in human organizations, it is a useful starting point to assume a certain level of messiness and complexity.

If human organizations were not messy, complex or muddly, then it is probable that information systems work could itself be automated, with fairly rigid or algorithmic activities ('if x condition, then do y' etc.). If organizations were simple and predictable, then simple rather mechanical formulae or methods could be applied. For example, in information systems practice there have been technologically driven 'solutions' applied into human contexts with a lack of understanding or knowledge of the specific characteristics of a given situation. Typically, for example, there is an assumption about the desirability of technology, or of automation, or assumptions about the abilities of people to adapt to new ways of working (see also Ashby 1973; Flood and Carson 1993). Sometimes those involved in information systems work try to simplify their challenge by appropriate or inappropriate use of a formulaic interpretation of their role (e.g. by reference to prescriptive methods (see Wastell 1996)) or attempting to find generic 'solutions' with little or no reference to the 'problems' (e.g. selling technological 'solutions'). It seems that in the practice of information systems, the context, and its complexity, is sometimes (conveniently) ignored.

If organizational problems were not messy, complex or muddly, the 'problems' would be relatively easily solved, and there may be more probability of the successful use of the application of mechanistic thinking (as in a simple technology 'solution' derived from thinking about organizations as machines of some sort). However, in many situations, it seems fair to assert that this would be completely inappropriate. It seems that a mechanical or prescriptive set of actions is rather an anathema to the complex realities in which IS is practised. Yet sometimes it appears that this is precisely the starting point of much of the attempts at preparing for practice, because of the current orientation of the discipline and/or the IT sector. (Figure 3.1).

Perhaps the preparation for practice in information systems should not start from the 'prescriptive and mechanical' (left hand side of Figure 3.1), but the muddly and complex world of organizations (right-hand side of Figure 3.1). That is to say, the starting point should be the 'making sense of' the messy realities, and methods, activities and processes (see Figure 3.2).

Figure 3.2 depicts the relationship between the complexity inherent in organizations and the thinking about the complexity. This is not the traditional starting point for (i)

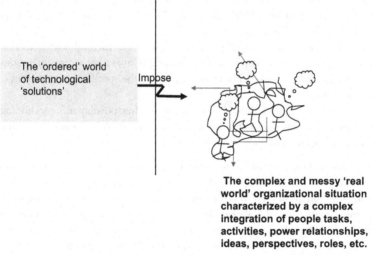

The complex and messy 'real world' organizational situation characterized by a complex integration of people tasks, activities, power relationships, ideas, perspectives, roles, etc.

Figure 3.1 Preparation for practice?

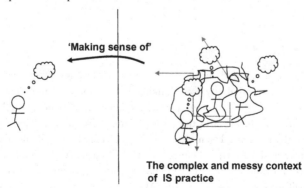

The complex and messy context of IS practice

Figure 3.2 'Making sense of'

IS practice, nor (ii) the starting point for the design of curricula activities, nor (iii) the design of typical research in IS. As a consequence, there is sometimes a tendency to oversimplify or ignore the complex, and thus it is not too difficult to identify instances in practice where inappropriate thinking for the problematic situation has precipitated changes that are equally inappropriate (e.g. in attempts to 'mechanize' complex human situations, or organizational processes, using computers).

If an organizational situation can be characterized by messiness, complexity or messiness, then the *process of* making sense of (i.e. thinking about) a given organizational situation is equally problematic (see also Weick 2001). This is because it involves at least a number of interrelated tasks. For instance, it may involve:

* analysis of the interconnectivity of a situation (e.g. human behaviour, tasks, processes, attitudes, power dimensions, social structure, communications, control, assumed goals etc.)
* observation and interpretation of humans' viewpoints, behaviours, perceptions etc.
* abstracting and clarifying during the process of analysis, observation and interpretation of a given organizational situation, and thus seeking suitable recognizable 'patterns' in that situation, which are sufficient to help gain insights without oversimplification
* evaluating how other cases, experiences, methods, methodologies, techniques, frameworks etc. might help in developing insight into either a 'current' or 'desired' organizational situation, without losing sight of the specific characteristics of the specific situation
* seeking suitable intervention of one kind or another, possibly using technology (or otherwise) to bring about changes in one or more areas whilst acknowledging the particular contextual complexities.

Since any of these activities involve 'thinking about' the contextual complexities of a given situation, it therefore follows that it is the 'thinking about' which is as much in question as the situation itself. It is the 'thinking about' that is required to be subjected to critique, because it is this that defines the 'problem situation' in the mind of the IS practitioner (the 'observer' of the problematic organizational situation). In other words, anyone describing a 'problematic situation' in an organization is at the same time expressing their 'mental construction' of it (see also Checkland 1981; Jayaratna 1994).

'Making sense of'

Bateson (1948) demonstrated certain lessons in 'muddles', including the notion that humans have limited capability for 'thinking of' complex or muddled states. For instance, it is relatively easy to demonstrate that there are far more 'muddled states' than 'recognizable patterns', and that the 'making sense of' is related to the 'lived experience' of the observer. For instance, if we select six letters of the alphabet and write them on each side of separate pieces of card, we can throw them into the air so that they land in a random fashion. On landing they will form a pattern. Throwing again, they will form a different pattern. After many throws (n throws), they might just land in a formation that is recognizable as a word, or a potential word. Notice that it is the human application of their cognitive process that determines a level of 'recognition' of patterns. After many more throws, (n*n) the cards might just land in such a way that there is immediate meaning attached to the pattern and there is a perceived recognizable 'pattern' to them (see Figure 3.3).

Sometimes 'making sense of' is easy and immediate because a pattern will be recognizable instantly. Other times it is necessary to search hard to find a recognizable pattern. If an observer were given an incentive of a cash prize every time a 'recognizable pattern' was identified, there is a strong likelihood that the constitution of 'pattern' might be manipulated to maximize the possibilities of 'pattern finding' and 'making sense of'.[1]

Using the example of six cards, it is easy to demonstrate that:

- there are many more 'muddled states' in the six cards than 'un-muddled' states
- one human can attach a meaning that another will miss, and this depends on their own background, experience, education and cognitions etc. For example, in the Polish language, 'apteka' is a chemists shop
- it is also possible to 'find a pattern' that is not immediately obvious
- humans have the capability to alter the rules (redefine what constitutes a 'pattern') to maximize opportunities (in this case 'to find patterns').

There are more than six variables, and more than six cards, in a problematic organizational situation. There are so many characteristics in organizational situations that it is impossible to recognize them or to 'represent' them all. There are too many characteristics in situations to analyze and, to compound the problem, 'problematic situations' in organizations are constantly changing. Therefore, it is reasonable that humans cannot account for all of them and keep abreast of the dynamics of the changes in a situation (see also Simon 1969). Patterns are *ultimately human constructions*, reflecting the process of thinking of those who are constructing them (see also Gadamer 1988;

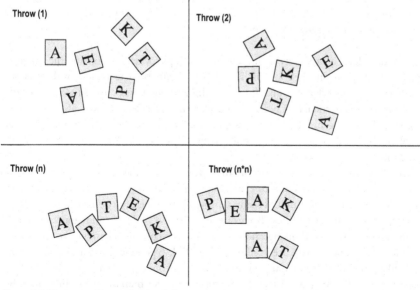

Figure 3.3 Patterns of meaning in six letters

Argyris 1990). The simple example given suggests that there are some key *challenges to reason* in information systems practice, which involves:

- analyzing the potential 'patterns' in a given organizational situation
- analyzing the reasons why certain patterns are selected over other potentially useful 'patterns'
- ensuring 'patterns' are found that are 'justifiable' in some way (i.e. it is easy for those involved in IS practice to 'find patterns' that they want to find).

Purpose and patterns

If we assume that human thinking is teleological (i.e. it is purposeful), each of these three activities, and the conclusions drawn from these activities, can be evaluated to try to determine the purpose that is attached by humans during the process of 'recognizing patterns'. This is true of all humans (e.g. information systems practitioners, as well as non-information systems practitioners). Since humans can only draw conclusions based on their own thinking process, the conclusions drawn are personal and are inextricably linked to the humanly constructed purpose. This means that the conclusions drawn will always be influenced by personal factors (e.g. past personal experiences, social-economic status, personal needs, personal ambitions, education, ethical codes of conduct etc.). For example, an information systems consultant's personal need to find a new contract can dominate their 'view of the situation', and can influence their construction of the problem situation, or the way they interact with their client(s). In this example, it would be easy to see that the information systems consultant may well develop a role that 'searches for' a problem to solve! This is not only true of IS consultants; it is true of any human undertaking such a task (e.g. researchers of organizations) and, from this, we can add to our list of challenges to reason in IS work:

- subjecting to critique the purposeful thinking about a 'problematic situation', and how it informs purposeful action.

Humans have a capability to analyze their own purposeful action and the thinking process that underpins their action. They have the capability to somehow abstract out of themselves, in order to think about why think about a particular situation, or how they acted in a particular way in a particular situation, and thereby also to change the way they think and act in future situations. This might be called 'thinking about thinking' and is depicted by the double arrows of a hypothetical observer (e.g. an IS practitioner) in Figure 3.4.

It is perhaps reasonable to assume that humans have the capability of subjecting their own thinking and action to critical appraisal and thereby learning about both their thinking and their action. It seems reasonable that it is pretty unlikely that animals have quite same capability. For example, it would be hard to imagine a goldfish thinking about its own thinking and action, and subsequently changing or improving it! Sadly for goldfish, they are confined to goldfish-type behaviour, and there seems little likelihood of too much improvement derived from developing their own inquiry into their own thinking as it affects their action. Sadly for humans, whilst they have the capability, they often fail to make use of it! Since humans have the potential to do it,

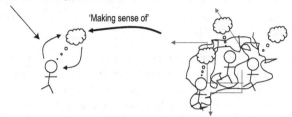

The double arrow is used to indicate a process of 'thinking about the thinking' that is involved in 'making sense of'

'Making sense of'

Figure 3.4 'Thinking about thinking'

there are some significant learning opportunities that may benefit humans, if they did do it, or were encouraged to do it, or learned to do it better. Since IS practitioners are human, they too are capable of undertaking such inquiry, in order to clarify their own purposeful thinking and action in their own practice.

Indeed, it is incumbent on IS practitioners to (or at least be willing to) subject to critique the purposefulness inherent in the patterns that they identify in a given organizational situation. In principle, IS practice must involve 'thinking about thinking' during the process of determining and developing their particular perspectives on organizations, and on what needs to change, and the opportunities afforded by technology to improve it etc. This is a challenge that is an intellectual process. It is highly challenging, and cannot be considered 'right' or 'wrong' in an absolute sense, but can be considered a necessary aspect of dealing with messy organizational problems, and one that can help to develop and heighten thinking in order to gain precision about what is taken to be 'problematic', and alter future actions (e.g. the actions involved in changing a 'problematic organizational situation').

Fads

The intensification of globalization has brought with it new challenges in working in organizations. The well known sociologist, Anthony Giddens, considered globalization as an interdependence of social relationships across the world considering it to be an 'intensification of worldwide social relations which link distant localities in such a way that local happenings are shaped by events many miles away and vice versa' (Giddens 1990: 64). The challenges are many, but may be conceived of as resulting from some widely accepted global trends, such as:

- There has been a significant increase in speed of the exchange of goods and services across the globe.
- Production, information, distribution technologies and organizational processes transcend national boundaries, and are enabled by rapid technological change.
- There has been a growth of highly competitive, complex and uncertain situations, brought about by global competition (e.g. providers of goods and services are often no longer confined to a certain geographic locality and are sometimes forced to compete internationally for local markets).
- There has been the emergence of a new 'flexibility' of organizational forms that allow teams to fulfil projects, activities and processes across geographic and

time constraints, and thus challenges the traditional career structures and other traditional organizational structures.

• There have been changes to the prevailing patterns of work and with them challenges to the prevailing organizational control structures (see also Handy 1994; Beck 2000a, 2000b).

The information and communications technologies are of course a key enabler of such trends. It is generally a common perception that global social and economic changes are having a profound effect on organizations (e.g. how they are organized, their development priorities, their values, management styles, employment conditions and the changes and pressures in which individuals enact their particular roles etc.). There is much controversy about how globalization is currently understood as it impacts on a given organization, and the validity of changes and responses that organizations undertake. For example, there are significant responses in differing contexts that are embedded in the practice of information systems that are commonly discussed, applied and expressed in some key terminologies (e.g. 'e-business', the need for 'downsizing', or 'outsourcing' or 're-engineering' etc.). These and others are commonly 'solutions' to, or to be responses to, global pressures and changes. Each of these advocate responses to perceived situations, often associated with changes in globalized social and economic relationships.

Some of these responses might best be considered to be 'fads' (see also Pascale 1995, Morris 1998). This is because many of the ideas that are considered 'solutions' often highlight some important issues and some complex social and economic changes, but ultimately *oversimplify* both the nature of the perceptions of the 'problematic situation', the process of 'making sense of' it, what the 'solution' is taken to be, and the actions that are needed to respond to its 'problems'. The 'fads' may attempt to give information systems practitioners prescriptive ways of thinking (i.e. they attempt to 'de-intellectualize' the process of 'making sense of'). Furthermore they often mean very different things to different people (i.e. there is often little consensus about how to undertake any 'solution' to the perceived 'problems'), and rarely integrate their messages to provide precision in terms of methodologically based guidance for changing organizations. That is to say, the fad-like responses are the result of poor quality thinking, poor quality guidance in the thinking, and weaknesses in the methods for problem solving. This results in a situation whereby fad-like reactions can themselves increase the uncertainties and messiness faced by those in organizational situations (e.g. information systems practitioners) and this can present additional challenges to reason for those undertaking organizational development work. Information systems practitioners are required to develop thinking that will enable them to move beyond 'fad-like' responses to perceived organizational situations.

A 'science' of sorts

One of the reasons that 'fad-like' responses are dangerous is that they are not underpinned by a set of principles that can guide an intellectual inquiry into 'problematic' organizational situations and guide suitable responses. Sometimes globalization is given to justify a particular 'solution'. Or it is a (convenient) interpretation (or misinterpretation) of a set of ideas or principles, which are then translated into a set of policy directives, or technology-based 'solutions'. It is as if it is possible to pluck a set of semi-defined ideas, and 'plonk' them into organizations, hoping that they may bring about something that can be claimed to be 'good' or 'useful'. In other domains of practice (e.g. medicine), there are sets of principles that can be used to guide investigation into the efficacy of certain 'solutions' (e.g. guidelines based on knowledge, experience and 'scientific' experimentation, which are situation and symptom specific). The guidance in medicine requires robust inquiry, which helps to formulate guidelines. Since IS practice involves taking responsibility for the formulation and testing of 'solutions' of sorts, i.e. by designing ways of working, changing organizations, evaluating the change etc., it also requires careful consideration about how to develop its own equivalent guidelines, inquiring activities, and equivalently robust methods of evaluating results (it needs its own 'science' of sorts, to guide and validate inquiring activities, during the process of organizational change).[2] By establishing such guidelines for information systems, it might be possible to avoid fad-like responses to perceived 'problems' in organizations, and to provide greater guidance in, for example:

- the intellectual and thinking skills that can are required by those involved in IS practice in developing appropriate and responsible actions
- the manner in which research is designed and operationalized in order to appropriately develop new methods, approaches and techniques, and to evaluate their effect in practice.

The first of these might be considered to be an issue for learning and development of those undertaking information systems practice. The second might be considered to be a concern for research and researchers in their quest for understanding and knowledge in order to help and guide practice.

'Science' and 'research' in information systems

The second of these bullet points might also imply that 'science' in IS is to help *in practice*. Such a position might be contentious to certain purists in the research community, because it might be interpreted to imply that all research has to be narrowly designed to 'solve problems in organizations' in some way (e.g. akin to a consultancy role). It might be considered that the intellectual questions and freedoms of academic research are too narrowly constrained or defined in that research 'must attempt to solve problems', which is perhaps only one style of research within the discipline. The purists might argue that it is essential to maintain the rigour of the research, and point to other highly successful disciplines which have a very distinct separation between the research community and the practitioners. The purist might argue that the research might be 'contaminated' if they played a part in 'organizational problem solving' during the process of research, or that there was little need to 'get involved in the messiness of real world situations'.

On the other hand, cynics and critics might retort by acknowledging that there needs to be a level of innovative thinking in research that can bring new ideas, concepts, methods, frameworks etc. into the field of practice (e.g. by linking with other disciplines). But that if it is to be termed 'IS' research it must ultimately demonstrate the usefulness to IS practice, which necessitates involvement in the practical difficulties of changing organizations, attempting to 'improve' them, or 'improve' our understanding of them by involvement in them. These same cynics and critics might point out some of the differences between inquiry in different fields, and that IS is uniquely different from certain other disciplines because:

• Some disciplines largely deal with natural phenomena that can be tested in a laboratory whereas the IS researcher has not got sufficient control over their 'laboratory conditions' (i.e. in organizations): research in IS cannot be done in anything that purports to be equivalent to a laboratory, which is separate from practice.
• In the natural sciences there are much better established processes of inquiry (e.g. identification of variables, measuring, testing etc.), that are not easily replicated in IS research.
• Research in IS is different from certain other disciplines (e.g. history, sociology) in that it is focused on action (e.g. to 'improve') and not simply observation.

The same cynics and critics might also point out the similarities between IS and, for example, engineering, since both have an applied component. And that a 'scientific' community who advocate methods with no applied component, or which 'observe' or 'critique' practice (as if from an 'ivory tower') is not necessarily sufficiently engaged in practice to make its research findings useful to practice. That is to say, it is a situation that can result in:

• Practitioners who are unable or who are unwilling to learn from the scientific methods provided by the research community.
• Practitioners rejecting the findings of the research community.
• Poor intellectual preparation for the task of preparing for IS work.
• Those who are charged with helping IS practitioners to prepare for IS work (e.g. course designers) failing to be guided by a sufficiently grounded 'body of knowledge', and thus their designs and actions are inadequate.
• The simplistic application of fads, as a social response or defence, because of the weakness in the intellectual preparation for the task in hand.

These are important debates in which our hypothetical cynics and purists highlight certain difficulties, ambiguities and challenges about, for example:

• the nature of what constitutes valid 'scientific' inquiry in information systems
• the impact and the relationship 'science' has on practice
• the practical problems of designing suitable inquiries in order to develop knowledge in the discipline.

Some of the challenges in the discipline arise from dominant epistemological assumptions that characterize certain aspects of research in the discipline. Information systems as a discipline has inherited certain epistemological assumptions from the natural sciences. Different disciplines use the foundations of science in different ways and, since information systems is a relatively young discipline, it 'borrows' its 'science' from a range of other disciplines. For example, many who are involved in the IS discipline, or who are involved in applying thinking to IS work in practice, may have as a basic assumption that there is a universal objective truth, knowable by rational, scientific approaches. Typically, research in the natural sciences assumes that the observer has little or no relevance to the observations being made. It would hardly be surprising if those involved in IS work have never thought about this. However, it also might not be surprising if the thinking that they are assumed to be applying is based on the same assumption. For example, 'business process re-engineering' 'borrows' engineering principles in its language and in much of the associated concepts. Those who are undertaking work in the area will commonly assume that the business processes that they are 'engineering', can be analyzed, developed, enhanced, designed and engineered in a similar way to physical items (e.g. building a car, robot, house etc.). However, the idea that IS can simply 'borrow' from the natural sciences could be considered to be flawed. For instance, the separation of the observed from the observer commonly results in:

- Responsibility for decisions being negated by the application or assertion that rigour in a selected 'method' is being applied (see also Wastell 1996), and thereby a relationship is denied between human thinking and the 'method'; in such circumstances, the method might be used to guide, and/or be used as a 'social defence'!
- Those involved in information systems work failing to develop the 'thinking about thinking' because they (e.g. the IS practitioners, consultants or researchers) are not seen as part of the problem-solving process.
- The application of scientific rigour in inappropriate situations, which demand flexibility of thinking, creativity, innovation and/or conceptual reasoning processes. These may not be considered to be compatible with the 'scientific rigour' found in the natural sciences.
- The inability to construct a justification of the thinking processes, because the 'truth' is seen to be 'out there', evidenced in selected empirical observations.
- IS practitioners, consultants or researchers taking on a role of 'expert' (supposedly with 'superior' knowledge derived from 'objective' and the rigours of 'scientific' research), and as a consequence failing to recognize their own or others' subjectivity

'Design-type' thinking

There are some significant differences in the work involved in the design of physical things and the design work involved in IS. Unlike designers of physical things (cars, bridges, buildings, robots, computers), IS practice seems to be increasingly involving the design of an 'organization,' which is both physical and non-physical (e.g. it involves physical things like people, technologies and machines but also involves activities, tasks, attitudes, data, knowledge and power – things that are non-physical, but might be considered to be of importance in achieving particular outcomes). Even the notion of 'organization' might be best considered a concept, which describes the integration of physical and non-physical things. Thus a given 'design vision' of the way people might work in the future (a requirement in IS work in practice) might be considered to be some sort of 'model' of the way both physical and non-physical things (people, tasks, activities, technologies etc.) could be 'brought together' in order to achieve specific purposes. As in a 'design vision' of physical things, a model of an organized set of activities must originate as a concept (i.e. a product of human thinking) and have some purpose (i.e. it simplifies and/or summarizes in some way the features of the designs that are involved). As in the design work of physical things (e.g. bridges, buildings, cars, robots), the process of deriving an organizational model might follow the consideration of alternative models, in a process of refinement of the models. By selecting from a set of alternative conceptual 'organizational' models, it may be possible to assess their desirability in order to meet desired outcomes, in a given situation. The models may be expressed as a set of explicit expressions, dialogues, arguments, prose or drawings (i.e. they can be communicated or written down), but they may also be implicit (i.e. they remain in the mind of a human (e.g. an IS practitioner)), but, nonetheless, they must aim to give clarity and purpose to the actions and decisions taken in everyday situations. The process of their construction, refinement and selection is a typical process of thought associated with teleological behaviour (i.e. it is purposeful) and, for the purposes of this book, it is termed 'teleological process modelling'. Undertaking this is a process that:

- In some way describes the characteristics of an organizational activity, or set of activities, and describes the elements (people, tasks, technologies, information etc.), which when they are organized in a particular manner, will produce outcomes.
- Attempts to distinguish (at a conceptual level) the difference between various alternative models.
- Assesses the various potential outcomes of each alternative model for a specific situation, in order to achieve a specific purposeful objective.
- Will have sufficient clarity in order that communication is sufficient so that others can understand it.
- Includes an evaluative analysis of how the modelling has informed the action of a manager in a given situation.
- Will attempt to develop general rules, abstractions or methodology, so to avoid the necessity of repeating the same thought processes when faced with similar goal-seeking activities (see also Churchman 1971; Checkland 1981; Wilson 1990, 2001).

If IS practitioners have a clear 'design vision', they may be able to articulate and justify the models that underpin their designs of organization and the technology and information that serves it. It is an interesting hypothetical question to consider the potential benefits of developing the IS discipline as (essentially) an *organizational design* discipline. The process also involves inquiry into any given designed organizational process, and to compare with the designed vision.

There are, however, certain challenges in design work where the artefact being designed is essentially non-physical. Indeed, it is challenging because it would necessitate consideration of the most appropriate form of modelling, which is inclusive of the essential set of elements that constitute a form of human organization (e.g. tasks, attitudes, beliefs, technologies, power, control, communication etc.). Any such modelling would be required to be evaluated in terms of how they help to develop precision of the thinking that is involved in undertaking IS work. It follows that:

- The view as described in the bulleted six points above might be used to try to 'improve' certain aspects of IS work (e.g. by developing precision about the organizational processes involved in deriving and justifying organizational designs, or intervention designs (or both)).

- There is a challenge in the development of the precision of thinking that might also be considered to be an issue of learning and preparing the thinking by those involved in IS work.
- Since the final bullet point in the above view is focused on generalized abstractions (i.e. applicable across different organizational situations), then it has the potential to contribute to the 'body of knowledge' in IS (i.e. it is pertinent to the discipline of IS as well as a given organizational situation).

If modelling such concepts is acknowledged to be more or less useful for the purposes of attempting to 'improve' organizational processes, then there are some further key challenges. For instance:

- Is it possible to develop guidelines into the construction of models that can be used to simultaneously provide insight, but which can also be used in a range of organizational situations?
- How can a design that is articulated in a conceptual model be said to be 'valid' in given situations?

These are very significant challenges because in design disciplines based on 'physical sciences' (e.g. construction, engineering, computer science) there are very clear principles, methods and techniques that can guide the designer, which is a situation that is significantly different to that in information systems, where there are relatively poor design guidelines (perhaps because the discipline is very immature). Further, in physical design disciplines, it is possible to be much clearer about how to evaluate the designed artefact (e.g. if a house is built badly it will fall down), but a conceptual model of an organizational process that includes both physical and non-physical elements requires extremely precise thinking and communication about both the construction of models and their evaluation. There are indeed further challenges in the development of the discipline:

- Is it possible to help IS practitioners prepare for their practice by providing them with the abstract skills that are necessary in making use of the models in their practice? (A challenge for those who purport to help with the development of current or future IS practitioners?)
- Is it possible to develop new ways in which designs can be communicated with clarity, for others to scrutinize and refine? (A challenge for future research?)

Systems

A most persuasive modelling type that has been used in managerial work is 'systems' models. These models can be used to help to structure inquiry into any given 'organizational process' (which are often referred to as 'systems'[3]). By using the systems constructs, it is possible to gain insight into an organizational process by considering its particular characteristics, e.g. boundaries, element structures and sub-components, the communication and control mechanisms of the operation of the 'system', performance measurements and their effects, and other characteristics and properties. Systems models can structure the inquiry into 'real world' processes, to conceptualize a range of options and alternatives in changing organizational processes. They have been widely written about by management writers (see, for example, Beer 1967, Checkland

1981), but rather poorly applied in the field of information systems (for the reasons outlined in the section entitled 'Systems Analysis' in Chapter 1). The use of systems ideas to help in information systems practice can provide the foundation for thinking about organizational processes (see also Chapter 6). For example, it is possible to model processes building on systems ideas, in order to:

- Develop an understanding of the nature (and limitations) of current processes that operate in organizations, and therefore draw conclusions about the effectiveness of the technology and the information that supports various aspects of its operation.
- Conceptually use 'systems' (and to integrate other types of models), to conceptualize future or desired processes (i.e. that are seen to not currently exist in a given situation), but which are considered 'desirable' in order to achieve a set of humanly constructed purposes and goals.
- Identify changes to the coordination or monitoring of current operations in order to meet specific goals or outcomes.
- Evaluate the models as a guide to thinking, in undertaking IS work.

However, there are some significant challenges in the use of such modelling. One of these is that it needs to be recognized that a model does not exist in the 'real world'. It is only a conceptual device (i.e. it exists only in the mind), and thus is a simplified view of certain aspects of the 'real world'. As such, it is only a concept. A concept may have implications for 'real world' activity, and may provide a rationale for intervention and change, but it is only a device that can be used to reveal certain characteristics of the 'real world'. It is akin to a rhetorical device, to learn about a current or future organizational process (or set of processes). It is to help structure inquiry. This is very significant for a number of reasons. For example:

- If an observer (e.g. somebody who is involved in IS work) attempts to use a model as a representation of a 'real world' human organization in an absolute sense, they will commonly have significant difficulty because of the messiness and complexity of that 'real world'. If the model is describing something very mechanical and relatively simple, it may be appropriate and effective, but since human organizations are characterized by human action (i.e. they are not quite like machines because humans 'change their minds', 'do things differently', 'reprioritize their actions', 'use intuitive thinking', 'react in unexpected ways' etc.), they are much more changeable, messy and complex. If models are used to represent that complexity, it can result in models that are unwieldy, and which are so complex that they do not seem to 'help'!
- If the model is seen to be a representation of what happens in the 'real world' then it is not necessary, or even possible, to differentiate the model from the 'real world'. This has very subtle but significant implications because it means that the model is justified by reference to observations about the 'real world' (sometimes termed observations or 'facts'). Thus, if something is observed then it should appear in the model, and this alone tends to be the criteria for its appearance in the model. The observer is forced to justify the model by observational 'facts', many of which are 'already known 'facts''. The danger is that there are so many 'facts' to choose from that the criteria of the selection of 'facts' are often unclear.

- If the model is seen to be 'accurate' and 'representative' of the 'real world', the model may have some uses, but can end up failing to clarify the thinking, and if it is seriously considered to be a representation, there are no opportunities to be creative about 'what could be' as opposed to 'what is'.4 There is no reasonably consistent guidance in how to model the 'what could be', and this limits the innovation in thinking that might be needed in problematic organizational situations.

On the other hand, the challenge is in finding suitable guidance on the use of models as a rhetorical construct within a process of learning and thinking, which is not only (or even primarily) derived from observations about the 'real world', but from a process of thinking that integrates a number of other elements in an inquiring process. This will be discussed in further detail in Chapter 6.

Information systems practitioners, consultants and researchers who are concerned with organizations, sometimes will allude to the 'current' situation, and the 'desired' or future situation of a given organization. Sometimes language is used such as, 'This is where we are now, and this is where we want to get to'. Sometimes organizational strategy is seen in rather similar terms whereby the 'strategy' is sometimes seen as (broadly), 'Where we want to get to, and how we are going to get there'. It seems reasonable to assert that beneath the language there are implicit models that are being used to depict both the current and the future states, and communicated through language and other media (e.g. dialogue, diagrams etc.). It also seems reasonable to assert that these models:

- may be very clearly communicated, or less clearly communicated
- may be justifiable or less justifiable, in much the same way as an historical discourse is considered more or less justifiable, by reference to historiography
- may be very precise and clear, or may be less precise and clear (there are varying degrees of 'fuzziness')
- may or may not include precision in the processes (and their designs) about how to achieve a shift from a current situation to a desired situation
- may be used for a 'hidden' purpose and the 'explicit' may be made overt in order to hide the hidden.

If we recognize that these implicit models are also concepts, they too can be subjected to critique in the same way as any of the explicit models. Since the discipline of information systems tends to be considered focused on the designs of technology only, there is often little guidance given on how to improve the precision of the thinking that underpins such activity in the context of organization. It is by no means the same. The challenge to reason is in the improvement of the process of modelling, and in the evaluation of how it impacts on the thinking process for both contexts.

The demarcation of 'current' from 'desired' organizational situations is useful in order to express desired changes. However, it is in a way subsumed into a process of modelling the organizational processes. This is because the process of modelling organizational processes will always include:

- the analysis of what is feasibly operable or what needs to be changed by reference to a 'current situation' (contextual analysis)
- the conceptual construction of models (design)
- the analysis of alternative designs to meet desired outcome (judgement).

As such, a process of modelling incorporates the possibility to reference a current situation and a future situation (sometimes simultaneously). Further, since the concern in modelling is to seek a design that is most suitable for a specific outcome, given a situation, then the process is simultaneously concerned with 'contextual analysis' of the current situation, the 'design' of models to help learn about current situation and future possibilities, and judging the relative strengths and weaknesses of alternatives in the formulation of action. Thus modelling involves consideration of the 'current situation' and 'future situation'. The use of systems models is one way in which to structure inquiry into human organizations and their processes.

4   Methodology

Abstract

Making homemade soup is easy! Even a novice cook can make great homemade soup. The first thing that a novice would typically do is to pull down the recipe book, open the relevant page and follow the instructions. Cooking might be considered to be a *human process*. The recipe might be considered to be some guidance on the *method*. The study of the methods might be considered to be methodology. This chapter is not about cooking, but it is concerned with human processes, methods and methodology in information systems practice.

Introduction

It would be rather inadequate to discuss the difficulties of a discipline, its ambivalences and its problems in both practice, curricula and in research, without proposing a change of some sort. This involves consideration of the core actions in practice, the methods that are provided by the discipline in undertaking the practice, and the methodology that can help to underpin the methods.

One of the core arguments in this book is that in IS problem-solving contexts, 'the problem' and the 'thinking about the problem' are inextricably linked. This was presented as a basic ontological assertion or position (for example, see Figure 3.2). It is a 'basic belief' that has very significant consequences for the discipline, its methods and its practice. It means that information systems practice is required to be focused on improving a given process of 'problem solving', but it also is required to be concerned with the improvement of the 'thinking about the process of problem solving'. For the discipline, this implies a need for continued improvement in the models and the modelling methods (e.g. 'systems' models). It also implies that an individual practitioner might want to move beyond 'as-given' models and modelling methods, but may also be concerned with '*thinking about the thinking about the process of problem solving*'. That is to say, they might need to be concerned about:

(i)   thinking about the process of 'problem solving' itself; but also
(ii) thinking about the (implicit) thinking that dictates the actions of the individual in undertaking 'problem solving', e.g. hidden motives, underlying politics of given situations etc.

Previous discussions have argued that 'thinking about the thinking' is a characteristic of the IS discipline in the future. As such, it is a requirement that it will be undertaken by (i) the IS practitioner, who is concerned to improve the thinking in order to improve the likelihood of effective change in organizations. But also, (ii) the same notion applies to those people 'in the organizational situation' (e.g. people in general, undertaking formal or informal roles in that situation – 'users', 'managers', 'operatives' etc.). It is their changing perception of 'problems', 'solutions' and 'actions to change', that ultimately will bring about change. It is the interaction between the IS practitioner, and these their 'client groups',[1] that is probably the most likely area that will bring about change in organizations. In principle, the solving of organizational 'problems' must be about improving the thinking about the 'problems' and how they might be 'solved' by human groups working in a variety of roles, in often heterogeneous teams (see the case material in Part IV). The discipline of information systems in the future will be (in part) concerned with helping to provide and facilitate those heterogeneous teams in 'thinking about how they are thinking' about their own processes, organization, situations and the possibilities of change, and of the use of technology in that change. It is this that will a key generator of change in organizations, fundamentally underpinned by a new approach in the IS discipline, whereby technology is harnessed by people and facilitated by IS practitioners.

Inquiry

Whether it is undertaken by the IS practitioner at an individual level, or by client groups facilitated by an IS practitioner, the 'thinking about thinking about the process of problem solving' is essentially an inquiry of sorts. It is of course not the only component of a process of inquiry, but since IS practice relies on a suitable understanding of organizational situations, the thinking about how and why the situation is perceived in the way that it is, is a key aspect of such inquiry. An inquiring process can challenge the assumptions of the inquirer; it can be harnessed to challenge the 'as-given' assumptions of the IS practitioner themselves, e.g. about the efficacy and effectiveness of the changes that they are bringing in a given organizational situation. It can challenge the client groups into thinking differently about their 'as-given' assumptions about the nature of a given human organization and how it is operationalized to produce outcomes. Inquiry informs the 'thinking about' and can involve (for example):

- Organizational situations, processes and activities in terms of what currently happens in practice or what should or could happen in the future.
- The validity of others' perceptions and expressions of what happens should or could happen.
- What constitutes a 'problem' and how a given 'problem' is interconnected with other 'problems', and can be considered a symptom.
- Analysis of the power dynamics of a given organizational situation.
- Clarifying how a given organizational process or set of organizational processes are served by technology and information.
- The frustrations, anxieties, attitudes, skills and knowledge etc., of those who are involved in the operationalization of an organizational process.
- The suitability of interventions and actions for change and improvement.
- The validity of monitoring, measurements, evaluation and control.

- The use of information and technology in monitoring processes.
- Analysis of the effectiveness of the team working in a given situation, in the undertaking of certain activities (e.g. in aspects of IS practice).
- etc.

Inquiry of course can be undertaken formally, underpinned by formal designs (e.g. as in a formal research proposal), or it can take a much more informal or implicit form, and be embedded into everyday contexts and activities. Any inquiring activity in practice can be considered to be valid or invalid, or 'more or less valid'. The validity of any inquiring process can itself be the subject of inquiry (sometimes referred to as 'epistemology'). Thus, the 'inquiry into the validity of the inquiry' is a source of continuous improvement. Researchers are required to be explicit about the process of such an inquiry; although practitioners are not necessarily expected to be explicit with the process of inquiry; it is probably desirable that they should be able to undertake suitable inquiring activities.

In undertaking the 'improvement of thinking' there will always be a requirement for inquiry of some sort. Without inquiry, the 'thinking about' cannot be improved. Improvement of the 'thinking about' involves preparation of the mind, in terms of developing suitable analytical skills, self-awareness, the selection, application and evaluation of techniques, tools, methods, ideas, principles, attitudes, values, ethics etc. These must be prerequisites of information systems practice in the future. Inquiry can occur to serve a variety of purposeful goals, but the effectiveness of action can, in many everyday situations, be improved by improving the effectiveness of inquiry, (assuming that the inquiry is designed for the purpose of informing action in practice).[2] Therefore, the preparation of the mind involves developing knowledge about the nature of inquiry itself, and what constitutes appropriate inquiry for the purpose of IS practice.

Inquiry is characterized by a process in which assumptions are challenged and tested, and new insights gained. In some situations in organizations, individuals will have their own assumptions about the current situation, or the requirements for change. A process of inquiry can challenge such assumptions and, in the process of the challenge, such assumptions can be refuted or substantiated. What is incompatible, in an inquiring process, is that the assumptions are not challenged in some way. If that were the case, there would be little point to the inquiry in the first place.

As might be seen, the 'thinking about' and the 'problem situation' is linked has very significant consequences: this ontological assertion has resulted in the inevitable position that *methods* in information systems must be considered fundamentally to be underpinned by a set of inquiring activities.

Teleology

A key starting point for considering the design of suitable inquiry for the purpose of improving organizations, is the relatively irrefutable observation that human organizations are teleological in nature (i.e. they are purposeful). That is to say, they have function, and do something. The purpose of a given organization, or a subsection of an organization might be explicit, or it might be implicit and hidden. But it will always have purpose, and the many elements that integrate together (e.g. people, tasks, roles, activities, technology, power structures, information, communication, control mechanisms etc.), will each play a role in the function and purposeful behaviour of the whole.

These simple statements conceal some important issues and considerations, which will be discussed in more detail in Part III. For the time being, we will take the obvious statement that organizations have human purpose, and are made up of elements that act together in meeting that purpose. Thus, it stands to reason that the study of human organizations involves the inquiry into the purposeful behaviour of humanly organized sets of people (or human organizations, or 'processes'), and includes the inquiry into the elements as they contribute to the purposeful whole. This is a familiar starting point for systems thinkers, who traditionally have based their inquiry on the study of the purposefulness of an operational 'system', i.e. the teleology of a human activity 'system'. Thus, the 'system' is used as a conceptual construct in order to learn about the purposefulness of the elements (including human action), within the 'system', or within a functional 'whole'.

It was Singer (1959) who formally outlined the 'science' of functions: his work outlines the shift in analytical methods and imagery, from the physicist's focus on cause-effect relationships, to the analysis of the function of the components within a functional whole, (termed a 'product–producer relationship'). Thus:

> objects falling within a class defined in terms of function, can exist in and only in a world of which all empirical observations can be adjusted to a mechanical image of some closed system constituting part or all of that world.
>
> Singer (1959: 324)

Singer's work grapples with the scientific basis of observations about the functional components of a 'whole', which on one level exhibits spontaneity, freedom of action, but can be considered to have a function in producing something 'Are we not then, invited to look deeper into that historically most interesting, but most obscure topic of a teleological interpretation of natural phenomena' (Singer: 341).

Singer's was an exploration of the movement in science away from observations of phenomena, which was dominated by the attempt to identify variables and the cause-effect relationships between them, towards the analysis of 'the whole'. This was a radical shift in scientific terms. It was in effect, to some extent, a redefinition of 'science' in a manner of speaking, because the dominant form, which focused on the isolation of variables and the expression of their relationships (normally expressed through the language of mathematics), was considered inadequate in some respects. For example, it tended to focus on the variables in isolation of the function of 'whole'. Singer was concerned that this did not adequately focus the mind on the varied conditions, and elements were required to 'come together' in order that the 'whole' achieved its 'explicit' or 'implicit' purpose.

This has important implications because it implies that inquiry can be underpinned by inquiring into 'purposeful wholes' (e.g. organizational processes). This is not simply something has important implications for practice. It has important implications for researchers in IS, because they can use these ideas to structure their inquiry in a way that moves beyond analysis of cause-effect towards the inquiry into transformations that occur as a result of the interactions between elements in a 'whole' process (e.g.

organizational process). Information and communication, for example, would be considered an element of the 'whole', not an isolated subject of study with relatively weak conceptual integration to the 'whole'. In order to make useful such ideas, there must be a particular orientation of the mind. As discussed in Chapter 1, information systems has embraced *some* systems ideas, but, as can be seen, it has not fully grasped the fundamental roots of systems ideas.

Modelling organizational processes

This theme was later taken up by Churchman (1971), who examined human organization as functional 'wholes'. If the functional 'whole' was considered as a starting point for inquiry into IS practice, then the inquiry would be concerned with, on the one hand, the models of the functional 'whole' and, on the other, the observations of components and elements that had some role in the function of the 'whole'. Rather than use the term 'whole' we will use the term 'organizational process', or 'process' for short. Thus 'systems' provides a set of constructs, principles and ideas, which can guide the inquiry into processes.

Inquiry is used to bring insight into a 'real world' organizational process, by reference to a *conceptual 'model'* of some sort. The conceptual model is one that is constructed in the mind, during a process inquiry, and which reflects and gives insight into a 'real world' process in practice. The model and the 'real world' process are inextricably linked: the model provides the lens through which an organizational process is analyzed. The model is a device and, in analyzing organizations, is essential as a component of an inquiring process into organizational processes.

Thus a 'process model' will need to be something that is heuristically useful to develop understanding of a functional process in an organizational context in practice. Indeed, any observer who expresses aspects of a function of an organization can be considered to have an implicit model of that function in their mind. As such, a model can be used to explicitly explore the 'real world' process, or it can be used implicitly, in everyday language (i.e. a model will exist in the mind of an observer, to express aspects of an organizational process). Any model (implicit or explicit) itself has purpose (e.g. it could be used to shed light on the 'problems' inherent in a process; it could also be used to whinge, demonstrate the failings of somebody or something etc.). That is to say, the implicit or explicit model, in application, will itself be teleological in nature.

We can therefore conclude that (i) the formal and explicit purpose of a model might be considered to provide an IS practitioner something that can shed light on certain 'real world' human processes, the activities and their functional (or dysfunctional) elements, as they contribute to an assumed explicit or hidden human purpose, and (ii) by exploring the implicit models, and the purpose for which they are constructed, they can reveal much about the constructor and their attitudes and beliefs. Thus:

- Whilst human organizations and processes are not natural, mechanical or biological (see Boulding 1956; Vickers 1983), they can be usefully considered to be purposeful 'wholes'.
- These 'wholes' can be expressed implicitly in human language; or they can be outlined explicitly by using diagrams, discourses, verbal communication, to consciously express process models.

- The process using the models (whether implicit or explicit) will have purpose.

The principle characteristics of human organizational 'wholes' is formally outlined in 'Anatomy of Goal Seeking' (see Churchman 1971), which also includes a discussion about the nature of the design and conceptualization of human organizational systems. Churchman (1971) articulates some key components of a model of a human organizational process, which gives us a starting point for an inquiry into any 'human activity set' (or, in this book, 'process'). The formal principles are paraphrased as follows:

- A human process will have purposeful characteristics, although the 'purpose' may often be hidden, or assumed, and human behaviour of those who are in some way connected to the 'process' may or may not be acting in accordance with the assumed purpose of the 'process'.
- The purposefulness of a process does not imply that it is easily achievable, or even achievable at all but, nonetheless, can be perceived of as an implicit or explicit mission.
- A process will have measures of performance, by which the process is judged. The process, the measures of performance and the judgement can be done explicitly (stated, written down, formally applied etc.), and/or can be implicit (unsaid, implied in actions, attitudes, beliefs etc.).
- The measures of performance will affect the process both explicitly (i.e. they can be designed explicitly to affect the process), and also can affect the process implicitly (i.e. they are often undetected by those who are involved in making judgements about both the measures of performance and their affect on the process).
- A process may be considered to be serving a particular identifiable group (i.e. 'clients'). However, there are certain potential ambivalences in the identification of the clients and the way they are served (or otherwise) by the process.
- The client group of a given process might be a homogenous grouping, but may also not be homogenous. Often there are multiple 'client' groups, and therefore the process must serve multiple groups. Sometimes this situation can cause difficulties in identifying choices, priorities, decisions and actions in the operation of the process.
- A process can be considered to have components that are purposeful, and these components can be judged as contributing (or otherwise) to the purposeful process as it attempts to achieve certain explicit outcomes, or operates to produce other (often hidden) unwanted outcomes.
- A process operates in a context (social, economic, political etc.). The context may be considered to be interacting with 'other processes'. The context may be considered to be teleological or ateleological. The context can be judged as contributing (or otherwise) to the purposeful process and how it is measured.
- A process must be designed. It can be designed informally (i.e. it is implicit in the mind(s) of the designer(s)) or formally (i.e. with an explicit 'design' that can be expressed or written down). The designer's concept of the design influences actions by the decision makers, who are involved in the operationalization of the process.
- The formal and 'as-given' design intention, with regard to the process, is assumed to maximize benefit to the client of the process.

- The operation of the process will include decision points and the decision making that will make the process evolve and change, which causes it to deviate from its original design intention. The deviations can be in the components of the system, or in the way the system is to be judged. The deviation may or may not be 'desirable', and/or may or may not be necessary, but judgement on the deviations is desirable.

- The design and the operationalization of the process must be sufficiently stable to enable the designer's intention to be realizable, or to allow deviations to be judged, without having to undertake a complete redesign.

The above are a paraphrased subset, expanded in a variety of ways from Churchman's 1971 original. They have also been considered by systems thinkers in a variety of forms (e.g. Checkland's (1981: 174) 'formal systems model'). These principles could be considered to be a generalized set that can guide the thinking about any 'human process' that can be modelled. The 'process models' focus on the purposeful 'whole', and the particular set of circumstances, elements, components and conditions that enable the 'whole' to fulfil its purpose, and the above can help to structure the inquiry into any given process in practice. *This includes the way information is used in achieving the purposeful outcomes of the whole process; this also includes the way the technology is used in achieving the purposeful whole.* Thus technology and information, which has been the central concern of the discipline and practice of IS, cannot be separated from the inquiry into the purposeful whole. It is this conceptual separation in the discipline and the field of practice of information systems that might go some way to explain some of the failings in practice (see Chapters 1 and 2). Using Churchman's principles, it is possible to structure inquiry about the function and elements of human processes, and the role of technology and information within it. These of course are hugely important for the inquiry into organizations and processes. That is to say, organizations and their elements can be analyzed by reference to system models. In the language of the previous section, this is the inquiry that informs the 'thinking about organizational processes'.

In a further intellectual reflex, this inquiring process itself can be considered to be teleological in character, and thus is itself a teleological process (or 'system'). Thus, both (i) the subject of inquiry (concerned with inquiring into human processes and human organizations) and (ii) the inquiry itself (concerned with the efficacy of the inquiry) can be considered teleological human processes. It is here that we close the loop, so to speak, by linking the notions of teleological models to our earlier discussions on '*thinking about thinking in undertaking organizational problem solving*'. That is to say, the principles of teleological processes can help to frame the inquiry into *the models of organization*, and the same principles can help frame inquiry into *the thinking about the models of organization*. In the language of the previous section, this is the inquiry that informs the 'thinking about the thinking about organizational processes'.

It is this that is the role of 'systems' within the discipline of information systems in the future. It is subtle, intricate and intellectual. It is also difficult to grasp and apply, but is an essential ingredient for the future of the discipline of information systems. The discipline of information systems relies on 'systems' ideas; 'systems' provides the thought structuring for two key inquiring activities that underpin practice – into the organizational processes, and into the thinking about the organizational processes!

We will expand on how this fits together in conceptual terms in Part III, and will demonstrate the operationalization of this in Part IV of this book (see also Churchman 1968, 1982).

Inquiry into processes

If cooking a homemade soup is considered to be a human process, then it is possible to develop inquiry in order to (i) clarify the purpose, (ii) characterize the human process (the making of homemade soup), and (iii) characterize the methods utilized in undertaking the human process. In cooking a homemade soup, the purpose is not cooking per se. There can be multiple human purposes in a process of cooking. For example, 'feed the family', 'impress the girlfriend' or 'provide a service to the restaurateurs'. If the purpose changes, the judgement on whether or not the process has achieved its goal also changes. Thus, each of these purposes will have different measures of performance. Further, if there are different purposeful goals, then each will involve different activities in meeting the purposeful objectives etc. This is the fundamental principles behind teleology. Each different purpose will mean that the underlying model of the process is different. That is tantamount to saying that the methods to achieve the purpose will be quite different. The skills and knowledge required will be different. The clients will be different. The tools and techniques used to achieve the purpose will be different. Expectations of the results of the process will be different. Since the purpose is different, the process characteristics are different. A well-developed understanding of the purpose will give us insight into the appropriateness of the process. And analyzing 'real world' processes, and the associated human behaviour, can give insight into the (often hidden) purpose. The inquiry into purpose is often simple, but sometimes it is quite difficult. This is because, in a given 'real world' process, there are multiple (often conflicting) purposes, each of which can be represented on a different process model.

In the example, 'cooking' is the general descriptor of a process, not the purpose. 'Cooking' is only a language construct and, in a sense, it generalizes about many of the characteristics of the process in practice. But the process is radically different because the purpose is different. From this, it may also be possible to generalize about certain aspects of both cooking and human processes (e.g. those typically found in organizations). For example:

- Any human process may be expressed as having a method for the attainment of a specific purposeful goal, and this is the role of the model (which is sometimes expressed explicitly, but often it is expressed implicitly).
- If, hypothetically, a 'real world' organizational process was said to have only one purpose that was easily definable (generally an impossibility for an organizational process), then the model would be relatively simple to express and would be directly 'representative' of it.
- No model can give insight into a whole 'real world' process. For example, in the case of cooking, it is the recipe that is an explicit form to represent the process, but there is much that is implicit in the human process in practice.
- The process of *outlining the method* and the *use of the method* are different processes, often with differences in purposeful behaviour associated with them. They cannot be assumed to be the same thing!

- It may be easy to articulate the method of some human processes. Others may be more difficult. Mechanical processes are probably easier to articulate than are intuitive, innovative or creative processes. For example, the mechanics of sailing a boat is probably easy to articulate, but sailing a boat is not!
- A well-understood process (such as cooking) will have tried and tested methods, derived from a situation of relative clarity. In organizations, the purpose of many of the processes will be open to interpretation, and a process may have many purposes. As such, there may be many process models pertinent to one organizational area of work. Thus the definition of certain human processes can be highly problematic! But models act as an 'inquiring machine'.
- It is probable that it would be possible to evaluate how changes in one organizational process can effect changes in another area or human process. For example, it is quite easy to see that failure in the human process of cooking can also affect other processes, e.g. of eating! The point is that in organizational problem solving, we need to develop inquiry about human processes and their interconnectedness before we can make changes or improvements.

Some human processes are easily characterized because they are easily structured into stages and steps, and are well tried and tested (e.g. there are standardized measures, protocols and language that are communicable and 'adequate for purpose' – such as in a recipe). In such situations, the application of 'work studies', or certain principles that are often associated with scientific management, can be applied (see Taylor 1947) to optimize and change the processes in question. These types of organizational processes are called 'systematic' (see also Chapter 6). Other human processes might not be so easy to characterize (e.g. they are much less routine, subject to human judgements and interpretation, there are less standard terms and measures, there is a hidden purpose etc.). However, just because certain human activities are not as easily characterized, it does not mean that it is not possible to characterize them! Nor does it mean that they are not purposeful and cannot use the same sorts of inquiring activities to help to understand them.

It might be that some processes can be characterized in a mechanical manner, in stages and steps etc. (e.g. insight into aspects of them can result from the use of traditional IS techniques such as role activity diagrams, data flow diagrams and the like). Other processes may require a discourse and deep analysis in their characterization, and significant effort in understanding their hidden characteristics and implicit structures etc. In order to characterize any process, however, there is a need to undertake inquiry. Certain characterizations can use simple diagrams and structured charts quite effectively as part of the inquiring process, (e.g. process flow charts, data flow diagrams, materials flows, recipes etc.); others are much more complex and require a discourse about goals, priorities, conditions, standards, ethical concerns, hidden and explicit control structures, the values that underpin them and so on. For example, if we were to consider the human process of 'management consulting', it is not possible to write it down in a simple recipe-type form without losing much of the implicit aspects and intricacies that make up the activity, and different priorities and viewpoints in conducting the process. In such a process, it is not easy to identify some of the hidden purposes within the process.

In a similar manner, the human activities of 'managing change', 'researching' and 'inquiring' are equally difficult to explicitly state in a rule-based form (such as a recipe), but they are nonetheless analysable, and can be characterized by subjecting their characteristics to human inquiry using systems constructs (see for example, those presented in the section 'Systems Constructs' in Chapter 6). This inquiry is a necessary part of information systems work in organizations. Analyzing processes has long since been a key aspect of the discipline, but the integration of a teleological approach has not as yet been integrated into the mainstream of the discipline. In doing such an exploration, whatever methods and tools that are used, and whatever the stream of thinking used, it is inevitable that it will include interlinkages between the 'element characteristics' that constitute the task, e.g. behaviours, task, control mechanisms, information, methods, informal hidden aspects, as well as the explicit etc. By analyzing and considering how to undertake particular activities within the process, we are likely to make inferences and assumptions about the justification of the aspects of the methods used in context. It seems that the exploration of these aspects (e.g. the characterization of the process, the methods involved in the process etc.) may be able to help develop knowledge about any humanly organized process that is adapted to a variety of contexts. Further, the way we undertake an inquiry into a human process depends on the way the inquiry about the process is constructed, and this is an issue of epistemology and of the inquiring process.

The inquiring process

The notion of teleology, as discussed in the previous section, can help to structure the inquiry, and to help to focus the mind on some important questions that are required of one or more organizational processes. They are, however, only constructs, used within a *process* of inquiry. There are other characteristics of a process of inquiry that are required to be considered during the process.

In other words, a process of inquiry is itself a teleological human process, and there are characteristics of that process that should be analyzed (and continually improved). The continual improvement can only be undertaken if the inquirer is thinking about the process characteristics and evaluating the impact that such characteristics are having on the process. For example, the process of inquiry is radically different in information systems practice than that of an inquiring process undertaken by, for example, a chemist, or an ethnographer. An inquiring process into chemical reactions may include the testing of chemicals in given conditions in a laboratory. The conditions, actions taken, the chemicals, the outcomes etc. are documented along with implications, generalizability, new hypotheses etc. Since information systems practitioners do not work in laboratories, but in organizations, the process of inquiry is bound to have rather different characteristics. For example, in information systems practice, the variables cannot be isolated, nor can the conditions be controlled as in a chemist's laboratory. But human inquiry does not necessarily require a laboratory. For example, in the social sciences, phenomena can be studied outside of the controlled conditions of the laboratory. An ethnographer, for instance, will typically study human behaviour, human belief systems, human organization, social groups etc., and abstract lessons and learning from observations (i.e. from the application of observational methods). However, this is not to argue that a process of inquiry that is essentially ethnographic is the same thing as the process of inquiry undertaken in information systems practice. Nor is it necessarily correct that skills in ethnography are appropriate for an IS practitioner. It just means that the two might be worthy of comparative analysis in order that we might establish a better understanding of one from another. For example:

- Ethnography is normally considered to be a relatively long *observational* study of human social groups in order to abstract new knowledge. However, an IS practitioner is not purposely abstracting lessons for generalizable new knowledge (that is not the purpose and therefore there are teleological differences). The IS practitioner is attempting to inquire about problematic issues and 'help' to solve them; the purpose is significantly different and this will result in some significant differences in process.
- Both the ethnographer and the IS practitioner are concerned with human actions, activities, assumptions, belief systems, power groupings, attitudes, knowledge etc. However, whilst these things are important to both the ethnographer and the IS practitioner, there are different issues that are of interest. For example, IS practitioners will concern themselves with aspects that would not be considered by an ethnographer, e.g. resources, procedures, processes, monitoring activities, efficiencies, information etc., which may be of less interest to an ethnographer.
- The reason why an ethnographer is undertaking ethnography is a different from the reason why an IS practitioner is undertaking an inquiry, which is to be used as a basis for intervention and change, (or organizational 'improvement' of some sort). Intervention is not normally important or a consideration in an ethnography.

There are some learning points that can be drawn from such a comparison, not least that the ethnographer is attempting, at least temporarily, to observe social phenomenon without imposing himself onto that social situation. Normally, the aim of the ethnographer is to become a 'fly on the wall', or to observe people and attempt to avoid becoming part of the social situation under examination. During an inquiry, *sometimes* the IS practitioner also needs to avoid imposing himself on to a given situation. The inquiry should be able to reveal issues of concern, expressions of anxiety, frustrations, the power politics, the human activities, structures, technologies, the characteristics of organizational processes etc., all of which are required in order to develop understanding of the potential options for change and 'improvement'. However, the objective of IS practice is ultimately to make change, and thus ultimately to 'disturb' the organizational situation.

There are some further learning points that might be drawn from this discussion. For example, in ethnography there is an attempt to negate the effect of the inquirer. This is also true in the process of diagnosis in IS practice. However, this is not true when an IS practitioner attempts to make changes happen in any organizational process. For example:

- in any given operational process
- in the process of undertaking an IT project
- in the process of application development.

In a way, the IS practitioner is in effect required to iterate between analyzing and observing to 'disturbing' and purposely changing something. We will discuss the principles of intervention in organizational processes in Chapter 9 and evaluation of intervention in Chapter 10. These are both elements that are not necessarily in (for example) ethnography.

The interactional sequence

The *interactional sequences* are a central component in IS practice. It is a social interaction, denoted by (I) in Figure 4.1, in which an IS practitioner engages with others (e.g. client groups etc.).

The interactional sequence will play a fundamental role in determining what is and what is not possible in the process of IS practice, including (i) the possible interventions, (ii) the effect of interventions, and (iii) all the inquiring activities and actions. For example, the expectations of client groups of the role of an IS practitioner will determine, to a large extent, what aspects of a given organization is available to be subjected to inquiry and change, the access given and expected norms of behaviour etc. Sometimes IS practitioners need to work hard to intervene in changing such expectations before work can begin! For example, in IS practice, it is common that a client group will consider the role as being concerned with only computers, and thus an IS practitioner will be given access to the computer applications, but may not be given access to the wider problematic issues that face the client organization. This is a result of how the role of IS practitioner is conceived in the mind of the client group and/or in the minds of the IS practitioners themselves. In effect, the IS practitioner can end up being 'boxed-in' and confined to a narrow role because of his own, and/or others', beliefs and expectations. Thus, it is essential that an appropriate interactional sequence can be developed to challenge client groups' expectations.

Any inquiry into the nature of social interaction might be informed by the field of study that is sometimes referred to as 'social psychology' (see, for example, Bruner 1990). This is a component of psychology that deals with the thoughts and feelings of individuals that is informed by the actual or imagined presence of others in a situation (Allport 1968). Commonly, the field is divided into the analysis of behaviour of one or more individuals, and the social context that influences or determines individuals' behaviours, e.g. social structure (see also Lindesmith *et al.* 1975). Such ideas rest on the assumption that humans, even when working in isolation, are social beings, simultaneously shaped and shaping their social structures by their own social action (see also Giddens 1984). Allport (1968) uses the analogy of a stream to demonstrate this:

> Just as the bed of a stream shapes the direction and tempo of the flow of water, so does the group determine the current of an individual's life. This interdependence of the ground and the figured flow is inescapable, intimate, dynamic, but it is also elusive.
>
> (Allport 1968: viii)

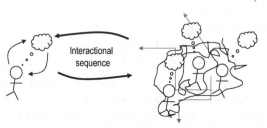

Figure 4.1 The interactional sequence in a process of inquiry

In social psychology, social interaction is commonly seen as the source of social experience, and from birth it is instrumental in the construction of an individual's awareness of the world. By interaction with other humans and other 'things' (e.g. social structures, norms, common beliefs, concepts, knowledge, values, ethical codes of conduct, power structures etc.), humans develop their consciousness. As such, human consciousness is related to experience. In order to interact, humans must be able to communicate their experience. By communication, consciousness can be enhanced because an individual can relate their own experience to that of others. Mead (1934) argued that psychology, as a discipline, failed to make sufficient linkage between the thinking process and interaction. It was argued that psychologists tended to assume that people were capable of self-conscious thought, which determined interactional sequence. Mead, however, proposed that this starting point was erroneous, arguing that we should assume that thinking processes were the result of interaction: 'Mind arises through communication by a conversation or gestures in a social process or context of experience – not the communication through mind' (1934: 50). This is significant in IS practice, because it implies a need for the IS practitioner to become aware of certain *social processes*, in order to be able to recognize and explain why certain conditions and constraints exist and, to some extent, to gauge the possibilities of changing those conditions and constraints.

The notion of 'gestures' is used by Mead as a basic component of interaction. To illustrate the meaning of 'gestures', Mead used the analogy of a dog fight. Thus, when one dog makes moves to attack another, its 'gestures', such as aggressive movements and postures, stimulate another dog to respond. The 'gestures' are the relatively automatic responses of both dogs to a changing situation. There is no imagination involved, nor awareness of any explicit 'rules' of behaviour. In that sense, Mead's notion of 'gestures' is similar to Bateson's (1972) analysis of the relationship between animal behaviour and human dreams, in which feelings are not controlled by the conscious mind, as in many other human situations. Thus in Mead's dog fight, it is not *human interaction* in a human sense, because a dog does not imagine what responses its gesturing will bring, and the 'tactical' aspects are only ever automatic responses to a situation (see also Lewin 1935, 1947).

IS practitioners may 'automatically respond' to situations, as in a dog fight, but, because they are human, they are also capable of interpreting the meaning of their gestures for the other individuals, and can choose their actions in terms of such meanings. Therefore, clearly, humans do not only react to situations, but interact on the basis of their construction of the world. As such, action is justified on the basis of the meanings of the objects and events encountered. Further, interaction is not only a matter of *responding* to objects and events encountered, or responding to the activities of others. It also involves responding to the inferred future intentions of others. This is possible in human interactions by use of analyzing significant 'symbols' and constructs through language. Thus, interactional processes must focus on the interpreted meanings of the 'symbols' (see also Rose 1962; Lindesmith *et al.* 1975).

In Mead's work, gestures are clearly not substitutes for language and other symbols. They are 'automatic responses' – or non-symbolic interaction, or 'without conscious mind'. To be 'symbolic', interaction must be something much more than innate reactions. For instance, there may be 'significant gestures' (see Natanson 1973), where the individual is able to place him or herself in the position of the individual to whom the gesture is addressed. Further, and in that case, the gesture is recognized as significant, and with meaning, by those making the gesture, because they are anticipating the response by the recipient. This, termed a 'significant gesture', is the first stage in consciousness – a first stage in a symbolic interaction. However, there are greater levels of symbolic interaction that can be carried out mentally, i.e. possible actions and consequences can be analyzed prior to acting (see also the 'Cycle of Control' in Tannenbaum 1968). In order to achieve this, language plays a key role in a 'system' of significant symbols (see Mead 1934). Thus, language use involves the mind, to express thought. Further, with the development of symbolic interaction through the internalization of the conversation of significant gestures, mind is also able to evolve. Hence, Mead's original argument that mind does not precede interaction, but evolves from and with it, and is a point made by a number of social psychologists 'Human beings interpret or define each other's actions instead of merely reacting to each other's actions' (Blumer 1962: 180).

The notion of symbolic interaction has some important implications in the IS practice. For instance:

- Effective interaction involves evaluation of the changes that the interaction makes on the 'mindset' of 'client groups', e.g. during the early stages, the interactional sequence is required to set up roles and relationships in order to enable subsequent work to be effective or possible.
- Often, an effective interactional sequence must be developed in order to help client groups to take responsibility for change.
- At times, an interactional sequence will be designed to avoid influencing the mindset of client groups, e.g. when undertaking diagnosis work but, at other times, it will be designed specifically to influence the mindset of others (e.g. during intervention or learning activities).
- IS practitioners can use their intellects to evaluate the effectiveness of particular interactive sequences (which is a form of action), to meet certain goals and outcomes.
- The process of learning and knowledge construction in a situation (e.g. in a process of 'diagnosis of organizational problems') is inseparable from the experiences of the learner, and can be explored by the analysis of language and action in a given social situation.

Modus vivendi

Following from this, it stands to reason that each interactional sequence (e.g. between the IS practitioner and the client group(s)) will have a 'structuring component', which will have a highly influential effect on the behaviour of individuals engaged in the interactional sequence. It is a 'structuring component' of an interactional sequence, norms of behaviour etc. For example, young teenagers playing, in the presence of adults, would be different if the adults were not there. There is a 'structuring component' that enables or constrains the interactional sequence by the presence of adults. A Catholic mass 'structures' behaviour in a very different way to that of a bar or a football match. Each social situation brings with it expected norms of behaviour, and will influence human behaviour and interactional sequence in different ways.

Further, there are 'as givens' that constrain the social actions. In a Catholic mass an 'as-given' assumption is the existence of God, and therefore questioning this type of 'as given' is not possible in the social situation. The '*modus vivendi*' is the unseen or 'as-given' assumptions that are not questioned and are not questionable, and which act to dominate behaviour and social interaction. For example, the 'social situation' of a courtroom has explicit structure and behavioural norms and roles. In a courtroom the 'rules' can be written down, and the process is highly predictable, and as such might be considered to display 'systematic' characteristics (see Chapter 6). Other situations, whilst exhibiting structuring characteristics, are less easy to formalize into explicit rules, and processes are much less mechanistic (e.g. the social processes in a pub). Nonetheless, there remains a *modus vivendi* that dictates what is acceptable and what is not acceptable behaviour. Even in conflict situations there is a mode of engagement, where participants will agree on a tone of voice – a vocabulary – and a method of structuring arguments and actions in an interactional sequence. In this sense, there is a structure to the interactional sequence, which has a controlling effect on behavioural norms and on behaviour itself. These are agreed upon and are sometimes quite explicit and at other times they are implicit, but they are always difficult to assess and evaluate in terms of their appropriateness, purpose and their role in achieving specific outcomes and goals.

In an organization in which the IS practitioner operates there will be a *modus vivendi*, which can dominate the interactional sequences, providing a set of 'as-given' assumptions and behavioural norms, assumed into the social situation. There are dangers when outsiders (e.g. IS consultants) enter situations where the *modus vivendi* is unclear or is strongly dominated by one party. Commonly, an outsider may feel uncomfortable or constrained, to the extent that this dominates the process of interaction by defining the scope of construction or questioning of ideas or knowledge etc. In IS practice, it may be necessary to question the assumptions of the 'as givens' in order to enable new thinking processes to occur, but it must be carefully handled. This may be a powerful weapon at intervention stage, but it may be considered to be something to be avoided during diagnosis-type activities of problematic organizational situations. During the diagnosis, or during the modelling of processes, the IS practitioner may include the characterization of the *modus vivendi*.

Props

In his analysis of social interactions, Goffman (1959) uses the analogy of a play in which actors use a set of 'stage props', i.e. the decor and setting, or the icons in which an interactional sequence is enacted. For example, in a ceremonial coronation there are a multitude of 'props' that are set to enhance the aggrandizement of the new monarch and associated personnel and institutions. The props in this case also include a staged decor of the subservience of others (e.g. military parades, the common people ('serfs') waving flags of support etc.). Other 'props' include the multitude flag wavers who enact a role which simultaneously aggrandizes the monarch by demonstrating subservience. Other situations have similar 'props' (e.g. football matches, pop concerts, political demonstrations, consulting situations, IS project meetings). In this sense, situations are characterized by roles that humans undertake, in a teleological social process, and there are 'stage props' that have certain functions during a 'performance'.

The outcomes of a 'performance' may be explicit (e.g. the coronation), or they may be emergent outcomes of the performance (e.g. a feeling of subservience to the monarchy etc.). The emergent outcomes are those that are outcomes that may or may not have been intended (e.g. the feeling of dislike of the monarchy after the ceremonial pomp of a coronation). As such, the process of enacting a 'performance' may or may not have the desired effect on an 'audience' (i.e. it fails in its intended purpose).

Every situation can be analyzed for its 'props', and how they act to influence the perceptions, behavioural norms and outcomes of a situation. IS practitioners themselves can be considered to have props, which in different situations can be considered to have various levels of effectiveness in influencing or changing perceptions and influencing action and outcomes of an interactional sequence. The 'props' that are available to the consultant may seem rather limited at first sight (for instance, a consultant cannot take an entourage of people, as in a coronation, to act as stage props on a consulting assignment). Nonetheless, there are certain 'insignias' that consultants commonly use to stage an interactive sequence, e.g. personal characteristics such as clothing, size and looks, posture, age, sex, race, speech patterns, facial expressions. The branding of a consultancy firm is also a prop, and this is in-built in the training schemes, brochures, research reports, the gate-keeping administration personnel. For example, these may be specifically designed to portray certain symbols (e.g. 'orderliness', 'integrity', 'competence') to outsiders. As in any prop, the emergent characteristics might not have the desired effect. The effectiveness of, or requirements for, specific types of prop can be subjected to critical analysis, and could be considered to be a component of an inquiring process.

Group processes

Since IS practice is normally undertaken by practitioners and 'client groups' coming together to perform actions and tasks, then the process is essentially a form of 'group process'. If we asserted the rather obvious point that the outcome is only as good as the process, then it can be seen that the effectiveness of any group processes has a determining effect on the outcome. This is a general statement about any purposeful action, and is as applicable in diagnosis and organizational problem solving as it is in any other human activity. One key aspect of process is the way in which groups of individuals work together in 'teams' of sorts. In IS practice, there are always interactions with the others, in purposeful group activities, as depicted in Figure 4.2.

One of the most important elements of the 'background' of the social situation is the perceived membership of groups. Groups might be formal and explicit (e.g. a working group set up to manage the implications of a new IT application), or informal (e.g. the girls who go to the pub on Friday evenings) and sometimes set up without its members being explicitly aware of its existence. The actions of groups will display behavioural norms, a *modus vivendi*, and there will be contextual 'props' in the situation in which the group process is enacted. There will be interactional sequences, each of which will influence the 'mindset' of those in the group, to the point that it may significantly influence members' actions. To a large extent, the effectiveness of the group process can determine action, and the informal perceptions of action, as well as the explicit rationale for action. It is for these reasons that in undertaking IS practice, and in undertaking the inquiring activities, it is important to simultaneously be able

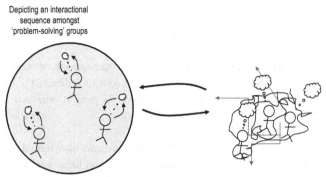

Depicting an interactional
sequence amongst
'problem-solving' groups

Figure 4.2 The group process of the IS problem-solving team

to evaluate the group processes that may have a significant bearing on the outcomes. If a group of IS consultants, for example, undertake work in a client organization, it is reasonable to assume that the consulting group will be able to organize themselves, and this means being able to explicitly evaluate their own process, and take action to improve it, if it is to achieve its purpose; if they cannot, then it seems rather inappropriate that they should be helping others to organize themselves!

Lewin 1935, 1947, 1951 discussed the relationship between group membership, informal and formal roles, and behaviour. One individual may play a role in a number of groups simultaneously. For example, a person may belong to the upper middle class, be a member of a small family, and part of a larger family group, and belong to political and religious groups, and on the committee overseeing the new computer installation. Generally, the group membership influences much of their behaviour within that context. There are, however, occasions when their belonging to a group is less clear for a given individual. For example, on joining a group, an individual may go through a period of uncertainty as to whether they 'belong', or are socially accepted within the group, and this leads to uncertainty in behaviour. The individual will become more or less self-conscious, inhibited or inclined to overact. Uncertainty of this kind is derived from the fact that the individual is crossing the group boundaries. Uncertainty in the movement across boundaries can cause certain behaviours that cause an individual to emphasize or repress certain characteristics in order to gain acceptance into a group situation.

People stand at the margins of some groups and this sometimes affects their behaviour; for example, attempting to gain acceptance into a group, or to become a passive observer, are interactions that are constructed from a personal response to a group situation. In social situations, there are individuals who see the need to cross from one group to another, and act to negate the boundary, or even attempt to destroy it (see also Lewin *et al.* 1939). For example, a member of the working class who aspires to be part of the middle class will act in ways to demonstrate their membership of the middle class (another social grouping). When outsiders to a group are making an attempt to gain acceptance to an unfamiliar group situation, they may enliven their manner with movements that express membership (e.g. by displaying outward signs of proficiency, integrity etc.). This also often occurs where the group roles are ill-defined and it is necessary to define a role (e.g. a newly formed IS consulting group formed to undertake a problematic or ill-defined task). Further, experience of membership of one group is sometimes transferred inappropriately to another. This can be characterized by aggressive or intransigent gestures, which demonstrate membership of one group, but is not responsive to the new group situation.

> If an individual always acts as a member of the same specific group, it is usually symptomatic of the fact that he is somewhat out of balance, for he does not respond naturally and freely to the demands of the present situation.
>
> (Lewin 1935: 148)

Established groups will have a history that will sometimes have roles that are largely predefined. This will influence relationships, attitudes and behaviour (e.g. a workers' union group will consist of members, shop stewards, management representatives etc., each of which will have a particular role). Whilst there are formal roles in group situations, there are also informal roles that are undertaken. For instance, in a group meeting, there may be one who takes on a 'joker' role or a 'serious doer' role or an 'analytic intellectual' role or an 'organizer' role etc. Sometimes people use the same or similar informal roles in different group situations. In situations where the formal roles in a group situation are not well established, their members will tend to search for both formal and informal roles. Both formal and informal roles will have impact on the group process, influencing and changing the 'mindsets'. For example, a change in role can change the mental construction of some of the characteristics of situations (see also Schutz 1972).

Roles can be defined formally, and they can also emerge from the experience of fulfilling a role. For example, a general practitioner fulfils a well-understood role as somebody who will serve a situation by applying expertise to aid the health of others. This is a well-understood social role. However, even in the most well-understood roles there are many competing interests and interactional sequences that influence behaviour. For example, when a particular patient complains of flu-type symptoms, the doctor might reach first for the sick leave forms, rather than searching for the best cure. The action is confused by the competing role of the general practitioner, which is to provide independent judgement on the ability to work. Role conflicts can exist, e.g. the role of providing health care will also involve managing budgets, liaison with other health practitioners (e.g. chemists, professional or practitioner bodies etc.), and this will often involve conflict of interests (e.g. does the doctor search for the most effective remedy regardless of cost?). The same conflicts of interest, and the prioritization of tasks, processes and relationships that are associated with roles in practice, exist in everyday group situations, which can be subjected to critical analysis.

There are a number of key abstractions from this discussion. For example:

- Information systems practitioners work in group situations, with formal and informal roles that influence behaviour, action and relationships.
- Sometimes it is important to analyze the group processes with the purpose of improving them, because they are very important in determining outcomes.
- Facilitators can be used to observe and improve group processes, and these can be very important in facilitating the groups involved, particularly where their decisions and actions have major consequences.

There are many dimensions to inquiring into group processes. For example, we could focus the analysis on:

- Who holds power, how is pressure exerted from one human or human group to others.
- Communications and information sharing within the group, and the resultant effect that it has on coordination and control of tasks, discussions etc.
- The *modus vivendi*, or the 'as givens' that constrain or control the behaviours of the group.
- The use of props, insignias, gestures etc.
- The roles that are 'played out', which might be formally and explicitly constructed, or informal group roles that evolve with the group.
- The 'mindset' of those within the group.
- The relative personalities of the group, and their strengths and weaknesses.
- The 'successes' of the group process and its outputs that were planned for, and the outcomes that were not planned for.
- A combination of all or several of the above.

Such criteria outlined above might be essential for the monitoring of the group process. Monitoring can be done implicitly but, in the process of learning about the group process, it is appropriate that it is done explicitly. Being explicit can help in determining the rationale for the selection or exclusion of the criteria that are to be used in analyzing the group process.

IS practitioners must be able to monitor and evaluate group processes, as an essential skill in analyzing human organization. If, for example, they cannot analyze the organization of their own group processes, it is hard to see how they can help in changing human organizations (i.e. organizing others' group processes).

Principles of method

Since the perceptions of a problem solver, the 'problem' and all actions undertaken to solve the 'problem' are all interconnected via the thinking process, it stands to reason that a large component of problem solving entails inquiry (and learning) in order to inform action. It is of course essential that an IS practitioner is able to avoid paying lip service to the seriousness of the inquiring tasks. Otherwise, he will be unable to outline the *intellectual* basis of his actions. For example, if there is not a process of explicit or implicit inquiry for the purpose of diagnosis, actions are likely to only ever be 'solution oriented', because they will have superficial clarity of the nature and context of the 'problem'! Indeed, an information systems practitioner may often use language to suggest that a 'diagnosis' has been undertaken (they 'espouse' the method that supposedly guides them) but, in reality, it has been done superficially, or not at all. If there is not intellectual basis upon which action is undertaken, the information systems practitioner is limiting themselves in terms of the intellectual basis for action.

It is inevitable that people *espouse* a method, purporting to inform action. For example, IS practitioners might say and think that they are using SSADM (Structured Systems Analysis and Design Method) or PRINCE (PRojects IN Controlled Environments) or another method but, in practice, their actions are informed by something much more subtle (e.g. their 'gut feel', experience, beliefs etc.). This is not to say that the espoused methods have no relevance to action. Rather:

(i)   Acknowledging the difference between espoused and the action 'in practice' can help the IS practitioner to engage with such methods with a greater sense of awareness, sensitivity and discretion, and not feel constrained by them, or feel the need to justify action by reference to them.

(ii)   By analyzing the 'gap' between the 'espoused' and the action 'in practice' can be a rich source of learning.

For instance, an IS practitioner is faced with complexity and pressures (as discussed in Chapter 3) and, as such, it is impossible to control conditions (as in a chemist's laboratory). Sometimes a role–relationship between a client and consultant can result in an IS practitioner not being given the licence to undertake a thorough set of inquiring activities. As such, the social process is dynamic and changeable and, thus, 'what is intended' or that which is espoused, is never quite the same as what actually happens, i.e. the complexity and social pressures can never be predicted or controlled. An IS practitioner might intend or espouse the undertaking of a robust diagnosis of a given situation, when in practice it was not undertaken, or not undertaken robustly. Subjecting such a 'gap' to critical analysis is a necessary aspect of working in organizations.

The idea of exploring the espoused and the method in practice, as a source of learning, is a *general principle* that would be true of any organizational problem-solving process (i.e. not just the work of the IS practitioner). From our discussions, there are of course many such principles. For example:

- All actions that aim to be 'problem solving' are directly linked and related to the implicit or explicit thinking of the problem solver (and hence the information systems practitioner). This means that the starting point for improvement in IS action, must be in the improvement of the thinking process that underpins that action. Improvement of the thinking process will sometimes involve making explicit aspects of the subconscious and implicit thinking.
- By becoming more aware of the implicit drivers of action, the IS practitioner can become more aware of their own assumptions, biases, knowledge limitations, motivations etc. In other words, in undertaking action and developing greater awareness of the implicit drivers of action, the IS practitioner has the potential to improve his own thinking, i.e. an IS practitioner must be able to think about the way he thinks!
- The interactional sequence between different humans will determine what is and what is not possible in the organizational situation, and thus will have an instrumental effect on the process of IS practice.
- IS 'problem-solving' actions need to be initiated as a result of both (i) the perceived needs of someone connected to the situation, and/or (ii) a perceived ethical imperative to act. They cannot be initiated based upon the problem-solvers' own needs.
- All IS initiatives involve change, and evaluation of the change must be undertaken in conjunction with the interventions that are designed to instigate change, otherwise the effect of interventions will remain unknown. Evaluation will be required to consider the unforeseen outcomes of the change initiative.

- IS improvement initiatives always necessitate ongoing consideration of ethical dilemmas, and this includes the choice to act in the first place.
- An IS practitioner must be able to provide a rationale for his methodology, and seek to reconcile the espoused methods with the methods used in action, or in practice; in doing this 'reconciling' there may be great opportunities to abstract lessons for methods, and it might be a particularly rich area of exploration for researchers.
- IS problem-solving activities will involve conceptually modelling organizations. This is not to say that the models used are 'reality': they are and should be considered intellectual constructs in order to learn about the 'real world' situation, possibilities and intervention options.
- IS problem solving is characterized by a process of developing learning, thinking and inquiry on the part of both those who might be considered to be 'in' the problem situation, and the problem solvers themselves.
- Information systems practitioners generally do very little in terms of actual change, but they can be considered a catalyst for action undertaken by those in the problematic situation.
- In the process of organizational problem solving, there must often be a 'shift' of ownership of the problem from the IS practitioner towards 'those in the situation' (i.e. client groups). This is because 'client groups' are the real change agents: the IS practitioner is only a catalyst.
- No organizational processes, no changes to them, nor interventions to 'improve' them are value free: they will always reflect certain values of the humans who are involved in their construction, design or operation.
- Organizational processes, and the models used to inquire into them, will be a requirement and precursor to the inquiry into the role that information and technology plays, or might play, in that process.
- In undertaking IS practice, it is useful to identify certain 'activity sets', which would be expected to be undertaken in a given order. We will term this a 'structure' (of sorts), which can help to guide the activities and actions that are involved, and also to help structure the discussions about those activities.

There are of course many such principles. These are some abstractions about the nature of the underlying principles of method for IS practitioners, into which other knowledge will be required to be integrated. For example, knowledge of technology products, techniques such as entity relationship modelling, entity life histories, role activity diagrams etc. In other words, these are principles that are required when working in organizations, but not a substitute for other, more traditional knowledge of the information systems discipline. But the traditional knowledge must be embedded into these types of principles, if the discipline is to lead practitioners in changing organizations.

A set of inquiring activities

Above we have discussed, in general terms, a number of very key ideas and constructs. For instance, (i) the use of teleological process models to help structure inquiry into organizational processes, and (ii) the need to apply such models to the human process of inquiry itself (epistemology). The integration of these are considered to be an essential aspect of the rethinking of the IS discipline, if it is to be considered one which centres on organizational problem solving. However, there are certain assumptions that are being made here, which are worth reflecting upon. For instance:

- that improvements in inquiry can in fact be achieved by greater awareness of the teleology of the inquiring process itself
- that the inquiry into the validity of the inquiry (i.e. epistemology) can and will improve future inquiring activities
- that improvement in the inquiring process can have impact on guiding action.

This last point is worth particular attention. In the human activity of 'information systems', it might be rather over-mechanical to prescribe action (e.g. 'do this' then 'do that'). To do this would be to assume that the actions are mechanized and, perhaps, are equally appropriate in any given 'situation'. Such an approach might be appropriate in activities such as 'mending a motorbike' or 'making homemade soup'. However, there is much more complexity and variation in the constitution of 'information systems practice'. As such, it might be better to consider that suitable inquiry into a variety of aspects of 'organizational problem-solving' activities, and actions appropriate in a given situational context, may enable improvements in the precision of thinking. This, in turn, may improve action. However, it would be wrong to assume that it does influence action in practice, or that it determines action. However, it would be reasonable to assert that there is a requirement to 'improve inquiry', and to evaluate its 'effect on action in practice'. These are areas of academic research that are required for a practical discipline such as information systems.

If we recognize that inquiry has a role in practice, it does not imply that it is infallible. As in academic research, there are many complex characteristics of a process of inquiry, and the subsequent actions that are undertaken as a result. For example, (i) the motives for the inquiry in the first place (!), or (ii) the ethics of the actions taken, or (iii) the 'basic beliefs' that inform priorities and decisions, or (iv) the values that 'drive' the inquiry etc. Further, the evaluation of an inquiry ('epistemology') cannot relinquish the human responsibilities that individuals have in improving their thinking! Or, to be more precise, it cannot relinquish the responsibilities that an IS practitioner has in developing precision of thinking in informing actions in practice. Nonetheless, a *discipline* is in existence to promote continued improvements in thinking in practice, whether it is ultimately achievable or not.

Human action involves subconscious and conscious thoughts. For example, humans can undertake action in situations, with:

- relatively little consideration of the validity, rationale or justification of those actions or
- weak analysis of the possibilities of 'success' in those actions (i.e. the actions are fit for purpose), or the nature of what constitutes 'success' etc.

Humans have the capability for carefully considering their thinking before, during and after they undertake action; it is likely that humans, more than any other known living animal, have the intellectual capacity for evaluating aspects of their own thinking process, and thereby improving it. This is probably a characteristic that differentiates humans from any other animal. It is a characteristic that enables humans to learn and organize themselves. This relates to both the subconscious and the conscious thinking process that influences action. From this, it is also probably reasonable to suggest that, whilst they have the capability, they also:

- often do not think carefully about their thinking as it affects their actions
- may benefit from more guidance on how to think carefully about their own thinking as it informs action.

From these conclusions, it is probably also reasonable to suggest that:

- humans probably will sometimes undertake 'thinking about thinking' intuitively and with little conscious thought, but often will not use this capability much at all; and
- where humans do not use this capability, they are limiting their own learning possibilities, in which action is undertaken without critique of the thinking behind it.

Since information systems practitioners are human, they are capable of developing more precision in their thinking as it informs their action. In organizational problem solving, it may be considered useful to develop inquiry about (for example):

- the motives for the 'information systems' activities and actions
- the political (power), social, historical and economic context of a given set of organizational processes
- the nature, structure, elements etc. of existing or future organizational processes
- the monitoring and controlling one or more organizational processes
- future or long-term organizational needs based on inquiry about long-term policy objectives, goals or circumstances
- intervention options and opportunities, and the consideration of likely outcome
- evaluation of the effectiveness of the interventions to change an organizational situation
- etc.

It would be perfectly rational to think that inquiry into some or all of these would be ongoing in the process of IS practice. For example, inquiry into the social politics of the context would be undertaken at all times, not just at the beginning! Similarly, modelling new organizational processes will require consideration of future or long-term policy priorities and options. But, in practice, the modelling will inform the practicalities that will be required to be considered in the thinking about policy options. It is, nonetheless, useful to divide the inquiring tasks of IS practice into a number of 'chunks' in order to cognitively simplify the discussion about them.

Although the inquiring 'chunks' might be temporarily separated from each other, they must integrate in order to fulfil the purpose underpinning the actions that are required in 'solving organizational problems'. That is to say, such a set of inquiring activities are required to help to inform and justify change actions in practice. IS practice is itself complex and messy, reflecting and mirroring the context in which it is undertaken. The whole activity (of inquiry and action) underpins the actions of the information systems practitioner. Since breaking the inquiry into sub-components is probably a good way of discussing the nature of the inquiring activities, and how they integrate with each other, then it is useful to outline some form of 'structure' that in

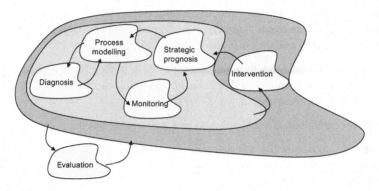

Figure 4.3 A sketch of a set of inquiring activities

some way characterizes the nature of those inquiring activities. For example, inquiry could be considered to involve:

- An exploration of the various perceptions about the 'problems' of a given organizational 'situation'. We will term this an 'inquiry for *diagnosis*'.
- Developing an understanding of existing organizational processes, and others' perceptions of them, including the potential priorities, interlinkages and element structures of them. We will term this an inquiry into organizational processes that involves modelling organizational *processes*.
- Making a judgement about the degree to which a process is considered to be working effectively or otherwise. We will call this an inquiry into '*monitoring and control* processes'.
- Inquiring into the process of organizational policy priorities and (for example) the long-term implications for a set of organizational processes. We will call this inquiry for 'strategic prognosis', which is an essential component of a process of 'strategy'.
- Inquiring into different intervention options, the practicalities and possibilities of different sets of actions and role–relationships designed to help make appropriate changes in organizational processes. We will term this the inquiry into the 'process of *intervention*'.
- Evaluating the process of organizational problem solving itself, in order to learn about future organizational problem-solving activities and actions. We will term this the inquiry for the '*evaluation* of an IS problem-solving process'.

Each of these will be discussed in detail in the following part, and they will be demonstrated in the process of information systems work, in the case study in Part IV. Their interconnections and structure are sketched in Figure 4.3.

Part III

Inquiring activities in organizational problem solving

For many years, a de facto and dominant activity set for information systems has been based around the 'waterfall' stages of application development, e.g. feasibility study, systems analysis, systems design, implementation, post-implementation review etc. Today sees a very different context in which information systems is practised. The 'waterfall' is not irrelevant, but as the discipline moves increasingly from being centrally concerned with application development towards organization development, the 'waterfall' cannot remain the centrepiece of the discipline of information systems. In the future, it may be that the design of technology applications disappears entirely from user organizations. This would leave information systems practitioners the task of applying a variety of technologies and pre-constructed shells, to improve organizational performance. It is not difficult to see that this is a general trend. Currently, however, it is probably reasonable to argue that application development, and more generally the application of computing technologies, will be embedded and integrated increasingly seamlessly with organization development: that is to say, application development may be considered a component of the 'organizational problem-solving' process that increasingly characterizes information systems practice.

This part outlines a the principles of a number of core inquiring activities that might help to provide a new 'wrapping' of sorts, which might help in the reorientation of the information systems discipline and to help it to integrate other knowledge into organizational problem solving. This is based on the assumption that the discipline is required to incorporate organization development as a key aspect and focus. However, as emphasized elsewhere in this text, this does not imply that the discipline must ditch application development and technology. Rather, the application development aspects, and the technology, remain important knowledge. But for reasons already given, it is the organization development that provides its fundamental raison d'être. As such, integrating technical knowledge into the process of organizational problem solving is essential in information systems practice.

In this part, the nature of inquiry for organizational problem solving is discussed. This inquiry is essential if there is to be an intellectual basis for changing organizations. If inquiry is not present in a method of organizational problem solving, then it is reasonable to suggest that any change initiative will be based on things other than an intellectual and reasoned thinking (e.g. 'gut-feel', 'fads', 'organizational politics'). In this part we will explore some of the most fundamental characteristics of inquiry for organizational problem solving. The practical operationalization of these inquiring activities is outlined in Part IV.

Part II

Inquiring activities as organizational problem solving

5   Diagnosis

Abstract

It is reasonable to argue that any information systems action to improve or change an organization in some way would be expected to be based on some sort of implicit or explicit 'diagnosis' of the 'problems' and the 'problematic context'. Undertaking a diagnosis can be considered to be an inquiring activity that focuses on perceived 'problems', social, political and economic issues, revealed through a variety of expressions of anxiety, frustrations and concerns etc., of client groups in a given organizational situation. A diagnosis may be undertaken intuitively, or it may have been the result of an explicitly designed analytical inquiring process. It may be more or less justifiable. But one aspect of information systems work is (i) the consideration of, and putting into practice, diagnosis-type inquiring activities that can in some way reveal some of the contextual challenges, and (ii) be able to critique the diagnosis upon which actions are planned, or have been taken.

Introduction

The term 'diagnosis' is used here (for want of a better term), recognizing that it often has strong affinity to, and connotations with, medicine (e.g. the 'diagnosis' undertaken by a doctor). If we were to use the word 'diagnosis' to mean a human activity and a component of IS practice, we would not necessarily be saying that the role of the IS practitioner is the same or necessarily even similar to that of a doctor. However, since we are using the term, we may learn more about the nature of the diagnosis in problem solving by comparative analysis and contrasting the diagnosis as undertaken by a doctor and the diagnosis that is undertaken by an IS practitioner. Both roles, for example, involve:

- A process of investigation, inquiry and analysis.
- Discourses between those undertaking the diagnosis and others (e.g. patients, or in organizations, client groups 'in the problematic organizational situation' that is being diagnosed).
- The selection and interpretation of data.
- A process of making judgements.
- The application of specific types of knowledge.
- The requirement of high levels of responsibility, because the process of diagnosis can result in conclusions that significantly impact elsewhere (e.g. in drug

prescriptions, interventions and organizational change, the way information is used, technology choices, changes in methods of work etc.).

However, it is also reasonable that the analogy between the diagnoses that doctors undertake and the diagnosis that IS practitioners undertake must be carefully used. For example, a typical doctor has a particular relationship with the patient, where their 'scientifically' tested knowledge is brought to bear on the outcome, and the patient will normally have a rather passive or even powerless role. In IS practice, the body of 'scientific' knowledge is much less well developed: there is much less agreement on the nature of what constitutes 'science' in organizations than there is in the natural science (e.g. medicine), and this has an impact on what can be taken to be valid knowledge (see also Chapter 3). Further, in information systems practice, the 'client groups' may be required to play a much greater role, whereby there is a much greater shared responsibility both during a process of diagnosis and in subsequent actions. This is because ultimately, in organizations, it is the human clients who need to embrace and take responsibility for change. That is to say, it is they, ultimately, who need to change aspects of their own organizational processes (e.g. tasks, actions, attitudes, methods, techniques, technology, power structures, control mechanisms etc.), in collaboration with the IS practitioner. Further, the 'knowledge' from which the IS practitioner draws is not a defined body of knowledge that is 'scientifically' proven. They do indeed draw upon knowledge (e.g. they draw on methods, techniques, principles etc.). But since much of the knowledge is in part about human organizations, much of the knowledge is in fact inside the heads of the client group(s). That is to say, the knowledge that the IS practitioner draws upon is, in part, a process of 'making sense of' the knowledge given to them by client groups about the nature of operational processes and the specific organizational context. The knowledge in IS practice is much more dissipated than in the diagnosis in a doctor's surgery. Indeed, the IS practitioner does not have a 'pill' or a 'drug' to fix whatever is perceived to be 'the problem', but the 'pill' or the 'drug' in IS practice is a product of the combined human efforts and action to 'fix' or improve something. This involves sharing a vision of the nature of the 'problem' and the nature of how it might be 'solved'. The outcome is of course dependent upon the human interaction and the human process involved in which IS practitioner(s) and client groups come together. In principle, we can abstract that the role–relationship and interactional sequences between IS practitioners and client groups is a central determining aspect of a process of diagnosis in IS practice (see Chapter 4).

Thus a process of diagnosis in IS practice is of course a process that will be very much constrained and structured by the interactional sequences and relationships, and is often imbued with power dimensions between an 'IS practitioner' and 'client groups'. We will explore these aspects in this chapter, but also we will be also discussing the methods, constructs and techniques used in diagnosis, and the interrelationship between diagnosis and other elements of the process of the organizational problem-solving activities that IS practitioners are required to be involved in. We will explore these interconnections and how changes in one element can affect how others are undertaken.

In the discussions, it is assumed that diagnosis precedes action and intervention. Of course, this is not to say that it always does in reality! Sometimes the diagnosis of the problem (rightly or wrongly) is:

- not done at all
- done implicitly, without conscious thought
- done whilst doing other things (e.g. implementing 'solutions')
- done as a post-hoc rationalization of previously undertaken action, (e.g. interventions)
- undertaken as a social process by client groups and/or consultants.

Sometimes, each of these situations is perfectly justifiable, and appropriate. For example, there is often no time or need for undertaking a process of diagnosis in a way where the imperative of action is the priority and where a 'problem' is clear and agreed upon implicitly and explicitly (e.g. setting up disaster relief processes, technologies, information etc.). Another example would be where a post-hoc diagnosis is undertaken in order to learn about mistakes that have been made, i.e. a 'post-hoc rationalization' might be undertaken for the purpose of learning about how to improve a diagnosis-type inquiry. Nonetheless, it seems reasonable that in IS practice the process of diagnosis would *ideally* precede action and intervention, and that the resultant learning and thinking about it can help, even in situations that require instant action (i.e. the learning becomes absorbed into action in an implicit way). A diagnosis can help to identify problematic issues; it can also help in the understanding of the context of a process of organizational problem solving. Both of which are essential in IS practice. In this chapter, we will use the word 'diagnosis' as the purpose of the activity, and the process to be, in part, an inquiry of sorts, in order to inform action. Assuming that the inquiry can influence and 'help' in improving action, it is the inquiry that is the focus of discussion.

The problem of 'black triangles'

Given that a diagnosis is considered to be essentially an inquiring process, it is useful to consider some of the characteristics of such a process. The analogy of the diagnosis undertaken by a doctor has already been briefly mentioned. There may be other inquiring contexts that have similarities or dissimilarities, which are worthy of consideration. For example, in police detective work it is easy to amass considerable amounts of data, and the process of making sense of it becomes quite problematic. Indeed, the constitution of 'proof' of a crime is commonly underpinned by a process of iteratively working on scenarios (this happened, that happened, he was motivated to do X, and she did Y etc.). These scenarios are used to simultaneously collect further data (e.g. 'we must interview X, to get better understanding of her movements on'), to make sense of the complexity and varied data. This is also true in a diagnosis in IS practice. For example, it is impossible to collect data about a 'problematic situation' in organizations, without being careful about how to 'make sense of' it. As in police detective work, an IS practitioner must iteratively verify, refine the precision, develop the accuracy and question assumptions.

It is easy to see that humans in any investigatory or inquiring process can very easily tend towards seeing what they want to see! It is as if humans take their own assumptions about the nature of some aspect of the world, and try it find evidence for them. As in detective work, in organizational problem solving, it is easy to see how humans can make assumptions about what a 'problem' is, and find evidence that it is

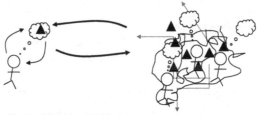

Figure 5.1 The problem of 'black triangles'

a correct assumption. In a sense, it is easy to see how humans can, in a way, impose a 'problem' onto an organizational situation (see Figure 5.1).

Diagnosis might therefore be considered to be a process of inquiry, where assumptions are explored, in which:

• A priori knowledge about issues, events etc. in an organization is utilized, but at the same time is questioned for applicability for purpose.
• Some sort or set of explicit or implicit 'scenarios' or heuristics might be used to question and refine understanding.
• The purpose is to develop a refined understanding (as opposed to selling a 'solution', or 'imposing a set of black triangles').
• There is no absolute certainty about conclusions drawn, but there are possibilities of developing greater understanding of a given situation.

Thus, diagnosis should be considered to be a *process*. It is easy to see why many might want to ignore such a process, because (i) it is quicker to ignore it, or (ii) they do not want to undertake the process because it does not fit with their purpose (e.g. to sell 'solutions'), or (iii) simply learning about undertaking an organizational diagnosis is difficult. There may be a range of other reasons why effective 'diagnosis' of organizational situations is not done in practice.

Many of those who are concerned for organizational improvement can often assert the nature of 'the problem' because it is convenient for them to do so. For example, many IT consultants will bring with them 'IT solutions' and will or may identify problematic issues or situations to fit the solutions! Some IT consultants will often advertise themselves as 'solution providers', and the danger with this is that they might provide solutions without a well-developed understanding of (i) the problem(s), and (ii) what needs to change to solve the problem (the IT may indeed need to change, but other aspects may also need to change to make it work (!)). They also may advertise themselves as IS specialists and practitioners! Of course, bringing 'ready-made' solutions, or bringing sets of assumptions about the nature of the 'problem' *may* be appropriate and useful in certain situations. For example, in situations where human processes are not in need of changing (!) However, there are some dangers and contentious issues when the process of diagnosis is either fragmented (i.e. the diagnosis is not linked strongly to the interventions), or not undertaken at all. For example, in situations where:

• An IS practitioner can end up providing preconceived solutions, and therefore can end up searching for problems to fit those solutions; in such circumstances the role of IS practitioner becomes 'selling' rather than solving problems!
• There is a strong likelihood that a 'solution-oriented method' will result in an IS practitioner constructing his reality to fit whatever solution he has available;

client groups and their organizations can become a frustrating nuisance when they challenge that construction of reality!

- A solution-oriented method means that those providing it may espouse that they have undertaken a process of diagnosis, when they may have, in reality, only undertaken selective diagnosis work, which they subconsciously know will lead them and others to the solutions that they can provide.

- A solution-oriented method can result in narrowly defining the 'interconnectedness' of a problem situation. For example, in an IT 'solution' there is often a focus on information, but there are many interconnected issues that are related (e.g. attitudes, knowledge, skills, processes, tasks, power groupings, control features, organizational hierarchies, roles etc.). A solution-oriented method may ignore the interconnected elements of the problem because they stand in the way of a desired goal (i.e. applying whatever the solution is perceived to be, e.g. an IT product).

It seems reasonable to assert that a process of diagnosis will involve questioning assumptions, and be characterized by an attempt to suspend judgement and the rather natural human tendency to assert greater or a priori knowledge (i.e. provide a 'solution'). The starting point for a diagnosis must be in the perspectives of those in the problem situation, not in the perspectives or needs of the problem solver themself (see also Chapter 4).

This is not to say that the perspectives of those in a 'client group' who are 'in the situation' have any more 'validity' than those of the IS practitioner. Indeed, it is not that an IS practitioner will necessarily simplistically accept or believe the perspectives of 'client groups', or others who are in some way connected to the situation. This is true of 'users', 'operational managers', 'senior managers', 'powerful people', 'not powerful people', 'people who hold the purse strings' etc. Nonetheless, the process of inquiry for diagnosis will start with these perspectives, and this form of inquiry implies the interpretation of the expressions, concerns, actions etc. of human groups who are in or closely connected to the situation. These might be viewpoints, ideas, frustrations, anxieties, perceived solutions, emotions and a range of other expressions. These are not 'facts', but expressions and perceptions that are necessary to be considered and interpreted during the process of diagnosis. Most importantly, during diagnosis, the inquiring process must not start from the problem solver's perceived needs or goals; if it did that, there is a danger that the metaphorical black triangles will appear in the diagnosis, which will create a barrier to the subsequent activities and actions in the process of organizational problem solving.

During this process of inquiry, it is also possible to continuously learn, verify and question the validity of the observations and interpretations that are being made. For example, it is possible to develop a certain rigour in the analysis, by iteratively seeking patterns in the expressions of the 'client groups'. This is analogous to the activities undertaken by a researcher when analyzing his 'data', and drawing generalizable abstractions. In a diagnosis, when undertaken by an IS practitioner, the purpose is sometimes different, as outlined in Chapter 1. However, the process of data gathering, and analysis, sometimes can be quite similar. For example, an IS practitioner may be required to undertake formal, informal, structured or unstructured interviews in order to draw conclusions about the situation of concern. They may also benefit from the use of quantitative survey-based analyses. Analytical techniques (e.g. content analysis of qualitative interviews, quantitative analysis of trends etc.) may be incorporated into the inquiring process. Such techniques are well rehearsed in research methods texts (e.g. Easterby-Smith *et al.* 1990; Gill and Johnson 1991, 1997; Saunders *et al.* 1997; Bryman and Bell 2003) and can give a certain rigour to the inquiring processes undertaken in IS practice. However, it must be also recognized that, in practice, often the purpose of undertaking formal academic research and that of organizational problem solving are often (but not always) different (see (A), (B), (C) and (D) in Chapter 2). In both research activities and in organizational problem solving, it is required that (i) the purpose, (ii) the designs of the process of inquiry, and (iii) the inquiring activities in practice, are each conceptually clarified and interlinked. Whilst 'research' and 'IS practice' can share the same observation and analytical techniques, they are quite different in practice, although integration of the two is required as discussed in Chapter 1.

'Systemic' diagnosis

The word 'systemic' is usually taken to mean something fairly specific in scientific inquiry. It usually sits at one end of a conceptual spectrum, where reductionism sits at the other end. In a sense, its meaning is associated with an attempt at demonstrating the interconnections between elements, when undertaking an inquiring process (into some form of phenomena). Reductionism is normally associated with reducing phenomena into its constituent parts and examining the parts independently and in isolation. It is also commonly assumed that reductionism, broadly speaking, implies that variables pertaining to the phenomena being studied can indeed be isolated, and often (though not necessarily) represented in mathematical notation.

The notion of reductionism and a systemic inquiry are particularly difficult notions to grasp, but a few simple metaphorical examples may help. Biology is perhaps one of the most cited disciplines that use a combination of reductionist and systemic approaches. And we will describe metaphorically a scenario from the simple inquiry into a particular phenomenon, i.e. finding an explanation about how a frog's constitution makes it able to leap significant distances given its size and mass. The inquiry process might pinpoint that the capability is derived from the frog's unique back legs. The study of its legs commonly means that the poor frog is dissected after death, the leg is severed from the body, and the tendon and muscle structure is studied. The frog's leg, dead and severed, is analyzed (e.g. measured, weighed, examined and compared). This method of inquiry might be considered to be a particular process of inquiry where the phenomenon being studied is isolated and separated (the leg) and reduced to a set of underlying structures, elements and components.

On the other hand, we can observe that the dead leg, detached, is a very different item to that when it is attached, alive and part of the living frog. If it is analyzed when the frog is alive, there are interconnected items and elements (e.g. the central nervous system) that cause the leg to operate in particular ways, chemical reactions that are caused by conditions that sometimes are found outside the physical body of the frog (e.g. when the frog is in danger), and the metabolic processes that influence the performance of the muscles on the leg. The process of inquiry that is involved when the frog is alive is in some ways much more problematic than when the frog is dead, but may involve testing the frog's reactions in different conditions, using concepts to try to explain behaviour etc. The frog's leg is analyzed in an attached state and examined by changing environmental conditions (diet etc.), and using a combination of conceptual hypotheses, testing and observed behaviours, conclusions can be drawn. The function of the leg is studied as an interconnected component of a wider 'system' (i.e. the system of the frog!).

Whilst this analogy is a little simplistic, we can observe that the 'reductionist' approach and the 'systemic' approach allow humans insight using significantly different inquiring processes and methods. Both of which have strengths and weaknesses. But we can say that the two are profoundly different. In the first case, the leg is detached and the process involves reducing the analysis to component parts. In the latter, the leg is attached, and the analysis is focused on the integration of the parts within the living whole. The reductionist inquiring process focuses on a process of 'reducing' phenomena to their constituent parts (e.g. x amount of water, y amount of sodium etc.). Systemic, or holistic, is the study of the whole and the interconnection of parts, as they influence each other (e.g. in the living being).

If we use this as an analogy to help us think about the options for a process of inquiry for 'diagnosis' in organizations, the first is to take a 'component' of an organization, isolate it, measure it and study it as if it can be subjected to analysis in an 'laboratory type' inquiring process. For example, there may be a requirement to study sales trends, applying techniques to explain the trends (e.g. regression analysis). In a reductionist-type inquiry, the sales department might be isolated (metaphorically 'cut off' and 'disconnected'). The inquirer might be tempted to analyze isolated components (separated) of the sales department (e.g. the flow of tasks using, for example, role activity diagrams (RADs), and try to 'optimize' based on selected techniques, i.e. the inquiry is 'reduced' to the analysis of the flow of tasks, which it is hoped provides the key to solving a 'problem').

In a systemic inquiry, there is a focus on the interconnections of the 'living organization', which may include the above (e.g. regression analysis, application of role activity diagrams), but also the sales department might be observed, as well as the way it interlinks with other component parts of the wider organization (e.g. information systems, customers, purchasers, operations), or other issues explored (e.g. the changes resulting from postmodern or global markets, the organizational power structure that might be influencing the issue of sales performance, the attitudes, beliefs etc., of certain individuals etc.). This type of inquiry is one that is exploring the 'living being' of the sales process, focusing on the everyday issues, challenges, perspectives and attitudes, and how other areas are interconnected to and influence its operation etc. It requires a more discursive, analytical and iterative method of inquiry, in which exploration and interconnectivity are a key focus. There may be conceptual ideas introduced to help the inquiry, and various hypotheses and ideas considered. Further, changes might be introduced and evaluated for their explicit or implicit effect. This type of inquiry will of course be a very different type of process than that depicted in the above paragraph (e.g. applying regression algorithms, mathematical analyses, role activity diagrams etc.), and may come to very different conclusions. For example, it may find that the 'problem' sits very much outside the sales department etc.

It would of course be unfair to judge any one inquiring process as being better than another – each will need to be evaluated on its objectives and particular context. Just as in the inquiry into the characteristics of a frog's leg, an organizational analysis may benefit from both reductionist and systemic ideas! However, there are some additional considerations that are derived from the characteristics of the entities being studied (a frog and an organization). For example:

- A 'human organization' is a non-physical concept, with physical attributes (people, machines) and non-physical attributes (e.g. tasks, power dimensions, anxieties etc.).
- A frog is physical thing (which can be touched and felt), and all components are assumed to be physical.

This distinction has some major implications:

- It means that what is taken to be a 'human organization', being a concept, must be defined conceptually before its attributes can be studied.
- Concepts are much more difficult to 'gain agreement' upon amongst a heterogeneous human group (i.e. what they are, what they look like, what their attributes are etc.), because it is trickier to communicate with precision something that is abstract.
- A concept cannot be tested in a physical laboratory in quite the same manner as a physical item can be tested.
- A component of an organization cannot be 'separated' and isolated in quite the same way as a frog's leg, because there is a necessity for the organization to keep functioning, (it is not possible to put an organization in a physical laboratory).

It means that IS practitioners have little choice but to rely on a systemic inquiring process, to seek the interconnectivity of elements within the framework of the conceptual constructs (the 'organization'), and to use creative and conceptual thinking to analyze the interconnections of the 'alive' entity. There are, however, plenty of examples of 'scientists' in organizations attempting to take the principles of reductionist science and 'testing' as if an organization or a part of it were:

- Analysable in a laboratory, and that a part of it can easily be separated and subjected to analysis.
- Entirely physical (i.e. there is the assumption that the concept is absolute and clear).

It might be useful to ask some simple rhetorical questions to demonstrate how reductionism might be implicitly and erroneously applied to organizations. For example:

Are IS practitioners asked to look at a particular issue or department, but not given the licence to interconnect other departments together?

- Are IS practitioners only given the opportunity to inquire into the information or the technology issues and not given the licence to inquire into interconnected issues?
- Are narrow techniques used to 'diagnose' and to optimize, without looking how the techniques fit into a more holistic inquiring or problem-solving process?
- Is 'strategy' separated from 'intervention' or 'operations' (i.e. a form of methodological disconnectedness)?
- Is the inquiry assuming that an organization is a static or mechanical entity because of the assumption that a scientific inquiry needs to express its findings in a mathematical form (an ontological assumption)?

Attenuation in diagnosis

It seems reasonable to suggest that in undertaking an inquiry for the purpose of diagnosis, it is not possible to be able to 'know' everything about a given problematic situation. Every manager, consultant, IS practitioner or any organizational problem solver must: (i) interpret various perspectives and observations (data) about the nature of 'problematic' issues, (ii) be selective of issues that are considered 'priorities' or 'of significance', and (iii) deal with patchy data about a given organizational situation. These types of activities result in a form of attenuation (see also Beer 1979, 1985). Attenuation implies being selective of certain things, in order to reduce complexity, and is represented in Figure 5.2.

If we consider that the process of diagnosis to be a continual learning and inquiring process, we are also suggesting that it has no boundaries, i.e. that there are always more things to learn when inquiring into a human organization. By that statement, we are also implying that an inquiring process into a problematic situation:

• Must necessarily be selective with the data that it uses, because making all data available is an impossibility (i.e. it requires attenuation).
• Must have something that is operating to attach importance to certain observations and to reject other observations in the process of attenuation. This is something that is related to the observer's own thinking (implicit or explicit) and, thus,
• must not be confined to 'the organizational situation' but the methods and the social processes that are involved in the processes of inquiry itself (broadly speaking, 'thinking about thinking').

This implies that the process of organizational diagnosis requires that the phenomenon that is under the diagnostic knife (e.g. the organization) cannot be separated from the person undertaking the diagnosis. Doing so would invalidate a diagnosis, because it would assume that the 'problematic' situation is knowable in an absolute sense, and that the individual human IS practitioner plays no part in the *selection* of what is taken to be 'problematic' and what is not taken to be 'problematic'. It would imply that there is no human input to the attenuation process! Systemicity in the diagnosis exists not only in an attempt to interconnect the 'issues' in the 'live' organizational situation, but also to interconnect the observed and the observer.

An initial cursory glance at the concepts of 'systemicity' and 'attenuation' may give the impression that these constructs are in conflict with each other. How can we be 'holistic' in the inquiring process, and at the same time recognize that elements being investigated are selected from the 'whole'? However, systemicity does not imply that all elements are analyzed, as this is impossible, and would assume that all elements are absolute (i.e. there is no interpretation in the observations made). Systemicity does not

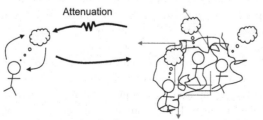

Figure 5.2 The concept of attenuation in the process of organizational problem solving

deny the inevitability of the attenuation process, but requires the observer (i) to recognize their own role in the attenuation process, (ii) to consider providing a rationale for the selection of certain elements, and, most fundamentally, (iii) to be able to explore the interconnected elements in their own purposeful behaviour, to produce the conclusions (in Chapters 4 and 6 we explore the use of teleology, process and systemic constructs).

In an inquiry for 'diagnosis', the selection of issues may focus on the interpretation of issues of (for example):

- tasks, procedures, rules
- formal and informal roles and responsibilities
- human attitudes, knowledge, skills, relationships
- control mechanisms, communication, information
- formal and informal power structures; and these can be derived from an inductive process of exploring the meaning of expressions of
- anxieties, concerns, frustrations, needs etc.

In summary, systemicity in a process of organizational diagnosis must lie in the:

- interconnection of the observed and the observer
- interconnectivity of issues in a 'problematic situation', and, most importantly,
- critical reflection on the rationale for certain things to be excluded, in the process of attenuation
- ability to work with the living organization, with all its quirks, contradictions and limitations, rather than separating a 'rationalized' (or 'dead') part of it and moving it into a metaphorical laboratory
- combination and integration of the above

Invariably, during the process of organizational diagnosis, there are group processes involving a variety of interactional sequences, and social dynamics (see Chapter 4). Systemicity implies that group decisions and actions are integrated into the diagnosis in order to interconnect the diagnosis to the process of diagnosis. In a group process, the individual members of the group may need to come to some form of 'agreement', which may involve a process of considering and reconsidering each member's perspectives in a process of learning in a process of refining a 'diagnosis'. Generally speaking, an 'agreement' is never possible in an absolute sense. Sometimes what appears to be an 'agreement' is not an 'agreement' at all, but is a set of concessions and 'agreed' actions, given a particular social process and set of power dynamics and roles etc. The group dynamic, and the operation of the group, is as important as the conclusions that it comes to. Indeed, the process determines the outcomes, and, thus, if diagnosis is undertaken involving groups and interactional sequences, it is important to include in the diagnosis inquiry consideration of the way in which the conclusions were drawn. It is obviously not possible to achieve this level of critique in all circumstances in practice, but it is very much required in the preparations for IS practice and, thus, is required to be embedded into curricula activity and applied (often implicitly) into practice.

The outcome of the inquiring process for diagnosis can be depicted in any form available (text, drawings etc.). The media for expression of the perceived 'situation of concern' may have important consequences for understanding, learning and communication (see McLuhan 1964 for insights into communication and technology, or Lewis 1992, 1994 for a much more specific discussion on the use of pictures in 'soft systems methodology'). The advantage, for example, of drawing pictures is that it can help link aspects of the 'situation of concern' together in ways that text cannot. Checkland (1981) and Checkland and Scholes (1990) advocate the use of pictures, calling them 'rich pictures', which is an attempt to interconnect graphically the issues of concern, and to express and communicate to others perceptions of the characteristics of a given situation (see Figure 5.3 for an example of a picture depicting the issues and expressed concerns in a large manufacturing organization).

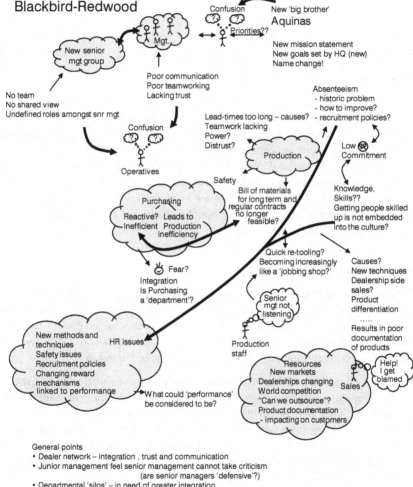

Figure 5.3 An expression of an organizational 'situation', an outcome of a diagnostic inquiry. The quality of the expression is, of course, only as good as the inquiry, and an IS practitioner may often be continually improving the diagnosis. This is always a subjective expression, often very imperfect, based upon patchy data. Despite the inevitable imperfections, the inquiry and an expression of this sort, can give insight into problematic issues, their interconnections and contextual issues and challenges in which IS is practised. It can also prove a basis for further inquiry, as well as other 'problem-solving' actions and activities.

6   Processes

Abstract

Modelling existing or future organizational processes is an essential activity in undertaking the inquiry into organizational effectiveness. Since information systems practitioners are concerned with current and future effectiveness, it is necessary that they are able to justify processes and/or changes to them. Using process models can help in the diagnosis of 'problematic' issues concerning the processes, in the construction of new processes, and the intervention in changing and improvement of existing processes. However, since processes in organizations are conceptual, rather than physical entities, there are some specific challenges in the modelling that is associated with this inquiring activity.

Introduction

If we are concerned with changing something, then it stands to reason that we need to know what we are changing. This simple statement is obvious, but it hides certain difficulties, and is one that sometimes seems to present some challenges for many involved in information systems practice, and other managers and consultants who are involved in organizational problem-solving activities. For instance:

- If we change something in a complex organizational situation, the change is an element in something bigger ('the whole process'). If there is change in one element, it has an effect on other elements and on the 'whole'.
- It is easy to articulate what we are intending to change, but not what actually changes; it is also common to see IS practitioners claiming that what they intended to change actually *did* change, and (to a greater or lesser extent) denying the unexpected changes (and consequences).
- Even if we can say that we intend to change something, sometimes our language and constructs are not sufficient or sufficiently precise. For example, if we are changing something that is designed to 'empower' employees through better information, it is often difficult to have clarity about the nature of 'empowerment', or what constitutes 'better' information!
- It is easy to find a rationale for a proposed change, but it is much more difficult to be certain that a given rationale is appropriate.

For example, many IS practitioners are, or have been, involved in changing manufacturing and related processes by the implementation of ERP applications, which cross the perceived 'boundaries' in a given organization. However, in undertaking a changes to processes, it is probable that changes are also occurring to aspects such as control activities, responsibilities, reporting mechanisms, information flows, departmental boundaries, cost or profit centres, the *raison d'être* of departments, power groupings, allegiances of human groupings, tasks etc. In other words, it is easy to say that we are changing one or more organizational processes, but not easy to say what, in precise terms, we are actually changing by a series of actions!! It is, thus, most important to subject the organizational processes to a form of inquiry in order to develop insight into the interconnections between processes, their assumed purposes, structures, perceived elements, context etc.

There are perhaps some further issues that can be drawn from this when we observe change programmes in practice in organizations. For instance, how often have we seen a 'change' in organization that essentially (i) brings no change at all, (ii) brings with it a change in something (e.g. reporting or control structures), but which fails to bring 'benefits', or (iii) fails to meet the objectives, or original rationale for the change? As a consequence, intentional and designed change often appears to be painfully slow, or non-existent, or changes that were intended to 'improve' can appear to make things worse in a variety of ways. Change initiatives often appear to cause a situation whereby organizations are in constant and often unsettling change and yet it also sometimes appears that the rationale and priorities of a change programme contradicts the rationale and priorities of another, previous or subsequent change programme. This amounts to a common feeling that the constant change initiatives sometimes seem to undermine the confidence in those instigating change! Is the thinking behind the different change initiatives so ephemeral and *ad hoc* that it can be simply swept aside in favour of some new promises, which themselves are subsequently swept aside? An inquiring mind would want to ask whether this is a condition that we want to have in our organizations, and whether there is something that could help managers, consultants and IS practitioners to gain greater consistency in their thinking and to look deeper into the challenges of change. For example:

- There must be a way to conceptualize the elements and their interconnectedness with other elements, in the function of the whole process.
- There must be a way to predict the effect that changes in one element might have in a given organizational process, in other areas (e.g. other organizational processes).
- It must be possible to provide some sort of language or schema in order that humans can become *more explicit* with elements and processes, and their predictions when changing aspects of them.
- It must be possible to organize complex projects (i.e. groups of human processes) in such a way that there is an attempt to develop conceptual clarity of the whole process and how it affects the 'whole' organization (i.e. not just a little bit of it).

In this chapter we will begin the exploration of developing inquiry into organizational processes. It is an inquiry that (i) questions the nature of existing processes in a given situation or organization, (ii) provides a way for a deep exploration of the fundamental transformative function of a given process or set of processes, (iii) can provide a way of inquiring into processes that are currently not in existence, (iv) can challenge existing assumptions about existent processes, and (v) can explore the interconnections between processes. The chapter focuses on the *use of* particular constructs that can help in the inquiry into any given organizational processes.

Explicit thinking about organizational processes

It seems reasonable to suggest that an organizational process is a concept that helps to depict a set of elements (organized or otherwise) that exist to achieve some human purpose. The elements can be a grouping of people, organized (or disorganized) in some way. The concept needs to help to think about chunks or groups of work activity; it needs to help to depict the tasks, activities, actions, power structures, information and technology; it is required to give insight into the *modus vivendi*, and purpose to 'coordinated' human activity in getting things done, for the attainment of purposeful human goals. Some processes in practice will be muddly, ambiguous and complex, in terms of their objectives, the work priorities, actions, tasks and control structures etc. And others might be 'simple', 'smooth', 'logical', 'as given' etc. The concept of process must be able to help structure inquiry into any type of process. Often, organizational processes are undertaken without being explicitly designed, and without being explicit about their characteristics; commonly organizational processes seem to work without the need for explicitly thinking about them too much! However, there is also a common need for explicitly inquiring, thinking, stating and communicating about perceived processes, their 'shortfalls' and attributes etc. There is often a need to critique aspects and characteristics of an organizational process or set of processes and how they are interconnected. This 'inquiring, thinking, stating and communicating' might be prompted by anxieties and concerns that things are not as they should be or how they could be (i.e. it is a concern to 'improve' some aspect of organization). There are a number of general possibilities and opportunities in this 'explicit inquiring, thinking, stating and communicating' activity. For example:

- there is the possibility of deepening understanding of an organizational process and the relationship between different organizational processes
- there is the opportunity for communicating perceptions of organizational processes to others and thereby
- building the possibility of agreeing or disagreeing about a processes and/or changes to it, for the attainment of human purposeful action.

By being explicit (or at least trying to be as explicit as possible), it is also possible to consider others' perceptions of organizational processes. If an organizational process is not explicitly explored, then it would not be possible to communicate and thereby gain others' perspectives about how it could, should or does operate. Invariably this means that an IS practitioner must be able to (for example):

- inquire into existing and future processes
- be explicit about the nature and characteristics of one or more organizational processes
- understand others' perceptions of constraints and failings of existing organizational processes and

- be able to translate others' expressions (such as frustrations, needs, anxieties, perceived solutions) into implications for organizational processes and the potential for changing them
- identify how the use of, or the changed use of, information and technology can 'help'.

However, making changes in organizational processes, or planning for the creation of new ones, demands significant care, because (i) any organizational process demands resources (human effort, time, money, technology), (ii) processes imply the use of resources that are often significant and which could be used for other things (i.e. there is an opportunity cost involved), and (iii) there can be many implications that might result from failure of any one organizational process. Indeed, changing organizational processes, or designing new ones, is a highly responsible task, demanding particular mental attitudes, and the application of methods and appropriate thinking. It means that an IS practitioner must be able to (i) access some underpinning constructs that can help, (ii) use a language of sorts, and/or (iii) use sets of robust conceptual ideas and principles (e.g. models). These are required to organize and ground their thinking sufficiently in order to communicate with others, and to others. The usability and robustness of such constructs is essential because often IS practitioners must be able to access this form of thinking in complex social situations, in which there are different interests and power groups and games being played out. The thinking must be very clear and precise and it must be practical, to help in a process of (i) understanding the different perceptions and the different power interests, and(ii) recognizing the particular situational characteristics in which action to change processes will ultimately take place. Therefore, there is high expectation and demand on a set of modelling constructs and principles, and their use in IS practice. For example, models need to:

- Be usable in situations where an IS practitioner is engaging with client groups who are much closer to the existing processes. That is to say, they can help to structure the thinking of the IS practitioner so as to contribute to discourse without the need for having intricate detail of the processes.
- Be applicable to systematic and non-systematic processes.
- Be sufficiently general, to aid communication in any context (e.g. in big organizations, SMEs, public sector, private sector, NGOs, government departments etc.).
- Be 'expandable' so that they are sufficiently precise to be usable in specific contexts for various purposes.
- Be usable to structure thinking about existing organizational processes, but also to conceptualize non-existing processes;
- Help the inquiry into such characteristics, in current or future organizational situations.
- Be applicable to operational organizational processes and other types of process (e.g. monitoring processes).
- Help model the teleology of the projects that can bring about change, including helping with the management of complex IS projects.
- Enable an IS practitioner to be creative and abstract about what is and what is not desirable for a given organizational process.

- Be usable in specific context such as the organization and control of processes that are subjected to outsourcing, or changes involving ERP applications etc. (see the case material in Part IV).

These are demanding requirements of a set of modelling constructs and principles. However, they are all necessary requirements in order to guide an IS practitioner to be able to dynamically structure informed discussion and inquiry without a priori knowledge of a given organizational process. If a priori understanding of the process was required, then the inquiry would have already taken place! In that sense, the modelling is required to provide a structure for inquiry in human discourses (see the case material in Part IV). The abstract constructs and principles are presented in the section below. In order to appreciate their power, continued engagement and exploration of their application is required, without which the appreciation of their power in dynamic human contexts cannot be discovered. Helping people access and use the constructs is perhaps one of the most difficult challenges for future IS practitioners and remains a core challenge for designers of curricula in IS, and other learning activities.

Systems constructs

From the above discussion, it can be seen that an inquiring mind would simultaneously ask questions about aspects of what it is that is being changed, as well as the thinking that might help to undertake and justify changes. Changing organizational processes relies on having a certain clarity in the thinking about the operational processes are that are being changed or designed, and what 'better' means for those operational processes in their own particular contexts. In that sense, it would mean asking questions about how a process might be conceived, evaluated or measured before or after the change has occurred. It implies a need for methods of sorts to unpick the nature, characteristics and element structures of organizational processes (e.g. a 'manufacturing' process, a 'marketing' process, an 'evacuation' process, a 'selling beer' process, a 'humanitarian aid' process etc.). It seems obvious from this that, without being able to ask certain questions about operational processes, we have no chance of being able to 'improve' them, except by serendipitous actions or from an intuitive 'gut feel' or lucky fluke. Often in current IS practice, there are *some* insights into the processes, e.g. to depict how a given process or set of processes will operate given the implementation of a given technology. But commonly these insights are not always particularly clear; often they are shrouded in jargon, and/or have not considered a range of alternative views of a process or group of processes. Even if change was deemed to be possible without the clarity of thinking (i.e. undertaken in a serendipitous or 'gut-feel' manner), it remains a challenge for the inquiring mind to know with some level of certainty whether such serendipity will indeed yield the desired outcome! In either case (whether it be derived from serendipitous action, or from explicit, premeditated and designed action), it remains that it must be possible to define sufficiently the nature of the operational process intellectually, and thereby be able to define what has changed and what has 'improved' from the change. This is central to the future work of the IS practitioner.

As already discussed, systemicity involves the analysis of the integrative components and elements that are the subject of inquiry. It seems that the same principles can help in analyzing and constructing organizational processes because systemicity involves the analysis of the integrated components as they 'contribute' to the purposeful action of 'the whole'. In organizational problem solving, the 'whole' will refer to 'the whole process', and 'process' may be a reference to a whole organization, or to sub-components of an organization. Indeed, the term 'process' may also refer to a group of organizations. Thus, 'process' is a concept that can be used in a non-prescriptive way, to describe a purposeful 'whole'; it is a construct that can be used to discuss a number of specific and integrated organization specific components (e.g. tasks, roles, power and control functions, coordination, communication, human attitudes and knowledge etc.). But although it is non-prescriptive in terms of what it can be applied to, it needs to be very precise in its application, its meaning and construction, and the application of its underpinning principles etc. Systems constructs can help to develop understanding of practical processes in organizations, because they offer some specific constructs underpinned by systemicity, i.e. broadly speaking, the notion of interconnectedness for the achievement of purposeful human goals (see Figure 6.1).

Churchman (1971) presents some foundational thinking in his chapter on the 'anatomy of goal seeking' and formally outlines the necessary conditions that must exist for something to be considered to be 'a system'. From his systems definition there are some core systems constructs and ideas, which may be applied to the inquiry about organizational processes. In doing this, we will refer to Churchman's articulation of a teleological system. We will do it in a slightly altered language, but the conditions as laid out by Churchman will help to structure the inquiry into organizational processes in practical terms. In other words, Churchman's ideas about systems can help to structure inquiry into organizational processes in practice, remembering that the systems ideas presented are conceptual constructs that will reveal numerous things about current or future organizational processes. We will discuss the inquiring activities in a particular sequence, which broadly follows the guidance given by Churchman, as shown in the table as outlined in Table 6.1.

Purpose

One of the core ontological assumptions that has been discussed in the discussion about muddles, and in the discussion about teleology in Chapter 4, was that human action is purposeful. Activities such as drinking, eating, smoking, driving, thinking, bungee-jumping etc. can be said to have some specific *human purpose*. The purpose might be

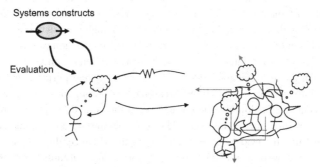

Figure 6.1 Evaluation of systems constructs in the process of improvement and change

Table 6.1 A number of constructs to structure inquiry into organizational processes

Systems construct	Explanation of the inquiring activity to guide the thinking process of the organizational problem solver
Purpose	The inquiry into the purpose of an organizational process (otherwise known as 'teleology' or 'the study of purpose').
Transformation, inputs, outputs	The inquiry into what could be considered to be changed by the operation of a process.
Boundary	The inquiry (often clarification) of elements that sit inside and which sit outside the boundary of a process.
Hierarchy and integrated elements	An inquiry into the elements of a process; how they can be considered to be organized in a hierarchy.
Beneficiaries	An inquiry into who is served by the process (expressed as a role) and what expectations for the process its beneficiaries have.
Decision makers	An inquiry into the process of making decisions in the operation of an organizational process; the effects and the degree to which the decisions 'fit' the defined purpose of the process.
Constraints	The inquiry into the constraints that might be considered to be outside the process but which determine or constrain the design or operational characteristics of the process.
Measures of performance	The inquiry into the measures of performance that are considered for monitoring the process, and to maximize its performance in achieving its purpose.
Unintended outcomes/processes	The inquiry into the effect of the operation of the process, i.e. that which is an outcome of the process, but not necessarily intentionally designed into the process.
Systematics	The inquiry into the level of structure, routinization and mechanical characteristics of the process, and its appropriateness in a given context.
Designers and design activity	The inquiry into the thinking and actions of designers who are involved in the organizational design activities of organizational processes.

deemed to be 'irrational' to an observer, but to the individual undertaking any activity in everyday life, it may be perfectly reasonable and they will be able to describe their purpose and rationale in their actions. In that sense, all human actions have a purpose that is 'rationalizable' by the person doing the action. Even though most action is undertaken without it being in the conscious mind, those undertaking an action can usually provide some sort of conscious rationale for it. The conscious rationale, and the actions, may be incongruent (i.e. the 'evidence' does not support the stated purpose). For example, a manager in an organization might give reasons for shedding jobs (e.g. 'it is the result of a need to cut costs'), although there might be, at the same time, a recruitment drive in other areas of the same organization! The conscious and stated rationale given does not seem to match the evidence. We could say, in this instance, there is incongruence between the stated purpose of action, and the action itself. But it must be noted, that the 'stating the purpose' will itself have a purpose!

If all human action can be considered to be purposeful, then all humans, therefore, might be considered to be 'purposeful beings'. Human action is imbued with purposefulness. Human thinking is imbued with purposefulness. The study of purpose is termed teleology.

If all human action has a purpose, then it follows that all human knowledge is also purposeful, because it is through action that knowledge is created. Even if nobody ever uses certain knowledge, it will be imbued with the purposefulness of its creator(s). For example, an unknown sociologist may make observations of the exploitative accounting practices of companies. The process of observing is purposeful, as is the knowledge that is created as a result. To the creator of the knowledge, it still has a purpose (e.g. to develop understanding, to develop new theory, to justify later actions, to obtain a research chair in a university, to add something to the author's curriculum vitae etc.). If that knowledge is then taken and used in other knowledge-creating activities and actions, or is used by somebody for some other purpose (e.g. lobbying the government to do something about exploitative practices in companies), then we could say that the knowledge is being used purposefully. As such, human action, human knowledge, and the human action to create knowledge, will always have purpose because humans are purposeful beings.

It stands to reason, therefore, that humans are able to organize themselves in order to achieve purposeful outcomes (i.e. human processes are purposeful!!). Further, it stands to reason that the designers of organizational processes (e.g. IS practitioners) will also be undertaking the activity of the 'design of organizational processes' purposefully. Furthermore, it also stands to reason that humans might state the purpose of their organized process, which is incongruous in some way with the actual action being undertaken within the process (e.g. humans might 'hide' or 'fudge' the purpose of an organized process both to others and to themselves!).

Generally speaking, organizational processes emerge over time, and their 'design' is often not clearly scrutinized. It is the continuous interactions between certain groups that enable organizational processes to emerge, e.g.:

- by those humans themselves who operate within the process (e.g. managers and workers who make everyday decisions, within the process)
- those who have designed the process to function in a particular way for purposeful outcomes (e.g. IS practitioners, consultants etc) and
- those who make use of the organizational process (e.g. the clients of the process whose feedback, expressed frustrations, threats of litigation etc., can change the operation of the process).

It also must be recognized that individual humans may not act in harmony or in accordance with the stated purposeful goals of an organizational process. Indeed, the notion that a process can be designed by a designer with a particular purpose in mind, and the actors who operate the process will act in accordance with the designed purpose in mind, is highly idealistic and naïve (and all too often occurs in IS practice). There are at least two quite simple explanations for this idealism and naïvety:

- First, in contrast to many texts in information systems, there are often multiple purposes in a single organizational process; there are informal and formal purposes in an organizational process, and these are often in conflict with each other for resources etc., and thus *no one model of the process is sufficiently definitive* that it can 'represent' an organizational process in a complete sense. There are, potentially, a number of different models that can help in inquiring about an organizational process. This is one very significant difference between human organizations and, for example, humanly constructed physical systems (e.g. mechanical devices). If one organizational process is deemed to have more than one purpose, it can be expressed as a different model, and if there is more than one potentially useful model, then there may be a range of different (and sometimes conflicting) purposes. We will explore this a little further later but, essentially, the design of organizations is perhaps a little different to, for example, designing a physical artefact such as a bridge, car or robot, because there is much more ambiguity of purpose in organizational processes compared to the purpose of a physical artefact.

- Second, designers of organizational processes sometimes can assume that people will share the same set of values, ideas, interests or sets of assumptions about how to make a particular operational process work effectively. We can see this in many organizations (e.g. doctors in a hospital will have a set of actual and espoused priorities associated with the care of patients, and not necessarily share the purposeful designs of the processes to optimize the resources spent on medicines). Thus, the values, ideas or sets of assumptions of designers are often in conflict with those of other decision makers involved in the operation of the process.

There is one very significant additional point that needs to be made here. Often, the values, ideas or assumptions that are embedded into organizational activities are the rationalizations of particular social groupings and represent the power dimensions in organizations. Organizational problem solvers (e.g. IS practitioners, managers, consultants) must need to recognize these, and may or may not be able to challenge them, depending on a number of factors (e.g. their own role, expected norms of behaviour defined by others, sanction by other powerful people etc.). They are, nonetheless, analysable, and can be integrated into models of an organizational process. The power dimension is a component of the inquiry into purposefulness, and therefore is an aspect of teleological inquiry.

Transformation

If we were undertaking the process of mechanical engineering, building physical artefacts from drawings, and designing physical elements and components that interact with each other, the definition of each of the subsystems or each of the components would probably be fairly clear and expressible. Indeed, in the design of mechanical things, the 'purpose' is often taken 'as given' and would not be the subject of inquiry. Thus, if we were designing a braking system for a car, its function would be relatively clear and well understood by the design team, even if its structure and architecture were quite complex, e.g. it has the purpose of slowing the car down! We will depict the process of slowing the car down by a simple systems diagram with arrows depicting an input state and an output state (see Figure 6.2).

This depicts a physical system, and generally braking systems are a product of mechanical engineering. On the other hand, in organizations, the organizational

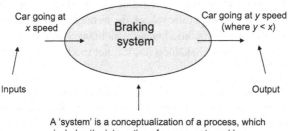

Figure 6.2 A model of the *purpose* of a braking system

processes, and their functions, are often much more ambiguous ('fuzzy') and problematic to explicitly state and define. For example, there are often varying viewpoints on the function and purpose of an organizational process; there are explicitly stated purposes, but there are also implicit and often hidden human purposes. As a consequence, there is often a lack of agreement amongst the people about what the process is transforming, or even how it could be seen to be transforming something at all! There is also an explicitly assumed purpose, but the explicit hides the implicit and rather hidden purposes of the process. Human systems are of course different from mechanical systems because of this ambiguity!

It might be possible to further hypothesize about why the function, and consequently the design of organizational processes, is rather different to those of physical or mechanical things. Perhaps one of the reasons is, for instance, that it is, perhaps, a little easier to relate to physical items because they can be touched, felt, prototyped and tested in varying conditions. Human organizations are much more problematic in a sense, because they cannot be touched, felt, prototyped or tested in quite the same way. It is reasonable, therefore, that the methods applied in the design work in organizations are rather different to that of engineering physical things. For example:

- There may be more effort required to define the function and purpose of an organizational process or set of processes, whereas in a mechanical system it might be taken 'as given'
- Since a human organizational process is made up of people, generally they will not have a single purpose (see Vickers 1983). The multiple purposes of organizational processes can exert pressure on humans by imposing contradictory expectations at a single point in time
- There may more scope for different viewpoints, ideas and priorities etc. about the nature, purpose and priorities of an organizational process, whereas a mechanical process is not subject to such variation.

In mechanical engineering, there is of course a social and human aspect of the design process, because the design teams themselves are made up of humans, but the artefact being designed is often perceived to have (i) no human element at all, or (ii) the human element is very much limited to the interaction between the artefact being designed and the human operator of it. In IS practice, that which is being designed (i.e. a human process) is very much a human affair, in which humans are organized together to achieve outcome, and mechanical and physical items play a role, but are not themselves the sole focus of design activity. For example, information technology has a role in a human organizational process, and whilst the role of the technology in that process may vary markedly, the process usually remains a human affair imbued with human purposefulness, ambiguity, ambivalences and muddliness (i.e. it is not mechanical). These observations imply that:

(i)   There is likely to be much more human involvement, interpretation and other human traits (e.g. culture, politics, power dimensions, collusions, purposeful misinterpretations etc.) in the work of an organizational problem solver (e.g. an IS practitioner) than in the work of the designer of physical things (e.g. a computer engineer).
(ii) There is likely to be much less consensus, and a greater number of different perspectives, over what it is that is being designed, the purpose of the designs and actions and interventions to make the designs work etc.

The comparison between mechanical and human systems also indicates that, perhaps, one of the biggest challenges is the inquiry into, and definition of, what a particular operational process is in the first place! For simplicity, we will give an example of a type of organization that is familiar. A university, for instance, contains many processes, and itself might be considered to be an organizational process. We can learn about it by modelling its implicit and explicit purpose in several different models. One starting point might be to take one of a university's explicitly stated purposes – that of 'transforming' students into graduates – and thereby viewing a university as a process informed by a tentative, and explicit, systems model, as depicted in Figure 6.3.

Lots of things will go on in the university process that involve transforming students into graduates, i.e. it will have lots of different sub-components and lots of different content, for example, lectures, examinations, resits, discussion groups, tutorials etc. In order for this transformation to work, it will have various support and administrative procedures, and a wide range of other things. It is possible to learn about what a university process could or should be by inquiry, using the various systems constructs. Even the general and high-level systems model given in Figure 6.3, can provide some key abstract constructs to help structure inquiry. For example, it may help us consider:

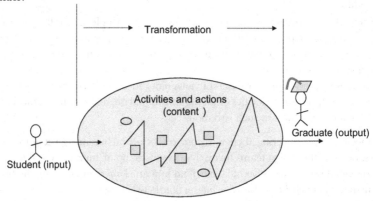

Figure 6.3 Towards a systems model of a university process depicting one of its (explicit) transformations

- Certain simple characteristics of a given process, e.g. an input (a student) and an output (a graduate). These may be required to be explored and defined. If there is no difference, then the process might be considered worthless.
- A range of (currently unknown) activities that can be further analyzed in order that the transformation is made. These further activities and actions may be subjected to analysis using systems thinking for the purpose of inquiry, and can lead to some sort of action to 'improve'. In doing this, there may be identified sub-components or 'subsystems'.
- The relationship between a given systems model, and a given 'real world' organizational process. For example, we can learn that a systems model can be constructed to represent and help us structure our thinking about what goes on in practice (the organizational process), and to see how 'improvements' or alterations can be made.
- The purpose of systems modelling itself, i.e. to develop insight, as a basis of intellectually justifying changes to the 'real world' process.

The notion of inputs and outputs is of course not new. It is fundamental to systems thinking, and indeed has been extensively used in management. However, the management literature often gets tied up in knots over inputs and outputs. It gets tied up in knots partly because it does not recognize the link between input and output and transformation. So for example, certain literature would argue that we can provide some sort of similar model (of, for example, a company) by identifying inputs such as 'human labour', 'money', 'materials' etc., and the output for example could be 'products'. This is normally considered erroneous in a system (see Singer 1959). The problem is that it is much harder to understand the phenomena of transforming a given artefact or concept when dealing with multiple inputs and outputs. It confuses the inquiry. It makes it much more difficult. In practice, the resultant inquiry does nothing but state the obvious, and is characterized by lots of things on either side of the model, which are claimed to be inputs and outputs (see Figure 6.4).

Rather, a systems model should be focused on an aspect of what is being transformed. For example, 'dirty car' might be considered an input and 'clean car' an output (a car-washing process); or, 'no skills' might be considered to be an input

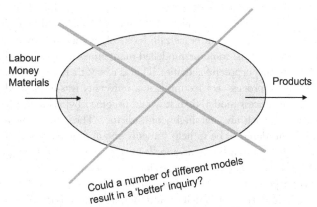

Figure 6.4 A rather difficult starting point for a systems model

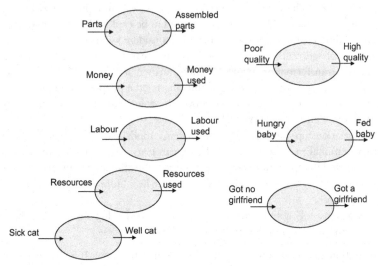

Figure 6.5 A variety of legitimate transformations

to a systems model, and 'skills' could be an output (some form of skills acquirement process); or, 'dangerous criminals' an input and 'non-dangerous criminals' an output of the systems model (a form of rehabilitation process) (see also Wilson 2001). In other words, the starting point of a systems model is a matter of trying to develop precision about the nature of the transformation, i.e. the thing that is being transformed (Figure 6.5 shows some examples).

In the above examples, something that is an input is being transformed into an output, and thus the nature of the transformation becomes explicit. Any organizational process must have transformational characteristics, which can be modelled using these simple systemic constructs. Careful consideration about what these can be can help develop clarity, e.g. for the IS practitioners and various client groups. Sometimes the transformations are 'hidden' or are implicit. They are always open to human interpretation and any process will contain elements and will have certain characteristics that are used to 'transform', i.e. it will always have an 'integrated content'! What that content is perceived to contain, what it should contain or do, and what it does contain or do, are questions that can be subjected to further inquiry but, in most situations, there will be certain levels of ambiguity. Any activity in the 'real world', or any process, could be modelled many times using teleological process models, for each of its purposeful activities. That is to say, there may be many models of an organizational process. For example, if a university was to be modelled using such a teleological process model, then it would become obvious that it has multiple purposes, some of which are seemingly contradictory. The purpose of a university process can be considered to be to help students obtain a qualification. The 'obtain a qualification' system is not the same as a 'learning' system, and there are probably examples where the process of a university has to accommodate the two (sometimes contradictory) purposeful activities. Using systemic ideas, the modelling can help to identify the different purposeful activities, and the contradictions that the process must accommodate in practice. As such, there may be many transformations that can be

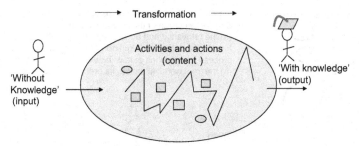

Figure 6.6 An alternative process model for a university

modelled and can be seen to be relevant. As an example, an alternative university transformation is given in Figure 6.6.

In the example in Figure 6.6, it might be claimed that a university develops knowledge, in which case we could create a second model, compare it with others (e.g. as in Figure 6.3), and develop new questions (e.g. what constitutes 'knowledge', what are the characteristics of a 'graduate'). There are some generalizable learning points that arise from this:

- There may be many models that are relevant for any one area of work activity, or one organizational process.
- The process of undertaking modelling helps us to explicitly state what these could be, and this in turn can help us understand why there are different priorities that sometimes conflict with each other.
- It helps to structure inquiry into organizational processes, the stated purposes and the unstated purposes, and the contradictions faced by decision makers etc.

There is of course a difference between the transformations as shown in Figures 6.3 and 6.6, and this difference could be the subject of inquiry into the relative merits of the different models and how they each help to structure inquiry. Thus, if we were to use the model as depicted in Figure 6.6, then there might be further questions raised, such as the assumptions about the nature of knowledge, and the constitution of the thing that is being transformed, i.e. a 'human with knowledge'. Such questions would be themselves part of a process of the clarification that is involved in defining a process, and may help to clarify certain aspects of 'real world' situations. This process of clarification is an inquiry and can help to communicate certain aspects within client groups. For example, it might be argued that the knowledge that a university gives a human is limited in some way, or could be 'made better' (e.g. more (or less) vocational, more (or less) based on experience, more (or less) focused on personal development etc.). Again, there are some generalizable learning points:

- What is conceived to be a transformation (i.e. input and output definitions) has significant implications for what is considered to be the nature of the organizational process.
- There is no one right definition of transformation but, with each definition, there is a need to explore and inquire about the nature of what is considered to be input and output (in our example in Figure 6.6, we could say that we need to consider

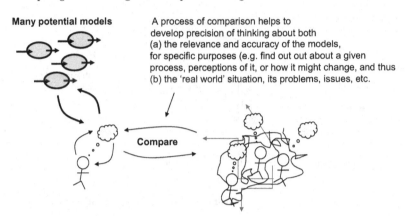

Many potential models

A process of comparison helps to develop precision of thinking about both (a) the relevance and accuracy of the models, for specific purposes (e.g. find out out about a given process, perceptions of it, or how it might change, and thus (b) the 'real world' situation, its problems, issues, etc.

Compare

Figure 6.7 The process of comparison (inquiry) for the purpose of learning

carefully what we mean by 'knowledge', how it is developed and its relevance for specific humanly constructed objectives).

- Since there is no one absolute or 'correct' answer, different people are likely to see each transformation differently and as such there may need to be a social process between people to use the modelling for inquiring purposes, and also (potentially) to find consensus or accommodation of viewpoints.

The process of definition, using systems constructs, is, therefore, an iterative questioning and inquiring process, used to refine the thinking. This involves a great deal of precision, and also may involve inquiring and thinking (e.g. as in our university example, 'what is the definition of knowledge?'). It also involves continual refinement intellectually, and since it is a conceptual process (i.e. it is in the mind), it need not be necessarily constrained by any reference to the 'real world' situation (i.e. it can be very creative and innovative). However, when applied to organizational problem solving, at some stage it must also make reference to the particular characteristics of the 'real world' situation that is the subject of change in which the models are to be applied, in order that it might provide the *intellectual* basis for change. The designer must, for example, question the 'do-ability' or 'feasibility' of the conceptual design within the context. This is not necessarily the same as an attempt of a designer to 'represent' the current situation in a model; rather it is seen as an intellectual basis to challenge current assumptions about the real world process. This is a significant characteristic of the social processes involved in modelling, because many who undertake different forms of modelling (e.g. in current IS practice) often start with questions about how accurately a model (e.g. a DFD) *represents* the 'real world' activities, rather than seeing it as a conceptual activity that helps to guide precision in thinking and inquiry *into* an organizational situation. The iterative, comparative process can enable innovation and creativity, and thus provide refinement to either (i) the models themselves, or (ii) the 'real world' human process in the situation. This can help structure the thinking behind proposed changes (see Figure 6.7).

Boundary

Since there may potentially be many models used to inquire into a given organizational process, there are of course challenges in making sense of the alternatives, and this will involve thinking about different inputs, transformations and outputs. As we go through a process of clarification and refinement (via inquiry), we are not just changing the conceptual thinking about inputs, transformation and outputs, as expressed in different models, but we are also changing the definition and the boundaries of the systems models. For example, the definition of the systems model will assume a certain content, and that the 'process' includes certain elements and excludes others. That is to say, certain activities will be inside and others will be outside a conceptual boundary, and the ability to consider what could be and what should be inside and outside the boundary can be intellectually challenging Figure 6.8).

Lots of items around us can be considered to have a 'conceptual boundary' of sorts, and when somebody describes something they are often implying a boundary. For example, a 'university' has a boundary that we conceptually imply when we use the word. The 'train station', the 'hospital', the 'production department', the 'solar system', the 'criminal justice system' are all terms that we might use in everyday life, and each can be considered to have a conceptual boundary in that, when we use the words, there is some hidden implication that it does something, has component elements, some of which are inside (and, thus, other things are outside) some sort of conceptual boundary. As such, when we are discussing systems boundaries, we are not doing anything that has not been done before: it is actually quite a humanly intuitive construction. Thus:

- When we say we are going to the X-ray department, it is not necessary to define the boundaries of the X-ray department, because it is assumed that in such a conversation there are similar 'boundaries' that are 'as given' between those who are conversing. In other words, the meaning of 'X-ray department' is sufficiently detailed for the purpose of the communication. However, when changing some aspect of the nature of the operations in an 'X-ray department' (e.g. when undertaking IS practice), there may be some requirement to define the meaning of 'X-ray department', and thereby consider explicitly the inclusion or exclusion

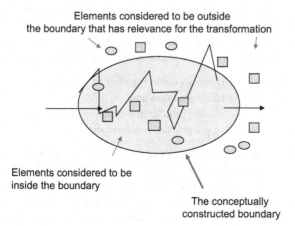

Elements considered to be outside
the boundary that has relevance for the transformation

Elements considered to be
inside the boundary

The conceptually
constructed boundary

Figure 6.8 Boundary construction

of certain elements within its boundary and how they contribute to the 'whole' process etc. For example, an 'X-ray department' may need to consider what it can and cannot provide in terms of its services.

- The boundary construction, whether it is implicit in a conversation, or explicit as in a model, is *entirely conceptual*. For example, it is pretty unlikely that on exiting a hospital, you will trip over the line of its boundary! In other words, it is a concept that is in the human mind. This is a very important point, because when we recognize that a boundary is in the human mind, and it is non-physical, it is possible to train the mind to question the boundary constructions that are implicit in our daily language and lives. It is the questioning of boundaries that has significant potential in thinking innovatively about processes, by defining processes in different ways.

Since the boundary construction is conceptual, it is possible that humans can construct the boundary in a number of different ways for a particular purpose. The purpose of the construction might be to clarify and refine the thinking about the characteristics of an organizational process. It also might be used purposely to confuse, because humans have the capability to change conceptual boundaries dynamically. Thus, humans can use a common language (e.g. the 'training system', the 'machine maintenance system', the 'e-business department'), but the meaning of the constructs being used is often variable because the boundary is being drawn in different places. Thus, different conceptual boundaries are being used, even if the words are the same! Furthermore, it is possible that boundaries are constructed dynamically, and sometimes manipulatively, so that there is a level of ambiguity. The ambiguity in boundary construction can be seen as purposeful, although the purpose is not necessary explicit. In some cases, questioning boundaries can become very sensitive, or 'political' in the social context, because people can sometimes feel undermined in a number of different ways when their assumed boundaries are challenged.

Integrated elements

If any organizational process can be considered to be purposeful, and transforms something, and the transformation is modelled using systems constructs, then it is reasonable and reasonably important to structure one's thinking about what the content of the process could or should be. This is, in effect, searching for potential answers to questions about how the transformation actually works! For instance:

- what components or elements come together to make things work to achieve a particular purposeful transformation and
- what is the best way to conceptualize the essential element structure that makes things work for different purposeful transformations?

Unfortunately, answers to these types of questions are like the search for the hen that lays the golden egg, as there is unlikely to be any perfect answers. Thus, it might be a search in vain, and a never-ending quest. Nonetheless, there may be some constructs and ideas that might be helpful. For instance, there must be a number of 'categories' of elements or components that integrate together and operate to make the process purposeful, and achieve transformation (e.g. tasks, activities, actions, technologies,

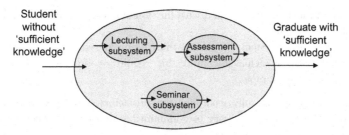

Figure 6.9 The content as a series of integrated subsystems

human attitudes, motives and knowledge, and will consist of power dimensions, communications, and controls). It is these that can form the core or the starting point of the inquiry into the integrated content. These components must integrate together, and they also might be grouped together to form 'subsystems', which service the 'bigger' system. If they are 'subsystems', then it is reasonable that each of the subsystems could be subjected to the application of the conditions that Churchman (1971) outlines, in order to refine the thinking about those subsystems, and each subsystem can consist of integrated content that transforms something (see Figure 6.9).

Each subsystem itself can consist of elements that can be considered a 'subsystem', giving the ability to model in a hierarchical manner, and to think and learn about both big and small systems, and how they integrate together, in achieving a particular transformational process. If we model any organizational process as a system (or subsystem), then we must be prepared to consider and apply the inquiring constructs. It might be, though, that an integrated structure can be identified without the formal application of such conditions, and in such cases we will use a different symbol (see Figure 6.10), which essentially is a 'chunk' of integrated human activity, which is a component of the whole, currently not subjected to the inquiring constructs.

It might be noticed that each element, whether conceptualized formally as a system or not, will involve some integrated elements as discussed (i.e. tasks, activities, actions, attitudes, motives and knowledge, power dimensions, communications, controls etc.). They will be a component in a bigger structure, and if that element fails to perform as intended, then it will affect the whole to the point where the whole may fail in its

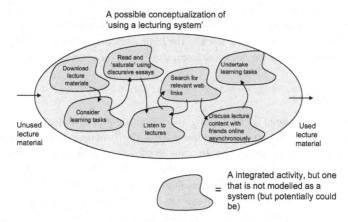

Figure 6.10 An example of integrated processes expressed as 'chunks' of human activity

purposeful transformation. We will discuss the system interconnections in more detail in the following chapter.

In a system or subsystem, its content must be organized in such a way so that the transformation is achievable, and this requires coordination, control and communication. For example:

- Certain activities can only occur after the satisfactory completion of others, and therefore, it may be necessary to communicate that one has been completed before another can commence.
- There must be communication about the coordination of human tasks, activities, actions, technologies.
- There must be evaluation of the effectiveness of different 'chunks' of human activities, or certain systems and subsystems, in order to make changes in them, and/or to control them.

Coordination, communication and control have always been the central role of organizational information systems. One of the problems in the domain of information systems is that there is often ambiguity about the organizational processes that are served by the information systems. The inquiring mind might ask about the realistic possibilities of being successful in improving the information systems, without modelling the process using systems ideas: how can an information system improve an organizational process without first inquiring about the whole process? This is also true in a number of other areas. For example, an inquiring mind might ask questions rhetorically such as:

- How can it be possible to change roles and responsibilities within an organizational process, without understanding the process?
- How can it be possible to change governance activities, procedures, or norms of behaviour that are required to make an organizational process achieve its 'transformation' without understanding the process?
- How can it be possible to change the power and control aspects of an organizational process without clarity of understanding the process?
- etc.

Thus, the inquiry into the process has importance in any area of organization (marketing, operations, finance etc.); it also has importance in any policy shift or change etc. It is central to the work of the IS practitioner, who is required to move into all areas of organization, and seek improvements in those areas.

Beneficiaries

If an IS practitioner is attempting to change organizational processes, then it is reasonable to assume that he must be aware of the 'beneficiaries' of the processes that are being changed or developed. In many IS consulting situations, the 'clients' are seen to be those who pay the consultant for their services. They are, therefore, sometimes seen as the beneficiaries of the consulting service that is provided. Whilst this may well be true, it also is true that there are other, possibly *more important*, beneficiaries. These are the *beneficiaries of the processes* that are being created or changed. Thus, if an IS practitioner is involved in changing a process, either directly (through action) or indirectly (thorough evaluation or consulting reports with recommendations), then the beneficiary might be considered to be those who use the product of an organizational process. Thus, the beneficiary can be considered to be those 'whom should be served' (Churchman 1979: 80) by the organizational process. Therefore, we can say that:

- If an IS practitioner changes a process, it may serve the beneficiary 'better' or 'worse' as a result.
- If the changes in a process in practice do not work 'effectively', then the client could be considered a *victim* of the organizational process, and the victim of the IS practitioner.
- The intervention of an IS practitioner will involve changing an organizational process and, thus, the client of the organizational problem solver is the beneficiary of the process (i.e. not the person or organization who pays for the service).
- If an organizational problem solver is being paid by somebody for their work, they can only be considered the secondary client and, thus, the process of consultancy serves the fee-paying client; if all goes well, the fee-paying client could be considered to be a 'beneficiary', albeit a secondary client.
- The process of consultancy may change an organizational process, and the clients of the organizational process are the users of it. If all goes well, then they can be considered the 'beneficiaries'.

It means that in IS practice there are potentially two different processes that are required to be serviced simultaneously (i.e. the consulting process, serving the needs of a fee-paying client, and the processes that are created or changed, serving the needs of its beneficiary). If the 'process of IS practice' was itself considered to be a teleological process, then they could be conceptualized as two different systems. If we were to consider the two as different teleological processes, it might be considered that they, in certain circumstances, and in practice, might be teleologically incompatible, e.g. servicing the needs of a paying client may act to the detriment of the beneficiaries of a organizational process. This of course can cause tensions, and sometimes it can cause decisions that are taken for expedience and are in the interests of the fee-paying client, rather than the beneficiaries of the organizational process that is being created or changed.

For instance, if the transformation of a university is taken to be changing 'students' to 'graduates', then the students can be considered to be the 'beneficiaries' (or 'victims') of the process. Changes to the university processes can be taken for a variety of reasons, and can be rationalized in a variety of ways. Whilst the beneficiaries of a university process can be considered to be students, the (fee-paying) client of the change might be another group (e.g. the management). The ethical concerns, and the resolution of conflicts of interest that can result, is an essential aspect of the process of IS practice.

The process of the university, when implemented, may or may not serve the purpose that is outlined in the transformation, depending on how the elements and subsystems work together in practice. In other words, if the design 'works' in that it 'improves' the value to the beneficiary, then the students can be considered to be 'benefiting' from the process of the university, but if it does not, then they can be considered to be 'victims'. It should not be assumed that changes in a process always will be beneficial to a beneficiary. Thus, we will use the term beneficiary in inverted commas, to denote the potential beneficiary, or the 'beneficiaries or victims' of the organizational process (see also Checkland's (1981) 'C' of CATWOE).

Decisions

It seems reasonable to assume that decisions taken by humans in everyday situations have a central role in (i) making the human processes work, and (ii) allowing human processes to adapt to new situations and conditions. As such, decisions and decision makers have a central role in making human processes 'work better' or 'work worse'. It also stands to reason that decisions can be made for 'good' reasons and for 'bad' reasons, and for a variety of reasons. These relatively obvious points highlight some less obvious, problematic and interrelated issues. For example:

*   How can decisions be judged to be 'good' or 'bad' in the particular circumstance or context in which they are made?
*   How can it be possible for decision makers to analyze their own decisions?
*   How can an IS practitioner make an intervention in order to 'improve' the decision-making process?

Within a particular organizational process, there are many decisions that are being made, often in dynamic situational circumstances. Decisions are made by 'managers' and by 'non-managers', and some of these decisions are very important to the current and future operation of a process, and also how the process will be able adapt to changing circumstances and needs. We can observe here that decision making is not the sole preserve of managers, or those involved in the design of organizational processes (e.g. IS practitioners). Rather, often the most important decisions are made at an everyday operational level by various human groups or individuals. It seems that, if improvements are to be made in the decision-making processes and activities, they must at some stage be subjected to critical analysis (or inquiry). If there were to be inquiry into decision making, then it would also be possible to consider the content of such an inquiring activity.

Since all human action can be considered to be purposeful, then it is also reasonable that any human decisions are also purposeful. The consequence of this statement is that improvement in the decision-making process must be a teleological consideration. The 'purposefulness' of a particular decision, or set of decisions, can be subjected to inquiry by both (i) the person or group who is undertaking a process of decision making, or (ii) an observer who wishes to judge the decision-making process and the decisions of others.

In undertaking an inquiry into a decision, or a decision-making process, then that inquiry itself could be considered to have an element structure. For example, the decision making may be subjected to critical analysis that:

*   Relates the decisions to the purposeful transformations of the process about which the decisions are being made (i.e. do the decisions support the purpose of the process?).
*   Relates the decisions to perceived changes that are occurring in the 'environment' of the organizational process, in which case both the decisions and the perceptions or rationale are interconnected.
*   Relates the decisions to the group processes from which the decisions emerged (i.e. the social dynamics of the decision makers are related to the decisions made, and often reflect the power dimension of the group).
*   Relates the decisions or decision-making process to the personal motives, values and objectives etc. of the human decision maker(s) (i.e. 'personal purposefulness').

It would be possible to consider further the element structure, and how to undertake each part of it but, for the purpose of the current discussion, it is perhaps sufficient to say that decisions must be evaluated in some manner of speaking, otherwise it is likely that there are decisions being made that have significant consequences, but which are 'good', 'bad', 'potentially dubious' etc. However, it is not the decisions themselves that can be isolated and evaluated; rather the decisions must be evaluated in terms of the human processes (and their purpose) in which they are made. The decision makers and the decision making are of course a key component of organizational process and can be included in a model of an organizational process; the modelling can include, as a component, an examination of the decision-making activities. As can be seen, this is a rich way of thinking about decision making, because it relates the process of decision making to the operational process in which the decisions are made. Commonly, in IS practice, there is the assumption that decisions are taken 'rationally', and the decision maker uses information as a way of determining the decision. Whilst this might be true to some extent, it rather simplifies the purpose of decisions, their context and effect; it also can tend to ignore the relationship between organizational processes and the decisions being made in everyday contexts, about its operation.

Constraints

Every organizational process will have constraints that are taken to be 'as given', within which humans must work and operate. For example, an organizational process may be being designed, implemented, modified or operationalized in a particular social culture, some aspects of which cannot be changed (see the section on *modus vivendi* in Chapter 4). Thus, certain aspects of culture are 'as given', and is assumed in the example that it is beyond the role of the IS practitioner to try to change it. Similarly, on a factory floor, there may be 'constraints' in the knowledge or skills of a set of operatives, which means that the process has to be designed, implemented, modified and operationalized within such constraints. Or, on the same factory floor, there are a set of machines that determine the way in which manufacturing is required to take place (i.e. a given technology determines the process, and therefore can be considered to be a 'constraint'). As such, an IS practitioner must be able to consider the design of the process within a given set of constraints.

It is reasonable to assert that organizational processes will always have a variety of such constraints. They can be constraints that are considered to be concerned with technology, human cultures, skills, knowledge, attitudes, procedures, law etc. Constraints can be considered to be something that are 'as given' (or cannot be changed at a particular point in time) but will have a significant impact on the organizational process. However, it is not the purpose of an IS practitioner to simply identify a set of constraints. Rather, it is the role of the IS practitioner to identify potential constraints that, if changed at a future time, could have impact on the design, implementation, modification or operationalization of the process. Thus, it is not a 'list' of 'constraints' that is taken to be 'as given'. Such a list would serve no function and would be benign. However, it can provide insight into new possibilities for the process at a future time. Thus, the inquiry into constraints can also be considered to be an inquiry into the things that, if changed, would change the process. Thus, the IS practitioner is not just identifying constraints, but modelling possible alternative processes. In the example of the hypothetical factory floor in the previous paragraph, if there was a 'knowledge and skill development' process of a set of operatives, then it would alter the nature of the constraint and, thus, alter the possibilities for the operational process. Similarly, using the same example, if there were alternative machines available, then by the process of their implementation, the constraint would be altered and, thus, change the possibilities for the 'factory floor' operational process.

The inquiry into constraints is, therefore, an inquiry into the possibilities for future processes. In order to achieve this, the IS practitioner will be required to be quite specific about (i) what is considered to be a 'constraint', (ii) the justification of the rationale for the identification of the constraint, and importantly, (iii) the consideration of the model of the process, if the constraint was not there, or could be in some way changed. Typically, this involves conceptual reasoning about the nature of the existing process and the possibilities of future processes, and also the pragmatics of how such constraints can themselves be changed.

Measures of performance

Humans are very quick to pass judgement on things, and indeed we tend to describe aspects of the world as 'good' or 'bad', or 'better' or 'worse' etc. In a sense, simple human judgements might be considered a very simple form of 'measurement', although it is not always clear what the criteria, units of measure, or the processes that are involved in such measures are. Nor is it always clear what the 'thing' that is being judged is, or what the circumstance of the situation of the thing is. Indeed, such judgements can become much more difficult in situations where the 'thing' that is being judged is a concept – such as an organizational process.

There are two rather significant points. First, that some things can be measured easily, with current technology and measuring devices (e.g. the length of a table, the weight of a bag of sugar). From this, it is also reasonable to state that other things are not easily measured (feelings, concepts, ideas, attitudes). In either case, however, human judgement is often applied in order to classify into 'good', 'bad', 'better' or 'worse' etc. There is of course a danger that inappropriate measurements are taken, e.g. we try to measure the weight of something in inches, or we apply a process of weighing to judge attitudes! It is possible to store such data and apply algorithms to it and to assume that it is logical to make decision choices or judgements on the data. The 'science' of measurement, sometimes known as 'metrology', attempts to develop a deeper understanding of the appropriateness of measurement as applied to different contexts. Since an organizational process contains many different things, and since it is a concept (i.e. it exists in the mind), measurement of it is rather challenging. Sometimes the challenges involved in measuring are not particularly well understood (it is sometimes assumed to be 'easy' and/or it is sometimes taken 'as given') and, thus, in practice we do see some erroneous or dubious practices. For instance, those undertaking the measurements may tend to:

•   Oversimplify, by the application of known measurement systems (e.g. weights, lengths, quantities, statistical analyses etc.) to measure things that are not appropriately measured in the way that the systems of measurements dictate. How often, for example, have we seen the application of quantitative measures applied to applications that are not suitable to the measurement system (e.g. quantifying human 'attitudes')?

- Use particular measurements to justify an action or strategy, which has been predetermined. Thus, sometimes the purpose of the measurements is not to help construct the action or strategy, but is to manipulate others into believing, for example, the efficacy of the action or strategy.
- Change the process of measurement. How often have we seen, in human affairs, regular and inexplicable changes in measures and measurement systems that imply a certain inadequacy of the original ones? The 'inadequacy' is often not analyzed, limiting the opportunities for learning, and is commonly attributed to changes in the 'environment' or 'circumstances', which are sometimes rather vague.

We will explore in more detail the issues involved in measurement, and specifically the measurement judgement of organizational processes (see Chapter 7). However, for the time being we will assume that it is possible to apply quantitative or qualitative criteria, to (i) help human judgement about a process or (ii) help explicit thinking about how a judgement could or should be made. Thus, the process of judgement may be considered to have a hierarchy and element structure, which consists of (i) the selection of the appropriate measurement methods and/or the appropriate criteria, (ii) the making of observations on the everyday activities by the application of the measures or criteria, and (iii) the use of the observations to make judgement about what to do or how to act. If the purpose is to make judgement and to 'improve' an organizational process, then it might be considered useful to term such a process a 'monitoring' process (i.e. the purpose of the judging and measuring of activities is to 'monitor' the performance of something, such as another organizational process. See Figure 6.11).

There are some important consequences of this. For example, (i) if a process is called 'monitoring' that involves quantitative and/or qualitative measurements, then the measurements are only an element in the monitoring process, but there are others that are equally important if 'monitoring' is to be purposefully undertaken. For example, there are issues of data collection and interpretation, decisions and actions in addition to measurements, and (ii) if monitoring is to occur, then it stands to reason that the operational process (that which is being monitored) must be well understood,

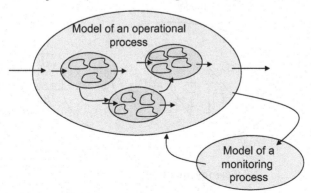

Figure 6.11 The monitoring process and its relationship to the operational process

otherwise any measures applied, any judgements and any monitoring activities cannot relate to the whole process.

In a sense, a process of monitoring is one that 'serves' another process. Further, it would not exist if the operational process did not exist. If we are attempting to model a process of monitoring, then it may also possible and useful to classify the principles and types of measures being used in it. One common type of measure used is that of 'efficiency'. For example, it is possible to conceptualize and apply measures of efficiency, which give us, in some manner of speaking, a way to analyze some aspects of the transformation of the process and how it is performing, given a set of resource requirements to undertake the process (e.g. manpower, time, money etc.). We will again use the example of the university process, and its 'transformation' of students to graduates, to demonstrate the concept and the issues of concern arising from the application of measures of efficiency.

One of the efficiency measures might be developed from the comparison of the inputs with the outputs in a given period. Thus, the number of students that enter the university process and the number of graduates that exit the university process might provide a ratio, which could be considered to be an efficiency ratio. For example, in year one, 100 students might have entered the university, but only 80 exited (or 'graduated'). Thus, we have an efficiency ratio as outlined in Figure 6.12.

In year two, it might be decided that 'improvement' in performance is required, and thus there is pressure (e.g. from government, funding bodies, sponsors or others) to achieve an 85 per cent efficiency ratio. In order to achieve the objective, those who are involved in the operational and everyday decision-making aspects of the organizational process may feel pressured to change the process, and change their behaviour and actions (i.e. this is the purpose of a performance measure). Thus, the measurement influences the operation of the system, and changes can come about that may sometimes be considered to be 'desirable' and sometimes 'undesirable' For example, if the monitoring metrics were used inappropriately, it might happen that

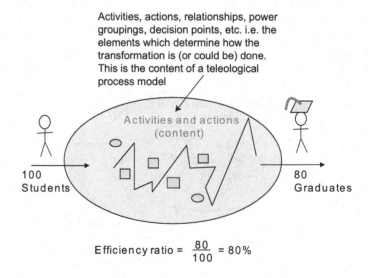

Figure 6.12 Deriving an efficiency ratio of an organizational process

lecturers might feel pressured to pass students that they would not have passed in previous years! This might be deemed desirable, or it might be deemed undesirable (again a human judgement). Indeed, an efficiency measure such as the one outlined may have the effect that it undermines the *raison d'être* of the operational process in the first place! For example, it may undermine its effectiveness to achieve one or more purposeful objectives (e.g. that of 'learning'). The notion of efficiency and effectiveness is demonstrated by this. Thus, an efficiency measure is taken to be a form of measure of inputs and outputs, and levels of resource to achieve the transformation of input to output. This is not the same as an assessment of the 'effectiveness', which must be considered to be the teleological aspects of the process (in this case, it might be considered to have the purposeful objective of 'learning'). In this example, the efficiency might be considered to undermine the effectiveness! The model, and the example of efficiency versus effectiveness, might be used to reflect 'reality' in order to learn more about the dangers of applying efficiency measures without consideration of the effectiveness issues.

Although the example is taken from the educational sector, the principles of efficiency and effectiveness can be applied in very much the same way to any organizational process (e.g. in the 'health sector', in private organizations, public sector, big, little, not-for-profit, NGOs etc). The point here is that the measurement activities are designed to affect operational systems, but they may not in actual fact be thought through in sufficiently precise terms to (i) predict or analyze the actual effects rather than the assumed or designed effects, (ii) analyze the rationale for the designed effects and to evaluate the possibilities of the design actually working, or (iii) evaluate the need for a balance between the striving for efficiency and the effectiveness of the process, in situations where efficiency drives may undermine the effectiveness of the process to deliver what it was purposely designed for! Further, neither efficiency nor effectiveness can be understood, or applied with precision, without a deep understanding of the process in the first place.

Unintended outcomes

Even if a human organizational process is relatively easily defined, because there appears to be general or common agreement about what it is and does, there does seem to be an opportunity to learn from being explicit and in deepening the inquiry into it. The process of definition can be achieved by utilizing the systems constructs. This process of definition serves a number of purposes. For example:

- It can help to justify actions that are taken in the performance of work.
- It can help to justify changes to an organizational process.
- It can help to 'iron out' or understand problematic issues associated with the organization process(es).
- It can help to understand the ambiguities, irrationalities and pressures that are imposed on people in everyday situations.
- It can help in developing diagnostics.
- It can enable better communication between human groups (e.g. between consultants, managers and other 'IS practitioners').

The definition can of course be integrated into the diagnostic inquiring processes. That is to say that the process of modelling can be used to gain insight into existing processes but it might ideally take place after the diagnosis of the 'problematic situation', as described in the previous chapter. This is because there are dangers in muddying the primary objective of the diagnosis inquiry, which should be focused on obtaining others' perspective and viewpoints on the nature and context of the 'problematic situation'. However, once done, the modelling of processes can be undertaken, and can be applied to different areas of concern as revealed by the diagnosis.

There is perhaps a further consideration, because we might argue that an organizational process can be modelled to consider transformations that are not necessarily expected or designed. By way of examination of this, we will use an example of a prison (after Checkland and Scholes 1990). A prison can be considered to be designed for different purposes, e.g. as a 'punishment process' (i.e. 'criminals' are punished for crimes). If a prison is considered to be a punishment system, then the general priority is to make it a rather unpleasant experience for the criminal. A prison also could be considered to be designed as a 'protection for society process'. That is to say, its purpose is to take criminals out of society so that they are unable to undertake criminal activity. In such a process, the general priority will be to hold the prisoner in conditions that might be a good deal more pleasant than in a 'punishment process'. Thus, we have two different models for the process of a prison (although there may be others). Often these two purposeful activities must, in practice, be operated side by side within a prison process, which can often produce ambiguity (e.g. in decision making etc.). Furthermore, in operation, there may be characteristics that emerge that are not designed. For instance, the actual implementation might be quite a different thing, and might give us unexpected or unintended outcomes, which are not part of the formal design but, nonetheless, can be modelled as a transformative system. For example, a prison can be considered to be an unintended but, nonetheless, excellent process that provides an 'education in criminal activity'! The evidence is derived from observation, logic and common sense: criminals go to prison, discuss their methods with fellow criminals, and emerge as better criminals! See Figure 6.13.

Now there are three potential systems models, for one prison process! In this last model, the principle systems construct of transformation has been applied to discover some potential areas that are unintended outcomes of the operation of a process. Using such a notion, it is possible to:

- Be creative with the notion of teleological process models, which are relevant to the situation of concern.
- Learn more about the intended and unintended consequence of the operationalization of an organization or one of its components.
- Abstract some lessons about the use of systems models. For example:
  - Apply a teleological process model to develop learning about a 'real world' situation.
  - Recognize that teleological process models are not used solely to help understand what a designer might want, or aspire to in an organizational process, but to model what actually can happen in practice.
  - Identify multiple teleological process models for one organizational process in practice, but this is not necessarily true in, for example, engineering.

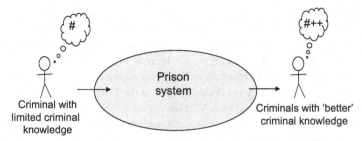

Figure 6.13 An unintended process of a prison, expressed in an outline systems model

Systematics

When discussing the characteristics of a human process, groupings of processes and how they interlink with each other, it would be quite easy to see that certain processes are characterized by levels of routine and programmable tasks, which are repeated with very little variance. For example, in some human processes, the expectation is that human behaviour is highly routine and regular etc. There are many such examples in modern organizations. In such examples, the human is repetitively undertaking work that is similar if not precisely the same. Or sometimes a machine can undertake such tasks in a similar manner. Thus, the process has a design that requires and assumes mechanical-type behaviour of some sort. It is a characteristic that is sometimes referred to as 'systematic'. There are routines in task structure that make a repetitive action appropriate in order to achieve the required outcome in the organizational process. The repetitive nature of routines can be explored and explicitly written down in rule-based type documents, sometimes using tools that are taken from or akin to engineering-type tools (e.g. data flow diagrams, role activity diagrams etc.). The word 'systematic' is used here to describe a generic characteristic of a human process. The words 'systematic' and 'non-systematic' are used in this book not to be mutually exclusive, but as a way of generalizing, and a way of communicating and thinking about the level of 'routinization' and the consequent outcomes (e.g. dehumanizing, deskilling etc.).

An example of a systematic process is that of an automated production line. The routines are such that they are often virtually entirely predictable and, thus, automation and robots can be used in this type of process. An automated production line is often entirely pre-programmable, and that is why machines can be used in such a process. Typically, the humans who are involved in a systematic process will use single purpose machine tools (i.e. there is only one way to operate them). There are many examples of processes in organizations where, in order that the process functions to specific objectives, people must behave in a rather programmed fashion, routinely repeating tasks. In extreme examples, there are disturbing (and unethical) dehumanization and deskilling issues associated with systematic organizational processes (see Braverman 1974). For example, in fast food restaurants, there are highly routine and systematic processes, e.g. there is no need for cooking skills.

Fordism is probably the most cited example of the development of 'systematic' processes (see Wilson 1992). This is probably because it was in the Ford factories that the production line was introduced and applied. Fordism is also closely associated with 'Taylorism', or 'scientific management', in which operations are analyzed 'scientifically' in order to optimize systematic operational processes. Taylorism usually involves breaking jobs, tasks and roles down, and analyzing the efficiency of each component part. It also implies a highly mechanistic method to the process, in which humans are 'deskilled' and 'dehumanized' (see, for example, Braverman 1974 or the mural painting of Diego Rivierra drawn in 1934 at the Detroit Institute of Art, which depict the workers and the machines that they used at Ford's River Rouge plant (i.e. not the car!)). In order to achieve a systematic process, it implies that the environment is stable and predictable. For example, on the supply side, there are regular, reliable and uninterrupted supplies, and on the demand side, there are opportunities for mass homogeneous markets for goods and/or services.

For those who are involved in organizational problem-solving activities, there are obvious ethical dimensions that are required to be considered. It seems reasonable to suggest that, in society as it currently is, the systematic process generates significant wealth and material goods. For example, the supermarkets would be a very different place if the systematic processes were unavailable or not operationalizable. The manufacture of goods would be very different, and the supplying process would be different. IS practice is often assumed to have a fundamental role in bringing about mechanical or mechanized human processes. This is possibly particularly the case in some of the sizable IT implementations (e.g. an ERP application). The technology can help to make processes more 'systematic' (see Zuboff 1988). It seems that there are dilemmas for IS practitioners and they must question certain aspects of their implementation of systematic process: for example, (i) are the gains that they bring sufficiently valuable? Or, (ii) how can compensation be given to the victims of the processes? Or, (iii) is 'more systematic' better in a given context? IS practice is concerned to change processes appropriately, to meet purposeful goals, but it must also integrate the ethical issues that are associated with the task.

In some situations there is a need to change an operation in order to make it more systematic and sometimes there may be a need in an organizational process to make it less systematic. For example, many organizations have been concerned to meet demand in mass markets. Mass markets demand operational processes that are routine and mechanical because the output can be the same, and can be repeated many times. However, with global changes, where mass markets are being serviced in other parts of the world, these same organizations are sometimes attempting to enter new markets that are specialized in some way, with high value products or services. Thus, in some situations, there is a need to increase flexibility, human intuition, skills and knowledge in the processes. This has resulted in such organizations attempting (i) to retain the systematic process in certain ways, but being expectant of greater flexibility, higher value products, less routine behaviours in employees and greater responsibilities given to operational employees, or (ii) to change the systematic process in line with new markets, by making certain processes less systematic. There are some key points that can be abstracted here:

- Intervention to change a process should not assume that it is a goal to make a process more systematic. A process being systematic is not necessarily a goal of an IS practitioner, but might be an outcome of a set of interventions and changes brought about by the process of organizational problem solving – but not necessarily. Indeed, the reverse might be desirable and might be a consequence of interventions. But,

- despite the fact that organizations can be considered to be demanding ever greater levels of human intuition, it would be erroneous to suggest that the systematic process is threatened in capitalist societies. In fact, it is continually being extended to new areas of work, e.g. in a call centre there are systematic routines applied to the process of conversations!
- IS practitioners have sometimes assumed or have 'taken as given' that developing systematic processes is inherently 'good'.

It is perhaps easy to see that there are sometimes underlying assumptions in organizational change methods that the goal is to make the non-systematic into a more systematic organizational process. Indeed, arguably, this is perhaps a basic (ontological) assumption behind many methods that have been associated with organizational problem solving. For example, in the 'modern' systems analysis and design literature (see, for example, Cutts 1991, Yourdon 1989, De Marco 1978, Gane and Sarson 1978), we see the use of techniques such as data flow diagrams, process flow diagrams, role activity diagrams, process flow charts etc., to model out either the current processes and/or future processes. In such literature, there are the assumptions that:

- The 'real world' process (to which the techniques are applied) has characteristics that are systematic in character, because the techniques often assume a certain level of repetition within the process that they are applied to.
- 'Improvement' is in the optimization of a systematic process, which is derived from making it more systematic by identifying and eradicating redundant tasks and activities.
- Not only do such methods and techniques make some significant assumptions, they are also sometimes used as if they can be separated from other important elements of human processes, e.g. 'systems analysis' is done, but excludes the power, politics, social situation, control, human knowledge, skills, attitudes etc.

There are perhaps some key challenges that arise from such thinking; for example:

- There may be benefit from embedding these type of techniques and this type of literature into a more robust debate about teleologically derived process concepts.
- It seems that 'systems analysis' needs to reach out in order to embed itself in organizational problem-solving methodology rather than confine itself to the task of application development, particularly considering that organizations are less concerned about development, but remain very concerned about the applications and how they can improve organization processes.
- The application of techniques needs to integrate their use with other significant aspects, such as ethical concerns etc.

Perhaps these points are worthy of further thinking, consideration and research.

Since systematic processes are characterized as being regular, routine and being rather mechanical in nature, it is hardly surprising that certain engineering principles have been used to depict or define them. Techniques such as those described (e.g. data flow diagrams, role activity diagrams, flow charts) are normally used in such a way

Table 6.2 Some differing (ontological) assumptions in organizational change methods

An 'inquiring' approach to human processes	An 'engineering' approach to human processes
Assumes multiple purposes in an operational process.	Assumes purpose is clear and 'as given'.
Assumes that organizations and human processes are problematic, complex and messy, but can be explored.	Assumes that the organizations and human processes can be 'engineered', often by the application of prescriptive techniques.
Assumes process models are 'intellectual constructs' used for the purpose of developing inquiry about 'real world' processes.	Tends to assume that techniques are representative of processes, and thus the model and the 'real world' are similar, if not identical.
Is oriented to inquiry about what the possibilities are regarding the 'problems' and the nature of possible 'solutions'.	Oriented to 'solutions', commonly taking the 'problem' to be 'as given'.

that they are assumed to 'specify' a human process. Such an approach commonly assumes that the purpose is clear, 'as given' and agreed (e.g. the word 'cooking' is the *purpose* of a process of cooking(!!), cf. the section 'Inquiry into Processes' in Chapter 4). Thus, the techniques are used to represent the process, rather than as a way to explore the process: the application of such techniques is assumed to closely reflect the 'real world' implementation. They also often assume that 'the problem' that is being tackled is easily definable, or that in the implementation of the process, as defined by the techniques, 'the problem' is in fact being solved. Such techniques are not normally used with a primary purpose of inquiring about organizational processes, or about the vagaries of the way they operate in practice, their form, structure and oddities etc. Rather, they are used as an engineering tool, as if what is being engineered is a physical artefact (e.g. building, bridge, robot). Table 6.2 depicts some differences in assumption that can be identified in the approaches.

It is easy to polarize such positions as outlined in Table 6.2. The reason for depicting the different approaches is to highlight some of the differences that can exist in underlying assumptions in the purpose and use of models and techniques. In systematic processes, the engineering approach can be useful and effective, but can also miss or oversimplify some of the subtle complexities, and often is not oriented to solving the variety of 'problems' within a human situation. Taking an engineering approach can result in a tendency to 'automate' and, in doing so, may solve problems, but in themselves are not problem solving in the wider sense or as a primary objective. However, in non-systematic processes (where there are significant elements of human intuition, variability in activities etc., or where wider problems are in need of consideration), an engineering approach can be largely inappropriate.

Design activity

In effect, when an IS practitioner considers the characteristics of a process, the model(s) that are used in the inquiry tend to attach a purpose to the process(es) in question. In effect, a model of an organizational process may assume a purpose (i.e. it will reflect some aspects of the thinking process of the designer). As such, it is merely a human construction, and is as fallible as the human constructor of it (i.e. an IS practitioner). Further, once created, it can be used to develop insight into an organizational process in practice, and its application during such inquiry is again as fallible as its user. Once it is used, and insights have been made about the 'real world' organizational process, the resultant actions (e.g. 'interventions') might be considered, and again these are as fallible as the human behind them. Since IS practitioners are humans, they too are purposeful beings, and as such their designs are not impartial or objective, and they too may learn about their own purposeful action, which may, in some situations, benefit from conscious or explicit analytical thinking. As a consequence of this, IS practitioners must be able to 'think about the way they are thinking' as discussed in Chapter 3.

The attachment of purpose to processes, whether implicit or explicit, demonstrates the contextual complexity in which IS practitioners work. Indeed, it demonstrates that whilst organizations can be problematic, the organizational problem-solving process is equally problematic. For example, in practice, the decision makers of a production process of toy trains may have significant ambivalence between the priorities involved in making robust toys that can give pleasure and learning to children, and a potentially competing priority of trying to develop efficiency in the production process. Similarly, an IS practitioner will often have ambivalence between the priorities involved in inquiring, modelling, making interventions in organizations etc, and other potentially competing human needs (e.g. their next project!). It seems, in both examples, there is a need to inquire, rationalize and prioritize, given the ambivalence and the competing pressures. The process of becoming increasingly aware of both the everyday competing pressures, and other factors that influence action in practice, has sometimes been termed 'critical reflexive practice' (see also Schön 1983), and is an essential aspect of organizational problem solving. In Chapter 3 we termed this 'thinking about thinking'. For example, it is possible to subject to critical analysis certain things that in practice can change human action. For instance:

- The competing pressures on an individual in everyday terms.
- Guiding methodological principles, (e.g. those being discussed in this book), and how they are being utilized (or not utilized) to influence thinking and action.
- The personal motives for undertaking the action in the first place, which influences thinking and action.
- The knowledge (or lack of it!), which constrains thinking and action in practice, etc.

We have depicted the notion of 'thinking about thinking', using the double arrows as shown in Figure 3.4 and considered it to be an integrated component of method when undertaking IS practice. Further, it is not inconceivable that an IS practitioner can assist in some way, through their actions and interactional sequences, to help and coach others to refine their thinking and develop for themselves a heightened level of critical reflexivity of their actions in practice (Figure 6.14).

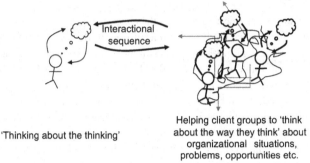

'Thinking about the thinking'

Helping client groups to 'think about the way they think' about organizational situations, problems, opportunities etc.

Figure 6.14 Coaching the 'thinking about thinking' in action!

Integrated elements

Undertaking process modelling aims to allow the clarification about the specific characteristics that make the process achieve some sort of humanly constructed purpose. It is possible to conceptually 'drill down' to analyze perceptions of the structure of components that could make a process 'work' or 'work better'. These components or elements can be conceptualized as part of a model that attempts to analyze the things that 'come together', to make the transformation. Literally speaking, the notion of the 'integrated elements' is one that integrates elements together in order to make the 'whole' work. It is non-specific in the sense that 'what is integrated', and 'how it is integrated', is not assumed by using the term. It means the term does not really give any indication regarding how to analyze the elements themselves, but to say that they are there! In that sense, it is a rather general term. But its generalizability is also a strength because it is possible to explore, within our inquiring activities, the 'things' that make the process work. Perhaps, rephrasing, we can explore conceptually the content of the workings of the process, and whether it is meeting the purposeful objectives, or whether the workings (or integrated elements) might be changed in some way. We can hypothesize about what the constitution of 'integrated elements' actually could be considered to be. For example:

- the 'coming together' of people, tasks, technology, actions etc.
- sets or 'chunks' of human activity
- subsystems
- roles, tasks and activities
- control, hierarchy, power dimensions etc.
- data and flows of data
- materials and flows of materials
- the way in which technology is used
- a combination of some or all of the above
- etc.

There is of course a choice regarding how to view and analyze the integrated elements of a process, and that view may need to be general, or it may need to be very specific, depending on the objectives of, (i) the inquiring process, and (ii) the discourses in which they are being used. However, there may be the necessity to take the same

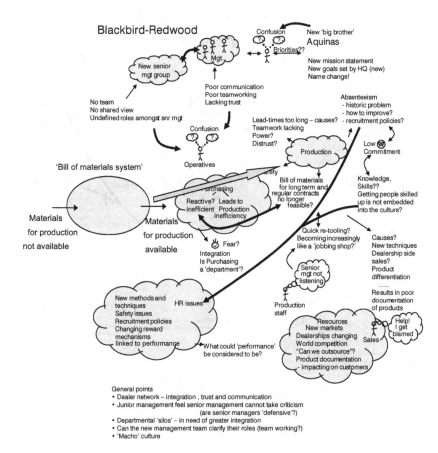

Figure 6.15 Selecting an area of concern, to subject it to iterative inquiry using process modelling

view of content (i.e. the integrative view), but be able to identify sub-component parts, which in some ways integrate to make the process 'work'. Hence, there is sometimes the suggestion that the sub-components are in some way a refinement of the original systems construct, i.e. it is possible to express the perceptions of an integrated set of components, as 'subsystems'. These are not elements per se, but subsystems with element structures (e.g. tasks, activities, controls, power dimensions, information, technologies etc). We could take some examples from a recent case and conceptualize the constituent parts or 'chunks' of human activity that make up one of the systems that have been defined previously (see Figure 6.15).

Of course, the diagnosis serves as a basis for justifying which processes are to be modelled, and there are commonly many possibilities (!) (See Figure 6.16.)

If we took one process and started modelling using systems ideas, having defined it, it is then possible to explore the various possibilities regarding how it can achieve its humanly constructed goals. For example, in a process where the objectives were defined to be to ensure that all materials are available to a production line, then it may be considered to consist of various sub-components. For example:

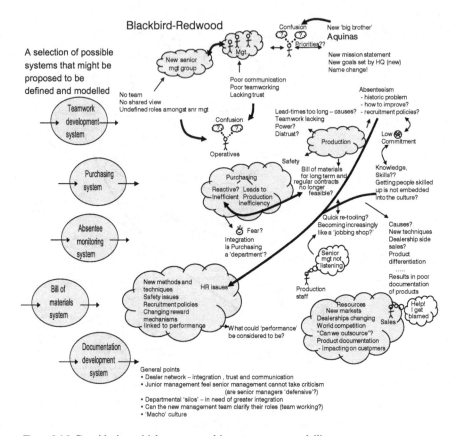

Figure 6.16 Considering which areas to subject to process modelling

- It may be considered to be important to ensure that there is up-to-date information about the lead times for the supply of materials and parts.
- It may be considered important to liaise with the sales team, in order to establish the likely differences between existing and future products, and/or what orders are likely to deviate from the standardized product.
- At the point at which an order is made, there may be a requirement for establishing the current levels of stock, or the forecasts of stock levels, in order to determine which material or parts might need to be purchased for the fulfilment of the order.
- The constraints of supply of materials and parts may be required to be considered in the overall production planning process.
- There may be a perceived requirement for setting up contracts for materials or parts with suppliers, and these contracts may be set up in such a way that the parts or materials are integrated into the production schedule (where or if possible).
- The orders of materials and parts must be sent to suppliers at the appropriate times.

Notice in this discussion, the 'bill of materials' is not seen as simply a breakdown of data about the materials and parts of a product. It is seen as a human process, which uses such data in the fulfilment of the process, as detailed in Figure 6.17.

In undertaking a definition of a given process, a great deal of innovation and creativity can be included into the thinking activities. If the 'real world' constraints are temporarily shelved, this would allow for a highly conceptual process into what 'could be' or 'should be' rather than 'what is'! It is easy, for example, to get lost in the details and complexity of failing organizational processes! In IS practice, *it is essential to avoid 'getting lost' in the complexity and muddliness, but to refine the conceptual schema sufficiently that it can help in defining 'what needs to change'*, in order that a process can successfully achieve its transformations and human purpose. In practice, 'what needs to change' will often involve information and technology, but not necessarily. Therefore, an IS practitioner must be able to make an intervention at a number of levels and in a number of ways, and not confine their actions to information and technology change.

If the integrated elements are explored in an inquiring process in the manner outlined, we might notice a number of key issues about the process of inquiry itself. For example:

- That the inquiry into the purposefulness of the expressed 'chunks' of a human process is, for the IS practitioner, an attempt to make sense of a messy human situation.
- It is not an 'engineering diagram' since there are many more uncertainties in an organizational design, because of likely changes in the situation; it must be a dynamic human communicating device!
- A conceptual schema as outlined recognizes that, within each component and sub-component, there is maintained the integration of humans, machines, tasks, control mechanisms, power relationships etc. It is remains integrative (and systemic) in that sense.

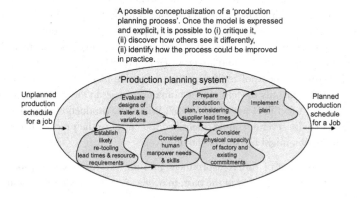

Figure 6.17 The 'chunks' of a human process, expressed as a human system

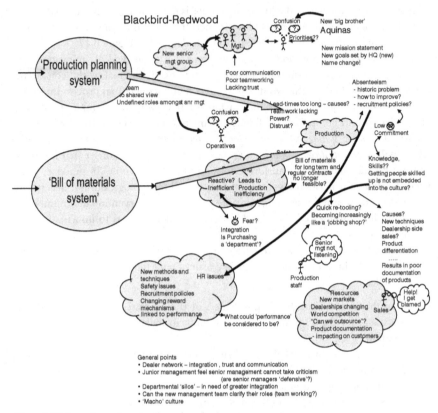

Figure 6.18 Locating a 'production planning' process

Interconnections between 'chunks'

The process of process modelling is typically characterized as one that is iterative, and one that refines, through the process of reconsidering and exploring the situation, as outlined in the diagnosis, and using systems models to structure the inquiry into processes. It means that different areas of the 'situation' are explored, and sometimes there are some surprising interconnections made during the process of inquiry. For instance, it might be considered that some of the problems in the production process, which might be located in failings in the production planning process, might be the subject of further investigation and analysis (see Figure 6.18).

In undertaking a process of modelling the production planning system, it might be seen to be useful to identify the 'chunks' of human processes in the same manner as has been discussed for the 'Bill of materials system'. Within the production planning systems model, there may be several 'chunks' identified as central to the process. For example, planning production might be perceived to involve:

- The identification of different products, and the variations in the product that customers have demanded in the past, in order to establish potential implications for the production process.

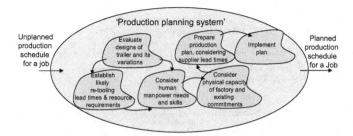

Figure 6.19 An expression of 'production planning' sub-components

- The assessment of the retooling requirements resulting from the variations in the products.
- Consideration of the human resources requirements in the production processes, and in the retooling requirements, including the skills required of the humans and the expected labour inputs required.
- An assessment of the existing capacity of the factory, existing lines and potential for new lines, alongside the need for existing expectations of spare capacity.
- The analysis of the constraints of the supply of materials and parts, and their lead times.
- The implementation of the plan, including preparing the line, contractual arrangements, checking appropriate health and safety guidelines etc.

The production planning system might be modelled as detailed in Figure 6.19.

As already discussed, and to reiterate, the primary objective of the process of process modelling is to prepare the mind (of the IS practitioner(s)), in order to help them develop precision, and engage in a debate with others (e.g. the client organizational groups). It is not the purpose to 'engineer' solutions per se although in the more systematic processes this could well follow.

Sometimes during the process of process modelling, it is apparent that there are some areas of 'overlap' and 'similarity', either between the systems under consideration or between the sub-components of them. For example, in both the Bill of materials and the Production planning systems, there is a sub-component process that is, for the purpose of planning production, considering the supplier lead times of materials and products, as depicted on Figure 6.20.

It is not the purpose of process modelling to 'standardize', because the primary purpose is to inquire into what is and what could be, in terms of organizational processes. Nonetheless, that inquiry might lead to the recognition that certain sub-components of the systems models are in fact similar in some way, (e.g. in function, purpose, structure etc.). It means that there are potentially, at least, components that might overlap and integrate, and with sufficient modelling in different areas of a situation, there are often opportunities to interlink the sub-components.

Hierarchy

So far, the sub-components of systems have been described as 'sub-components' or 'chunks'. This is for want of a better description, but one of the central characteristics

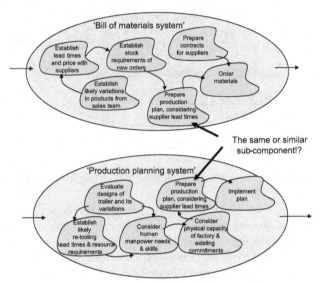

Figure 6.20 Similarity between sub-components in different models

is that each of the 'chunks' retains the systemic interconnectivity between elements that characterize human work. For example, they are not a list of actions (e.g. as on an 'action plan'), because in process models, the 'chunks' are integrated into other aspects, e.g. sets of tasks, knowledge, skills, information, control structures, human power relationships, technologies etc. It does not take much to recognize that these 'chunks' of a process can be themselves modelled as systems in their own right. Perhaps they could be modelled as 'subsystems' and can be defined using the same systems constructs to help to structure inquiry into them (see Figure 6.21).

As can be seen, the general model can be broken into components, which themselves can be modelled as systems. This can result in significant detail, because each of the sub-components can be continually broken down. The resultant hierarchical arrangement enables a structure around which to develop inquiry and as the inquiry progresses down the hierarchy, it is possible to develop increasing levels of detail. At each level, the inquiry process can engage social groups in their thinking about certain issues. For example:

- Communicating and exploring problems and potential changes to the organizational situation.
- Helping to uncover new problematic issues.
- Helping to explain why certain things seem not to work in the whole system, by recognizing failings in its constituent component parts.
- Providing a conceptual schema to help identify linkages and interdependencies between processes and sub-processes.

The iterative nature of the modelling can result in significant effort, and significant numbers of models, relating to many areas of an organizational situation, where interlinkages between systems can be indicated and the hierarchies can be expressed (see Figure 6.22).

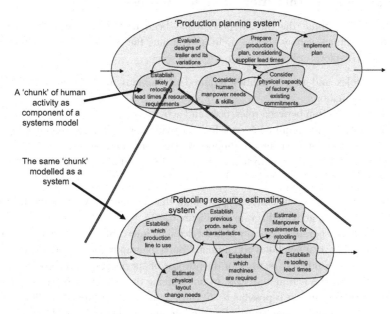

Figure 6.21 'Chunks' modelled as a system in a hierarchy

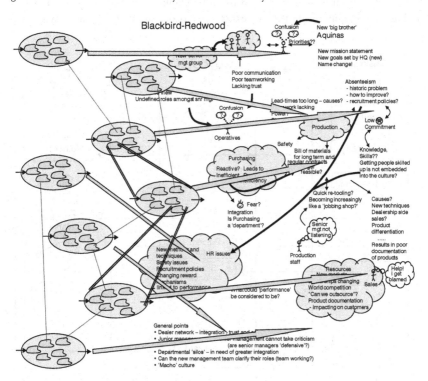

Figure 6.22 Many models, relationships and hierarchies

Integration of other modelling techniques

Once learning about the human process has been undertaken, and its systemic structure outlined, it may also be useful to continue the inquiry in other ways. For example, to explore:

- The roles and responsibilities required of humans in order to achieve the transformation.
- The relationship between roles, tasks and activities.
- The information required to coordinate activities, or support decision making.
- The data (and its structure) to support information processing.
- Control structures, monitoring, or, broadly, 'measurement' of current or future processes.

Sometimes a process is sufficiently systematic that it can usefully be modelled using techniques such an activity diagram (see Figure 6.23).

The activity diagram is typically used for detailing interconnection of activities that are required between machines and humans. Such diagrammatic techniques are well known and are assumed to be used for the purpose of specification of technology, and the role that it plays within a process. In undertaking the activity of modelling using activity-type diagrams, it is possible to: (i) clarify and refine an understanding of an aspect of an organizational process (i.e. the interlinkages between highly routinized human and machine activities), and to (ii) be explicit with the aspect of a process, and as such communicate the process characteristics to others. An activity diagram

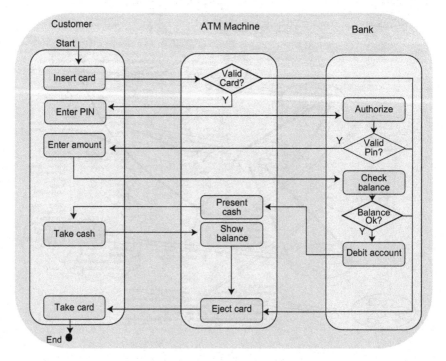

Figure 6.23 An activity diagram for an ATM (a very 'systematic' process!)

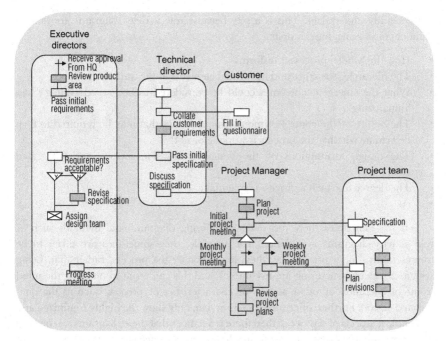

Figure 6.24 A role activity diagram depicting activities involved in managing projects

such as that shown in Figure 6.23 only shows the activities, interlinkages (as in a flow of activities) and the primary responsibilities of those undertaking the actions. Thus, activity diagrams may be enhanced to explicitly make interlinkages between the human roles in a mechanical organizational process, and their interconnectivity (see Figure 6.24).

Role activity diagrams and other similar diagrammatic techniques show only a component of a process. For instance, in the example given in Figure 6.24, there are five roles identified, with a number of activities that would be expected to be undertaken in each. The diagram explicitly outlines these roles and the interconnection between activities, but does not consider other aspects, for example:

- the power dimension of a process
- the attitudes of the people undertaking the process
- their knowledge and skills to undertake the roles identified in the process
- the hierarchy and interconnection between processes
- the data, communication and control elements of a process
- the non-routine, serendipitous aspects of an organizational process
- etc.

Nor is it, on its own, explicit about *purpose* (which, as in engineering physical things, is taken 'as given' (see the section 'Transformation' earlier in this chapter)). Ignoring the purpose would be appropriate in only the most mechanistic and systematic processes, and would not be appropriate when changing human processes. Unfortunately, in IS practice to date, the technique of applying role activity diagrams and integrating their use with the inquiring activities that are involved in teleological process modelling is not generally undertaken. This is a pity because role activity diagrams are limited without considering, for example:

- How the 'whole' process transforms.
- The hierarchy, structure and integrated elements in the transformation.
- What the emergent outcomes could be considered to be (e.g. 'deskilling', 'dehumanizing').
- The nature of the control or monitoring activities that may be required to help determine whether the process is working or not!
- The design assumptions of the designers, decision makers and integrated elements.
- The degree to which a process is systematic.
- etc.

Indeed, sometimes there are dangers in using diagrammatic methods such as role activity diagrams in isolation. For example, they sometimes are taken to be 'representative' of a process (i.e. they are seen *to be* the process, rather than being seen as a way of structuring inquiry into it), and this can result in blocking the mind from consideration of other aspects or characteristics of process (such as the ones bulleted above). Further, since these diagrams can only show the highly routinized and mechanical aspects of a process, then there is a danger that these diagrams can be used to instigate changes that attempt to mechanize the un-mechanizable. That is to say, they can guide the thinking and can result in action that attempts to make systematic, a process that is not suited to being systematic!

Other diagrammatic techniques are similar, but may show different aspects of a process, but themselves are limited in modelling human processes. For example, a data flow diagram can be used to detail the interrelationship between data and actions that operate or change the data as shown in Figure 6.25, but equally miss some very essential aspects of organizational processes in practice.

In a similar manner to the activity diagrams, the data flow diagram is highly selective of 'what it is looking at'. For example, it only depicts the flows of data between stores and processes and as such requires careful consideration about:

- How it can be utilized, and the appropriateness for modelling particular types of process (i.e. it requires the consideration of 'systematicness' of the process).
- What the diagram does not show about an organizational process. This is as important as what it does show but, unfortunately, is often lost by the mechanical application of such techniques.

The 'mechanistic' models (role activity diagrams, data flow diagrams etc.) would be useful only in highly regular, routine and semi-mechanical processes. In practice, they are usually applied without considering systems constructs such as those outlined in earlier in this chapter, and this may have some important consequences. For instance, it means that the purposefulness of the process has not been explored and, thus, is taken 'as given'. This may be appropriate in mechanical or semi-mechanical processes (such as an automatic teller machine) but, equally, it might not be appropriate in other types of process, (e.g. processes of 'providing humanitarian aid', 'developing strategy', 'learning how to sail', 'the process of a university', 'the process of managing a project'). As such, it is reasonable to assume that such techniques need to be used

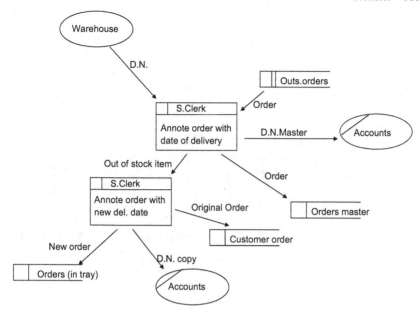

Figure 6.25 A data flow diagram detailing the flows of data in a sales process

carefully, because sometimes they can be used to model (and sometimes ultimately to 'automate') processes that are insufficiently systematic that they can be usefully modelled in such a mechanical type way (see Zuboff 1988).

'Process maps' or 'application maps'

In many large implementations of computing technology, there is a requirement to develop 'process maps' of sorts. These commonly vary significantly in their detail, but are required to help structure the inquiry into (i) how data is captured, (ii) how the data is used to update various integrated database applications, and (iii) the data sources of various reports (see Figure 6.26).

Although these types of models are sometimes termed 'process maps', the word 'process' in this instance applies to the process of the computer application, rather than the organization process, as has been discussed in the previous sections of this chapter. Sometimes a 'process map' is termed a 'systems flowchart'. This conveys the idea that a diagram is representative of the flow and architecture of the 'computer system'. The word 'system', in this instance, is used in a very different way than in previous discussions in this book. To avoid confusion with the words 'system' and 'process', perhaps the term computer 'application map' might be better. 'Application maps' are often constructed to show the flow of actions that are undertaken at various stages, by the computer technologies. These are often (unsurprisingly) mechanistic in nature, and rule-bound ('systematic'). It is unsurprising because the subject of study is an inanimate and physical artefact (a computer). An 'application map' can record both the flow of data, and the method of the flow (e.g. 'via FTP', 'batch update'). It will commonly include the characteristics and features of the technology platforms ('SAP GL Server', 'UNIX operating system' etc.). An 'application map' is often the basis

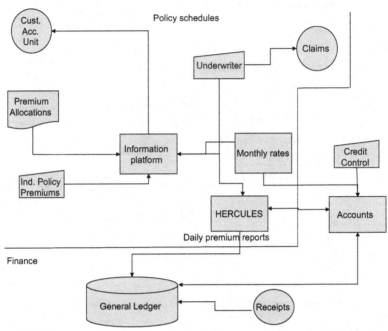

Figure 6.26 A 'process map' of a large application in an insurance organization

for inquiring into (i) security and integrity issues of the computer applications, and (ii) potential required changes that result from changes in organizational processes, or from legislation changes or conformance issues.

A key focus of the IS practitioner, in organizations with large computer applications, is often at the interface between 'application maps' and the role that computing technology plays in the various organizational processes. In undertaking such roles, it is essential to be able to relate the 'application maps' to organizational process models. This implies that this activity is underpinned by knowledge of both the human processes, and computer technology architecture (e.g. data structures, principles of algorithm construction, query languages, database security etc.). Such knowledge is essential if an IS practitioner is to be able to translate the organization rules, norms and expectations that are imposed onto organizational processes and the way they are structured and 'translated' into technology applications.

The construction of adequate 'application maps' is an extremely intricate and complex task. It is one that requires significant care. Organizations that have large and complex databases are rightly very cautious of making changes to the application architecture. The risks of making small changes to the applications can sometimes be very significant. Therefore, the development of 'application maps' requires significant care and precision. This inquiry is very much one that is underpinned by engineering-type inquiry (see also the section on 'Design-type Thinking' in Chapter 3). Unlike the inquiry into organizational processes, the 'application maps' are concerned with an inquiry into an inanimate artefact (the computer application). There are some very important ontological and epistemological considerations in such an undertaking. For example:

- An application map can be likened to any engineering drawing of an inanimate or physical object (e.g. robot, house, car).
- However, the process of inquiry into its structure and architecture remains a human process. Thus, the quality of the outcome is only as good as the quality of the inquiry.
- There are varied interpretations about the nature and function of an 'application map', as well as the methods used in its construction. These interpretations are human, even though the object is inanimate. The fact that the subject of inquiry is inanimate, does not imply that the inquiry is equally inanimate!
- IS practitioners are required to integrate engineering type inquiring activities, with the social inquiring activities that are required to change human organizations. IS is, indeed, at the cusp of the integration of differing inquiring methods and associated assumptions.

Social interactional sequences in modelling

In undertaking process modelling and the development of application maps, there are some important considerations regarding the social dynamics. There are, for example, social dynamics amongst IS practitioner teams and there are social dynamics amongst those with whom they interact. In other words, there is a social process in the activity of modelling, and this itself can be subjected to critical analysis. Thus, if we are considering a human process, then it may be possible to analyze it critically, in order to develop greater understanding of it and, therefore, potentially 'improve' it. It might be possible, for example, to apply the systems constructs to the human process itself! Indeed, if we consider the social processes that are involved, then it would be natural to consider (for example):

- The purposefulness of the group process (a teleological issue).
- The purposefulness of the actions taken by those involved the group process (again, a teleological issue).
- The 'thinking about thinking as it relates to action' of the individuals in the group process.
- The actions and activities of those involved in the group process.
- The formal and informal roles that individuals play in the group process.
- The power dynamics and defensive routines of those involved in the group process.
- The control and communication of the group process.
- The implicit or explicit 'measures of performance' upon which judgement about the relative success or failure of the group process that are being operationalized.
- etc.

As such, it is possible to take the systems constructs in order to structure an inquiry into the effectiveness of a group process. In undertaking the inquiry, for example, it might be necessary to question perceptions of purposeful actions and outcomes. For example, in IS practice, there may be a need to engage client groups into questioning the relative strengths and weaknesses of the processes that they are involved with. If this is considered to be the case, then the interactional sequences between IS practitioner and client groups may be, in part, 'to encourage the engagement'. However, this may not be possible, because of a particular role–relationship (see Chapter 4), e.g. the expectations of the client groups might be for the IS practitioner to 'provide answers', rather than to help them to 'find answers'. This of course is a role expectation on the part of a client group, perhaps motivated by an attempt at avoiding the pain of facing certain difficulties in practice, or the pain of having to think carefully about them! Therefore, the IS practitioner will need to be making interventions to help change the expectations about their own roles and relationships to client groups, before doing other things, e.g. changing processes, information, technology etc. For example, the IS practitioner may be required to make interventions in order to (i) change expectations, and once done, then they can (ii) make interventions to help the 'engagement' with the issues and problems of organizational processes. In this example, it is possible to abstract certain lessons about the social interaction between IS practitioner(s) and their client groups. For instance:

- Since it is the client groups who ultimately make changes (not the IS practitioner) then it is they who must themselves have a certain ownership of issues that are perceived to be problematic, and as such are required to engage with inquiry about existing or future processes.
- The IS practitioner must be able to direct the social interactional sequences in such a way that there are conditions conducive to changing organizational processes, and this may mean a very significant effort in managing expectations, roles and related interactional sequences.
- It may also highlight the need for IS practitioners to 'organize themselves' to undertake the task. For example:
  - An IS practitioner must be able to prepare his own thinking in order to prepare for his own purposeful action and behaviour.
  - Where IS practitioners are working in teams, the team process is required to prepare its own thinking in order to undertake purposeful action and, if it cannot, it would be reasonable to suggest that it is in no position to help others (i.e. client groups) to do the same!

In undertaking the inquiry into organizational processes, there is a danger of being driven by the imperatives of everyday concerns and anxieties, without having precision of concept. Hence the need for iterative evaluation or iterative inquiry about the validity of concept, as it relates to various perceptions of 'reality'. This iterative inquiring process also is concerned with (i) developing the detail of the models (as concept) and the interlinkages between different components and elements, and (ii) being able to enter a discourse with client groups, to demonstrate the various possibilities, whereby the discourse is a foundation for change. The iterative movement between 'conceptual' and 'real' worlds allows for the separation of conceptual construct from the muddliness of the real world. The argument is that there must be some way to abstract a concept without getting too embroiled in the muddliness. If we allow ourselves to do that, then our concepts will be muddly! Sometimes, it is useful to separate the concept of the system from the 'real world' imperatives, temporarily, and then to refine the inquiry into the 'real world situations', using the conceptual model to help construct new lines of inquiry. The conceptual model can, therefore, provide a structure that can act to guide the thinking about 'real world' processes. Putting it bluntly, if there is a difference between the conceptual model, and our perceptions resulting from the inquiry, then it is possible to either (i) amend or refine the model, or (ii) amend or refine the 'real world' process. One or the other must be judged to be 'wrong'! Iterative movement between the 'real world' and the 'conceptual model' is a characteristic of the inquiring process, in which further 'issues of concern' can emerge, and can be evaluated in terms of their importance for 'real world' improvement, development or innovation. The process is also a social process involving a number of groups and individuals (e.g. various client groups and IS practitioner groups).

7 Monitoring and control

Abstract

One of the most fundamental uses of information systems in organizations concerns the application of information and technology to 'monitor' aspects of organizational activities. The impact of monitoring and metrics has a profound effect on operations. Unfortunately, in organizations, the monitoring is commonly done extremely badly, often compounded by the power of the technology to hold huge amounts of monitoring data (commonly a 'scattergun' approach to monitoring). In this chapter we will explore a range of ideas about how to diagnose and improve monitoring activities. The discussion will outline how teleological systems models and constructs can help the human process of monitoring organizational processes.

Introduction

Humankind might be considered to be a highly judgemental animal. For instance, humans frequently pass judgement on things that surround them. They protest, complain, grumble, whine and carp. They also praise, commend, extol, honour and eulogize. In undertaking the whining and grumbling, and in their praising and commending, they are attaching some sort of value judgement to things (e.g. 'better', 'worse', 'good', 'evil', 'competent', 'incompetent' etc.). The judgements made can be based on an explicit process that leads to decisions or actions (e.g. an operations manager making a judgement about production quality, based on standard metrics regarding what is 'good quality' and what is 'bad quality'). Judgement can also be made on something very informal and implicit (e.g. a landlady in a pub discussing a regular customer, expressing her judgement by saying, 'she's "mutton dressed as lamb"… but she's very moralistic you know'). It is rare in everyday conversation, such as the one in this latter example, that the assertions, ideas and judgements etc. that are made are explored in an in-depth or analytical way. But if this was to be undertaken, it might be required that those undertaking the analysis might question certain things, such as:

- The criteria being used or applied in the process of passing judgement.
- The meaning of the terms and constructs being used (e.g. 'moralistic').
- Precisely what is the entity is that is being judged (in this example, is it the person, the person's attitudes, actions etc).
- The purposefulness of making the judgement, or of expressing the judgement; this would include:

- Why the person making the judgement has selected and used the particular constructs or criteria in the way that they have.
- The values of those making the judgement.
- etc.

Fortunately perhaps, everyday conversations are not subjected to explicit critical and analytical evaluation using criteria such as that outlined! If they were, we would have a world that might be dominated by long-winded and rather boring discussions about certain underpinning principles behind everyday judgement! However, it is of course important in *certain* contexts to explore explicitly the judgements being made, and the logic, or basis, of a judgement, and whether it could be 'improved'. In organizations, decisions are made on explicit and implicit judgements, and these form the basis of actions for improving organizational processes. If there is a need for improvement in organizational processes, it seems that there may also need to be improvement in the judgements made about the organizational processes. In human and organizational processes, the two are completely interconnected.

Challenges in judgements

Following the above introductory discussion, it is perhaps common sense to assume that if we are concerned with the activity of judging performance in a form of 'evaluation' or 'monitoring', then it is necessary to question (i) what it is that we are assessing the performance of, (ii) how it is going to be undertaken, and (iii) what the effect on performance is that results from the evaluative activities. It seems in this simple common sense statement, there lies some significant challenges for those involved in assessing the performance of human organizations for a number of reasons. For example:

- There are often ambiguities in what exactly is being monitored. Is it, for example, the whole process, or certain elements, objects or sub-processes that are components of the whole? For example, if we are to make judgements about an element of a process (e.g. the performance of a set of humans (e.g. nurses in a hospital)), there must be some account made of the process in which the human(s) work, and the purpose of the process, and the expected norms of behaviour of those who make the process fulfil its purpose. In other words, what is being monitored is not easily separated from other elements of the process, and it is perhaps both the process and the elements that are required to be the subject of analysis.
- There are often many performance monitoring activities that are undertaken simultaneously, but sometimes the results are contradictory. In undertaking each of these activities, assessment of how they each contribute to the whole is often not clear.
- There is often ambiguity about the (often hidden) purpose of the implementation of performance monitoring activities. For instance, the espoused 'performance monitoring' activity might be motivated by something other than 'monitoring performance', e.g. it might be instigated to control, change power relationships, bash a set of workers, deflect blame from one group to another etc.
- There is often significant contradiction in the process and purpose of performance monitoring. For instance, some would argue that 'data collection' about the process

being monitored is done in order to make decisions about what to do about it. Others might argue that the latter is overly naïve, and that a more realistic process would be that data is purposely selected by decision makers in order to justify their action, which often favours their particular political or power standing. It is easy to see that designers of a performance monitoring process might may be oversimplistic and naïve, which would cause their designs to be irrelevant.

• There are ambiguities about what measures are required (e.g. quantitative, qualitative), the way that they should be presented, and how these integrate with their role in the judgements and subsequent actions of decision makers.

• There are ambiguities in the *effect* that the monitoring processes have on various aspects of the operations. The monitoring may have purposely designed effects, but it also have some emergent effects that may not be immediately obvious, some of which may not be considered to be 'beneficial'.

• There is often no process whereby performance monitoring can be itself evaluated, and as such there is often no feedback to the performance monitoring process itself.

• When a human organization is being 'monitored' via the application of criteria or metrics, humans will change their behaviour to fit the monitoring metrics and criteria (which is exactly what the 'monitoring' is intended to do), but often if the criteria are not correct, or they are applied badly, there may be 'incorrect' (!) resultant behaviours.

As can be seen, there are some significant challenges in making judgements in organizations and about organizational performance (see also Vickers 1965), and these challenges are of *central importance* to the IS practitioner.

Models of the process of monitoring

If a human process is characterized by having elements and interrelationships between elements (such as people, power dynamics, ways of working, norms, beliefs, technologies, attitudes and a range of other things that make the activity operate in a particular way), then the assessment of the process must attempt to make judgement on both (i) what are appropriate elements, and (ii) their interrelationships. If we were to make a judgement on a process, it seems reasonable that the *process of judgement* itself should be subjected to inquiry, as outlined in the previous discussion. That is to say, for the purposes of our discussions we will term this the operational process that can be modelled (e.g. as a purposeful 'operational process'). It is also reasonable to conduct inquiry into the human process that makes a judgement about the operational process. Here we are separating into two components: the process itself, and the secondary human activity system that is designed to 'make judgement' about it (and therefore influences and affects the first in some way), and we can express this as two systems models (see Figure 7.1).

The arrow in Figure 7.1 labelled 'influences and affects' may be implicit, in that it can influence and affect without any conscious human action that results, or is derived from, the judgement. For example, 'nurses' on a hospital ward may be being monitored and judged on the number of patients in their care. In this example, we have a quantifiable measure ('number of patients in their care'). The fact that a given nurse knows the criteria upon which he is judged, naturally results in alterations

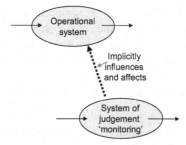

Figure 7.1 A systems representation of an organizational process and the process by which it is judged

in behaviour. This change in his behaviour can be conscious or subconscious but, nonetheless, is purposeful. The resultant behaviour might (for example):

* Be an attempt to maximize numbers of patients within their care.
* Be an attempt to maximize the numbers, perceived by others (such as those undertaking the monitoring) to be in their care, but actually trying to reduce the numbers.
* Be in becoming angry at being 'measured' in such a 'stupid manner'.
* etc.

An IS practitioner must be concerned to analyze the processes involved in the judgement of the operational processes, and the intended or unintended results of it, whether or not those results are desirable or undesirable, conscious or subconscious, explicit or implicit. In effect, the line between the two systems models as depicted in Figure 7.3 can help to explain the effects that may or may not be expected or wanted and, in that sense, there is an emergent effect arising out of the process of monitoring. The effect may also be purposely hidden by humans, because sometimes the process of monitoring is purposely designed to influence in ways that might be considered to be unethical or unwanted, and in such cases there may be alternative reasons and rationale given for the existence of the monitoring activities! For example, the 'measurement' of the number of publications as an indicator of commitment to research of a university process may be considered to have been designed purposely, to provide a mechanism for resource distribution, but it may have the effect of reducing the quality of research, because academics adapt to the way they are measured, and produce more research papers that are 'quick and dirty'.

If we were to use systemic constructs to help think about the monitoring process, we would consider the core systems constructs as outlined in the previous chapter. It would involve inquiry to define relevant systems models, and to consider the element structure of them. For example, it would be possible to consider the purposefulness of a system of monitoring: those who are doing the monitoring might be undertaking it for the purpose of control (i.e. to ensure that the operational process is functioning 'as it should', see Beer 1967). Since monitoring is a human activity, it is open to human interpretation, and thus 'monitoring' can be undertaken for other hidden purposes. For example, it might be undertaken to prove that an operational process 'works well', so that funding for it can be secured in the future!! Or it can be undertaken in order to prove to a wider audience (e.g. readers of reports that result from a process of monitoring) that a manager is deserving of a promotion or a pay rise! Or it may be undertaken to aggrandize the importance of an organizational process because of a power 'need' of certain groups. The point is that the process of monitoring can be subjected to critical analysis as in any other human process, using the systems constructs as outlined in the previous chapter.

The inquiry about the monitoring process involves a number of elements. For example:

• It may involve the human action of construction of metrics or criteria that are designed to be applied to a given operational process. In our example, a form of 'metric' is that of 'number of patients under the care of the nurse', in a nursing operational process. Decisions must be made on the criteria, although often, in practice, both the process of monitoring and the component set of decisions about the metrics and criteria are implicit (i.e. they are not explicitly defined). Nonetheless, in every monitoring process, they must be in existence, otherwise monitoring will have no meaning. Often the metrics and criteria may change, and the changeability is a characteristic of the process that must be of concern for the IS practitioner.

• The monitoring itself will consist of taking measurements, or applying criteria, and (perhaps ideally) these may be used in order to 'help' make a human judgement. This might involve formally measuring something (e.g. taking a random sample of patients under the care of nurses). As mentioned, this example is a quantitative measure or metric. The metric itself, and the method of data collection, must be subjected to analysis in order that it can be justified and is appropriate for purpose. The 'metric' may of course be qualitative (i.e. it cannot be measured). For example, the skills of the nurse cannot easily be quantified, but they nonetheless can be evaluated, and can form part of the process of 'monitoring'.

• The 'influencing and affecting' (as depicted in Figure 7.3) may also be purposely designed and action might be sanctioned and justified, depending on the results application of the criteria (if there is a condition x in the operational process, then it needs to be corrected by action y).

These elements themselves can be subjected to critical analysis. They are depicted in Figure 7.2 (see also Checkland 1981; Checkland and Scholes 1990; Wilson 1984, 1990).

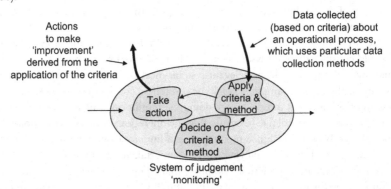

Figure 7.2 A possible element structure of a process of monitoring

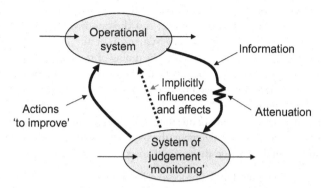

Figure 7.3 The interrelationship between the monitoring and the operational systems

The integrative content (elements, norms, activities, social structure etc.) of organization processes often cause the people within it to have or use constructs pertaining to their particular view of the organizational activity in which they operate an aspect of their lives. Nonetheless, the three component elements as depicted in Figure 7.3 will always be required in a monitoring process and, thus, can help structure inquiry into the effectiveness of the process of monitoring in practice. In terms of the purity of the concept, as a conceptual device, it does not matter that there are different interpretations, nor does it matter that there are different ways of undertaking monitoring. The systemic structure will always be a useful structure in which to investigate practice. These issues are very important in the inquiry about whether the operation of the process is effective; the systemic structure (Figure 7.3) is a construct that will be valid in inquiring into any organizational process.

Implicit judgement

In the same way that they make judgement about other things, humans also make judgement about organizational activities. For example, 'the deliveries are always late', ' this company will never improve whilst he's in charge' or 'the one-way system is nonsense in this city'. In other words, there is an implied organization activity set (or organizational 'process') in everyday statements and everyday language, which is constructed by those making such judgements (e.g. in this case, the 'delivery' process, the 'company' process, 'the one-way system'). This can be related to the role played within the 'process' of those making the judgement. There are not just implied 'processes' in everyday conversations, but often there are a range of assumptions made in associated judgements. For example:

• What is 'problematic' within the process involves judgement that is substantiable to a greater or lesser extent.
• One organizational process is often seen to be better or worse than another. For example, it might be that one hospital is 'better' or 'worse' than another, or one university is 'better' or 'worse' than another, or it might be assumed that the canals and waterways provided a 'better' or 'worse' transportation 'system' than the motorways.

We can notice a number of key points in this analysis. First, the nature of the 'process' is often ambiguous. For example, is it the one-way system that is poor, or the decision making about the one-way system? Is it the delivery process that is problematic, or is it something else, such as the timing of the orders? Second, often the expressions of the implicit processes are focused on the symptom, but not the cause, e.g. the one-way system may indeed be poor, but is this a consequence of something else in related human processes?

In making judgements about organizational processes, humans may wish to explore, in the same way as any other judgement, the basis upon which it was made. Thus, the same critical and analytical questions would arise, for example:

- The criteria being used in the process of judgement.
- The meaning of the constructs being used (e.g. 'nonsense', 'in charge', 'system').
- Precisely what is the entity is that is being judged (in this example, is it the person, the person's attitudes, actions etc).
- The values of those making the judgement.
- The purposefulness of making the judgement, or of expressing the judgement; this would include:
  - Why the person making the judgement has selected and used the particular constructs in the way that they have.
  - etc.

To which we could add:

- What is the organizational process that is being judged, and can systems constructs help in understanding the process (i.e. helping with its definition, or helping to understand how it related to other processes)?
- How can we construct suitable monitoring activities to ensure that the organizational process will work to fulfil its purpose?

Monitoring

IS practitioners are required to be focused, not simply on 'the operational process', but on the appropriateness of judgements on the process: judgement can be both informal and formal, but normally the formal 'judgement process' is considered to be some sort of 'monitoring process'. The process of monitoring may have criteria that in some ways are constructed and applied so as to assess performance of an organizational process, which must be able to take information from the process being judged. The information taken can only ever be a small amount of information, compared to the potential amount of information that is available about the operation of the process and, as such, there must be a form of attenuation in selecting information that is to be used in the 'judgement process'. The appropriateness of the attenuation is itself the subject of critical analysis in organizational problem solving. Further, if a monitoring process is considered to be the subject of inquiry, then it stands to reason that:

- There must the capability and capacity for the process to change.
- Human actions might be needed to purposely and explicitly change something in the operational process (see Figure 7.3).

If we said that IS practice involves evaluating, designing and changing the monitoring of organizational processes then it follows that IS practitioners must be able to inquire and make judgement about:

- The appropriateness of the monitoring process as it formally and informally affects the process that is being monitored.
- The appropriateness of the information to the monitoring process, and the appropriateness of the attenuation that is involved in selecting certain items of data for analysis over other potential data items.
- The actions taken, which are designed to purposely change the monitored system.
- The interconnections between the elements in the process of making judgements (e.g. the criteria and/or the 'metrics' that are used).
- The potential role of information and technology in the process, the sampling methods and algorithms that are used in the process.

Boundary considerations

In making human judgements that result in grumbling, complaining, praising and commending etc., it is sometimes an assumption that if something changes, then improvement might be made: 'if we had more staff then we could do it properly' or 'we should restructure the company, in order to modernize it'. In these examples, it might be that the 'judger' is not making the judgement based on an analysis of the process, but on a component of the process (i.e. the staffing levels, organization structure). It assumes that the components are analysable (or 'knowable'). It may make the assumption that changing an element or component of the process will improve the whole, and that the other elements of the whole are analysable. Further, in such judgements, there is the assumption that there is a correct diagnosis of the 'problem' and that 'improvement' will follow from some sort of 'correction' of the 'problem'. Such corrective changes may or may not bring 'improvement' and, in practice, it is often very difficult to determine whether or not claimed proposed actions for 'improvement' are justifiable; nor is it easy to justify that a given initiative or set of actions have provided 'improvement'!

It might be, also, that some 'improvement' might have been made in a particular area, but this improvement can cause other effects in other areas of work, which might be seen to have 'got worse'. Therefore the process of judging what is and what is not an 'improvement', the rationalization and logic upon which change is made, and the implications (possibly in 'other' processes) of that change are all potentially problematic and difficult areas for inquiry. Indeed, some would argue that humans are not able to rationalize sufficiently in order to make conscious improvement. This is because often small changes are not possible without impacting the whole. For example, the time of a delivery depends on the whole delivery process; or the arrival of a train at the correct time depends on the whole 'train transportation' process (e.g. the operation of the signals, the maintenance of the engines, the scheduling systems, the availability of labour and skills to drive the train etc. etc.). It is the process of understanding the whole that is the challenge, not only the identification of a 'problematic issue'. This is a significant challenge facing the IS practitioner, which stems from where to draw the boundary of investigation (see Figure 7.4).

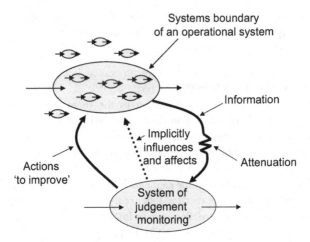

Figure 7.4 The systems boundary of that being judged

If it were hypothetically possible to 'know' everything about an organizational process (i.e. there was no ambiguity within the systems boundary of that being judged), then it might be possible to know (i) what to monitor, (ii) the metrics and criteria to be applied, and (iii) what to change. Unfortunately, there is often ambiguity. There are often different interpretations of the nature of a given process, and therefore this is a situation that is not possible. Consequently, it is only possible to select certain aspects of the whole process, to attempt to develop increased precision via inquiring activities and to use data collected about those aspects as a guide to inform the judgements regarding the relative performance of the whole process (i.e. that which lies within the boundary). However, it might be argued that certain processes might be, perhaps, 'more knowable' than others, i.e. some are 'more predictable' than others. We have used the term 'systematic' to depict a process that is one which is characterized by a high level of task continuity. For example in a highly routinized, mechanistic or mechanical process (i.e. one that displays highly 'systematic' characteristics), there might be more 'predictability' and therefore it is probably more 'knowable'. In certain circumstances, it is possible to construct a (more or less prescriptive) model for the specific purpose of predicting the behaviour of a given process (e.g. using role activity diagrams or various process flow charts etc.). Since factories often have highly mechanical routines, it possible to define specific criteria that are deemed important in the process, define qualitative or quantitative 'metrics' and therefore make judgement on the effectiveness of the process. Since not all processes in organizations are easily knowable and predictable, it is sometimes perceived as easier to define what is expected as an output, and measure those 'outputs', and (more or less) ignore the process characteristics that produce the outputs. For example, it might not be easy to model how a salesman undertakes a process of selling double glazing. Thus, applying metrics or criteria to the process of selling may not be possible, but applying metrics and criteria to the outputs of the selling process might be possible (e.g. how many windows have been sold in a given period). In such a situation, the salesman is 'monitored' on the number sold (an output measure). This metric and the subsequent data assume that high levels of sales indicates 'success' in the process. In other situations, on the other hand, it might be that the process characteristics are routine, mechanical and systematic and, thus, it is not only the outputs that can be measured, but many of the details of the process can also be modelled and measured with precision. For example, it might be easy to analyze the process and its elements of a process of assembling a golf trolley and, thus, process metrics and criteria can be applied to both process and output (see also Johnson and Gill 1993).

In either of these cases, there will be pressure exerted by the monitoring system. The exertion of pressure is exactly what a monitoring process is designed to do, because it is concerned to ensure that an operational process will meet its humanly constructed purposeful goals. It exerts pressure on the process, including the human actions, activities and behaviour, and it may also give an indication as to potential areas of 'improvement'. There is, therefore, a choice that must be considered as a component element of the decisions behind the choice of using and applying metrics and/or qualitative criteria to:

- certain elements within a process or
- the output of the process or
- both of these or
- none of these.

Commonly, monitoring that applies measures to the outputs of a process will be considered to be 'performance indicators' and will have attached a set of 'performance targets' associated with them. These can exert pressure on the operational process to conform and to perform in a particular way, but the pressure exerted needs to be feasible and realistic, otherwise they may adversely affect the attitude of the human groups affected by them. They must also be subjected to review and change, because they can result in unexpected outcomes. Unfortunately, decision makers who are in powerful positions to determine performance targets are often lacking in knowledge about the intricacies of (i) process modelling, which is a necessary underpinning for this type of policy decision, (ii) the processes in practice, and (iii) the unexpected outcomes and implicit impact that the changes in the indicators have on the process(es) in practice. As a consequence, the monitoring activity falls short of its intended impact. For example, the targets change behaviour in unexpected ways, or the targets get ignored and, thus, fail to apply pressure as they are intended etc. Information about the targets, the deviation from the targets, and the intended and unintended impact of the targets, are *central to information systems practice*. This aspect of the role of the IS practitioner are commonly not implemented or implemented so badly that it makes the operations 'worse', not 'better'.

If monitoring is applied to the process (as opposed to the output), then the structure of the process must be 'knowable' and 'predictable', and this normally implies that it must be characterized as systematic. Where monitoring is required on process (as opposed to output) and the process is not systematic in nature or character, then it may require somebody with a deep understanding of the purpose of the process to take a supervisory role of the process (i.e. the information and technology to control the process take a subservient role to that of the supervisor). In this type of instance, the criteria of 'success' are deeply embedded into the beliefs of those taking such a supervisory role, and information is very much linked to human cognitions of those undertaking that role. That is to say, it would be rather crass and simplistic to apply metrics (information in any form, perhaps enabled by technology) in isolation from the everyday observations and actions of the human supervisor. Further, the criteria being applied would normally be highly qualitative: people who undertake a supervisory role are normally expected to make judgements derived from close observation about the process including, for example, things that are not easily quantifiable (e.g. attitudes, skills of humans, task structures, work loading, power dimensions, responsibilities, formal and informal roles etc.).

The previous two paragraphs have depicted in outline the idea that monitoring can be applied in a variety of ways and, in particular, can be focused on process or on output. In either case, the purpose is to exert pressure, in order that the human operational process will be controlled. It stands to reason that control is the essential purpose, and without control the human organization is often likely to disintegrate! From this discussion, it follows that there are some generalizable principles that are essential to develop control of operational processes:

- The organizational process (the 'operational process') must have clarity of purpose, because without a clarity of perception about its aim or purpose, any controlling activity will have no meaning.
- In any controlling or monitoring activity the purposeful objectives and the degree to which the activity is attaining its objectives is assessable in some way and, thus, the non-attainment of objectives can be determined, and corrective actions determined.
- As a component of a controlling or monitoring process, there must be some capacity for taking 'corrective' actions so that deviations from the objectives can be reduced, e.g. change inputs, change aspects of process (see also Otley and Berry 1980).
- Information and its appropriate application play a central and pivotal role. However, in many situations, there is an overly simplistic application of information to a given organizational process.

Other control mechanisms

It might be noticed that the systematic process is one where it is relatively easy to apply monitoring controls. This is because they are mechanistic in nature, and tasks, activities and outputs can explicitly be monitored by the application of metrics and criteria to explicitly stated routines. Other processes are conducive to output controls in the same manner (e.g. selling double glazing is assessed on the number sold, not on the process of selling). However, it would be more difficult to judge the output of an administrative team in a hospital because it is much more difficult to identify a 'measure'. For example, it would be meaningless to try to control the process by output measures such as 'how many letters have been typed by the administration process today?'!! The process of the administration function of an organization can vary to such an extent that neither the process nor the output are easily measured for the purpose of monitoring.

There are situations in which neither output nor process controls are considered appropriate or desirable. For example, controlling the activities of a research process is much more problematic in terms of process and in terms of output. The activity structure of the research process is often very variable and changeable. It is not regular and routine, and is highly dependent on the interest and the professionalism of the researchers themselves. It is, perhaps, the opposite of being 'systematic'. Further, a research process cannot be controlled by output. For example, it would probably not be appropriate to measure the number of new discoveries made by a research team! If this were to be implemented, then it would be expected that there would be pressure exerted on the people in the operational process (in this case, the research operation). It might be expected that it may result in some 'unexpected' or 'unwanted' outcomes. For example, researchers may claim discoveries that are not discoveries at all (!).

In certain circumstances, the application of information, metrics and criteria as a method of control is not sufficient or effective, e.g. in 'administrative processes' or 'research processes'. In such circumstances, there are controls that can be exerted socially and behaviourally. Rather than focusing upon the process or the outcomes of the process, other controls are considered. For example, behavioural controls are sometimes considered to be more hidden and are based on developing an assumed value set, which underpins human behaviour, and the modus operandi of human groups. In doing this, controls are exerted by humans internalizing 'appropriate' norms, beliefs and values so that they then behave in ways that coincide with the stated purposeful objectives of the organizational processes. These are sometimes termed 'commitment-based' controls. Those who are undertaking 'actions to improve' will normally be concerned with the need to recruit people who share the same or similar values. For example, a research process will require a research team with similar values (e.g. they may value learning and knowledge development etc.). For example, a policing process may be considered to require individuals who have a value set conducive to catching criminals as opposed to joining in with criminal activity. The notion of ensuring that people who are involved in the operationalization of a process have compatible value sets, is often considered to be an important consideration in human resource policy, both in terms of recruitment policy, and in terms of re-socializing groups with the purpose of changing attitudes (see also Ouchi 1977, 1979).

It is, of course, of central concern to an IS practitioner that appropriate monitoring processes are designed and applied to organizational processes. When the principles of modelling processes are understood, it is possible to critique the failings of monitoring activities in practice. It is also possible to design and apply monitoring activities that can in some way complement certain (strategic) purposeful goals. It is also possible to recognize the limitations of information as a method of supporting the monitoring and governance aspects of organizational processes. The recognition of the limitations and, thus, the recognition of the most appropriate monitoring and control mechanisms, is an essential aspect of the role of the information systems practitioner. It is also a rather forgotten aspect of IS practice, because of the conceptual and practical challenges that this area presents.

8 Strategy

Abstract

Since Information systems as a discipline is centrally concerned to develop, improve and change organizational processes, there is the requirement that these changes are appropriate, given a set of (often ambivalent and contradictory) visions of the future situations and policy priorities in a given situation. As such, information systems in practice must be able to make inquiry into a set of possible visions of a future situation, and evaluate the impact that the resultant thinking has on current and future organizational processes. This is an *inquiry* of sorts, termed 'strategic prognosis' and is considered to be an underpinning component of the *process* of strategy in any given situation. This chapter will explore some of the characteristics and challenges in undertaking this in practice.

Introduction

From time to time, people in organizations may feel that they need to consider current direction, current policy priorities and the potential future consequences of various organizational change options and initiatives. This may involve the analysis of perceptions of what an 'organization' is now, at a particular moment in time, and/or what 'it' could or should be, given perceived changes in the context in which 'it' operates. Of course, in many cases, what 'it' is perceived to be now, and what 'it' is perceived to be in the future, how to change one 'it' into another, and the various perceptions and interpretations involved can all be quite problematic! Once there is engagement with an organization, the information systems practitioner is embroiled in strategy: sometimes the IS practitioner will be given 'as-given' assumptions about the efficacy of certain policy directives, and/or a set of given implications etc. Sometimes they may not be allowed to question certain assumptions about the process of strategy, e.g. policies, their formulation, priorities or the process of operationalization etc.; other times they may be able to play a part in its process in some manner. Sometimes it is essential that an IS practitioner must make an intervention in order to challenge and change certain characteristics of a process of strategy in a given situation.

Understanding and evaluating a current or potential 'strategy process' requires precision of thinking. The precision of thinking can be enhanced by a process of inquiry, which we will call the 'strategic prognosis', which may help to influence actions, policies, priorities and implementation etc., during the wider *process* of 'strategy'. That is to say, the process of strategy includes both a 'strategic prognosis' (an inquiry) as well as actions to change one situation into another, in a given organization. The inquiry would normally be assumed to 'help' in some way, to inform the actions for change in a given process of strategy. The nature of the inquiry, and the degree to which it serves to inform action, is an inquiry in its own right, and would be assumed to be a component of a strategic prognosis. In the practical everyday affairs of organizations, a 'strategic prognosis' may (i) not be undertaken, (ii) be undertaken in an implicit manner, or (iii) make unwarranted assumptions and assertions etc. Since IS practice is both affected by, and may have major implications for, a given process of strategy, it is important that the discipline of IS can provide guidance on: (i) understanding and evaluating a given process of strategy in a given organizational situation, (ii) becoming explicit about alternative process characteristics of strategy, and (iii) the underpinning inquiring activities that might be used to inform both (i) and (ii).

Following from this, it is entirely reasonable to say that a process of 'strategy', and the inquiry that (to a greater or lesser extent) purports to support the strategy, can be considered to be teleological in nature (i.e. they are imbued with 'human purpose'). For example, the formal and explicit purpose of the 'strategic prognosis' can be considered to be to develop the thinking about a variety of actions, policy priorities and interventions, for a given organization. For example, it could be considered to be an inquiry into:

- Current and future organizational situations.
- The likely changed circumstances in which organizational processes may need to operate; these may include consideration of the likely future social, political and economic contexts etc.
- The potential implications for current processes and the design priorities of future organizational processes.
- The *raison d'être* of the organizational processes in a given future situation (e.g. who is it going to serve in the future?).
- Future monitoring, control and governance structures of organizational processes.
- Future resources and capability for the operation of certain organizational processes.
- The values and ethical dimensions of a perceived set of change priorities.
- The social and power dynamics involved *during the process of inquiry* about current and future organizational situations (i.e. inquiry about the inquiry).

Since an inquiry (e.g. a strategic prognosis) is teleological, it may well have a hidden purpose. For example, in practice, the inquiry may be to 'justify a planned change or policy implementation' or 'to cut costs so that shareholders are happy' or 'to bash the xyz department because "they are a waste of time"' etc.). That is to say, an inquiry that purports to be a 'strategic prognosis' may not serve the goals of refining insights into new situations and circumstances in which future processes will be required to operate. Because inquiry is purposeful, the purpose may well be 'hidden', which may contradict the explicit purpose. It also stands to reason that, in practice, the quality of such an inquiry can be variable, i.e. it might be considered to be 'done well' or 'done badly'. The judgement of the quality of the inquiry will depend on developing a clarity of (and a defensible perspective on) the characteristics and elements that are involved in the inquiring process, and an assessment about the degree to which the inquiry serves its humanly constructed purpose (informal, hidden, explicit etc.). This chapter concerns itself with some of the considerations and characteristics of making such an inquiry. As such, it concerns itself with strategy as a *teleological inquiring process*, rather than a specific set of constructs, concepts or techniques.

Definition

The process of strategy and the process of a strategic prognosis has relevance in the field information systems for at least two interrelated reasons, which are somewhat tautologous. For example:

•   It would be reasonable to argue that an inquiry into current and future organizational 'situations' (i.e. an assumed element of a 'strategic prognosis') is, in part, dependent on a well-developed insight into organizational processes (see Chapters 4, 6 and 7), because its goal is to consider the impact on those processes (e.g. to determine their designs, investment requirements and change elements, governance structures, monitoring, priorities etc.).
•   It would also be reasonable to argue that during the inquiry into organizational processes (see Chapters 4, 6, and 7) it is necessary to consider their longevity given a set of changeable future circumstances, priorities and goals for them (i.e. a 'strategic prognosis' of sorts).

It is the close integration between these two that can make a process of strategy operationalizable. If organizational processes are to be conceptualized using systems ideas, then the integration of the two is, in a sense, a meeting of 'strategy' and 'systems'. In effect, this has huge potential for the field and discipline of IS for a number of reasons:

•   Since IS is both practical and has a highly operational focus (see Chapter 1), it is essential that there are ways in which to integrate the general policy-making processes (sometimes termed 'strategy') with the actions for the operational change of organizational processes.
•   IS as a discipline and a field of practice has the potential to become a leading discipline in formalizing the methods by which policy ('strategy') and process ('systems') can be integrated. This is because its recent history has required it to embrace *both* of these domains.
•   The practice of IS can start to mature in such a way that it can help to contribute to strategic work in organizations, and harmonizing the integration between policy and operations, which traditionally has been an area of severe haemorrhage in organizations in practice, and in the management discipline.

Challenges in 'strategy'

The reason why 'strategy' in information systems work is important is not because the computing technology is expensive to implement. Nor is it that information technology is inherently 'strategic' in nature; nor is it because technology brings 'competitive advantage'. Whilst all or any of these might be true in a given situation, they do not in themselves provide a generalizable reason why 'strategy' must integrate with IS practice. Rather, it is because changes to information and to technology always changes organizational processes; it can be central to the design of significantly new ways of working, and therefore it influences and affects organizational change priorities (see also the debate between Porter 2001 and Tapscott *et al.* 2006). It often determines the way organizational processes can be constructed. Furthermore, it is concerned, in some way, with the future, i.e. it involves 'peering into the future' to consider whether organizational processes are required to change in some way to meet the future challenges of certain perceptions about expected changes in situations and circumstances. It is the integration of, on the one hand, the current and future situations and, on the other, how those perceptions of situations are to affect organizational processes, their designs, characteristics, the priorities for improvement and investment, their demise etc.

Teleology of the strategy process

If we consider that undertaking 'strategy' is essentially a teleological human process underpinned by inquiring activities and principles, then its success can be considered to be associated with the degree to which it fulfils its humanly constructed objectives (implicit and explicit). This would involve a deep understanding of the humanly constructed objectives (i.e. teleology). However, in principle, since there is a 'hidden' purpose involved, the process evaluating the success (or otherwise) of strategy formulation and implementation, evaluation is in part concerned with the effect of the (often hidden) purpose in the actions that constitute the strategy formulation and implementation. This can be done during the process, by those undertaking the process, and can be considered to be a learning and inquiring activity. Unfortunately, evaluation in organizations, of their strategy, is normally done too late, i.e. after the undertaking of a 'strategy'. This is because it is not normally considered to be:

* a teleological process
* underpinned by a learning and inquiring activity.

In practice, 'strategy' is not necessarily considered to be an inquiry that can be critiqued in terms of its teleological process. Nor is it normally considered to be an activity that is largely underpinned by inquiry. Since it is not normally considered an inquiry, it is not critiqued from the perspective of its assumptions about knowledge construction. Since it is not normally considered a *process*, it is also not normally considered that it could be critiqued in terms of the social process that underpins the construction process.

Rather, 'strategy' is commonly seen as a set of constructs, models or frameworks to be applied; the 'answer' drops out of the application of the constructs, models or frameworks. There are of course a number of ontological assumptions that are often made in considering 'strategy' in this way. For example, the constructs, models or frameworks can sometimes be assumed to be 'value free'; their application gives a logical result; the process of strategy is in some way 'objectified'. This is of course impossible if we consider that the process of strategy is a humanly constructed one!

Thus, on the other hand, if 'strategy' were considered to be a teleological human process, then the activity cannot be considered to be socially value free. Further, it would be required to consider that the process of inquiry is socially constructed, to meet a variety of humanly purposeful objectives (implicit and explicit). It would also imply that the actions that arise from the conclusions drawn from such an inquiry may be used to impact on aspects of organizational processes and, thus, on people, tasks and activities etc. Broadly speaking, inquiry for 'strategy prognosis' is undertaken in a social context, and also has an impact on a social context (see also Mintzberg and Quinn 1996).

Integration of 'strategy'

Further, sometimes strategic choices, decisions and implementations of policy do not appear to be a 'one-off' or an occasional occurrence, but they are ongoing and evolutionary. These are often based on a set of assumptions about the future conditions and the potential impacts of changed circumstances. Thus, IS practitioners are often required to consider (and iteratively to reconsider) priorities and options, and also to refine their own thinking about, (for example):

- Their perceptions of the nature of the changing circumstances that require long-term policy decision and priorities to be made.
- The options and opportunities that might be considered for an organizational process, or a grouping of organizational processes.
- The feasibility of a set of perceived required changes, in a given social and economic situation.

Since undertaking the task of making strategic choices involves 'peering into the future', it involves inquiry into a 'situation of concern', albeit a future, or potential, situation. There is of course a danger that the inquiry or some of its results are taken to *be* the 'future situation' in an absolute sense, as opposed to an inquiring activity into that 'future situation'.

In practice, such a strategic prognosis is required to include consideration of the current and future situations and current and future processes simultaneously. In the discussion in this book, the 'diagnosis' and 'prognosis' are discussed separately in separate chapters, but this is not meant to suggest that they are not integrated activities in practice. Rather, in practice, it is necessary to integrate them. If a strategic prognosis was splintered and separated from other IS organizational problem-solving tasks, there can be some quite significant consequences. For example, it is possible that 'strategy' might be considered to be a form or expression of 'where we want to get to', which is fragmented from the operational issues of changing organizational processes. The consequence might be that there could be a danger that strategic issues, policies and decisions are not implemented (or implementable!). Indeed, a very pragmatic reason why strategic prognosis (the inquiry) must be integrated into (for example) (i) the diagnosis inquiry, (ii) modelling processes, and (iii) intervention, is that there is little point in attempting to fix an organizational process if it does not have a future! For example, in a photographic hardware manufacturing company, it might be considered that the traditional film camera has a limited commercial future, and that there are much greater opportunities in digital camera technologies. This conclusion might be derived as part of a formal inquiry, or it might be a hunch or an informal, intuitive inquiry.[1] In this example, don't fix the film camera production processes! Ditch them!

Then start modelling the human processes that develop digital technology, and those that can bring them to market. In organizational problem solving, there is limited value and limited benefit if the 'fix' does not consider future situations (i.e. there is little integration of strategy and systems).

Peering into the future

'Peering into the future' is a task that humans have always endeavoured to do and, no matter what their method, invariably they are surprised by the unexpected! It is hardly surprising that there are considerable difficulties in making major decisions that have significant long-term future implication in organizations. An inquiry, which consists of 'peering into the future', can never predict that future in an absolute sense, no matter how clever, cunning, insightful and perfect the inquirer's claim of their inquiry and their resultant 'insight'. Further, no matter how 'good' the inquiry, without linking the inquiry with organizational processes, there is bound to be selective and limited ability to translate the results into practical organizational process change.

Predicting the future is sometimes considered to be an impossibility. It is sometimes associated with the occult practices, e.g. of some sort of sage! It is also the domain of academics and scientists in virtually every discipline, because science has always been concerned to enhance human control over their future environments. For example, prediction can be associated with the mathematician, who uses data and sophisticated algorithms to predict future trends from past data. It is also the concern of the historian who might argue that it is through the study of history that we can gain greater insight of ourselves and the future, by learning from history. The sage, the mathematician and the historian may significantly differ in their methods and goals and, thus, there is significant variance about the types of things they would be expected to predict, and also their processes of prediction. For example, the prediction of the end of the world may be considered beyond mathematics, and a prediction of a quality control forecast might a little too specific for the sage! The prediction of the collapse of capitalism might be considered to be beyond mathematics and too uninteresting for the occult!

The activities of prediction, by occult practices, by the application of mathematics and by the study of history, have been around for a long time! Basing important decisions on the 'predictions' of the likely future situations of human organizations is perhaps a little newer than the practices of the sage, mathematician or historian. Arguably, it is an area of human activity that has emerged as a requirement in the twentieth century, as organizations attempt to 'smooth over' the 'destabilizing disturbances' that they have faced. Perhaps the task is made increasingly difficult by the uncertainties of the challenge of the 'postmodern' condition, and it is these 'destabilizing disturbances' that have caused this area of study and thinking to be considered as increasingly important (see also Chapter 3). Sadly, perhaps, the methods of the sage, the historian and the mathematician might be considered to be somewhat lacking (in different ways) for the purposes of considering future organizational situations, and the decisions, policies and actions that are required to deal with those situations (i.e. 'strategy' needs to create its own methods, and not simplistically 'borrow' from elsewhere). Indeed, there are some major challenges in doing this. In practice, the process of predicting the future is a highly fallible human process. It relies on an analysis of trends based on partial observations, patchy data and often 'gut-feel' and intuition (e.g. 'film technology does not have a future mass market'). In practice, 'strategy' is often based on little more than 'common sense'. It can sometimes be drawn from very simple assertions and value judgements about what the future holds. It might also be argued that the 'common sense' strategies are shrouded in a sort of pseudoscience for the purpose of justifying value-laden policy initiatives. Altogether, the domain of 'strategy' in practice is rather unpredictable, precarious and one that is fraught with dangers, but one that may have significant consequences.

It might be possible to gain a better understanding of the nature of strategic decisions and actions in practice, by careful thinking about the nature of its process. For example, (i) the purpose of the selection of particular 'evidence' (or 'data'), regarding perceptions of situational changes, and how that data is presented in justifying the need for 'strategic' change, (ii) the consideration of the selection and application of particular constructs in the process of understanding and evaluating an organizational 'situation', and (iii) the critique that is required to demonstrate the use of the constructs, and to analyse their assumptions and what they do and do not show. It might be beneficial to consider the strategy process to be teleological (e.g. it has an explicit and hidden human purpose).

Strategic constructs

Although the process and activity of organizational strategy might be considered to be relatively immature and often rather unsophisticated, fortunately there are a number of 'strategic' constructs that are claimed to help guide decision makers improve their thinking. These types of constructs can play a central role in the inquiring activities of those undertaking a 'strategic prognosis'. For instance, there are:

- 'Life cycle' or 'stages of growth' type frameworks, which can help to conceptualize the different stages that would be expected of a whole organization, or a certain grouping of processes in an organization (see for example Johnson and Scholes 1997: 114; or Nolan 1979; Galliers and Sutherland 1991). Such types of constructs assume that there are distinctive trends and characteristics that can be derived from them that are sufficiently well developed and generic that they can be applied to guide policy in a range of organizational situations.
- 'Environmental analysis' type frameworks that are considered to help structure thinking about the nature of a changing environment and its consequences (see for example the 'PEST' (Political, Economic, Social and Technological) analysis or 'Porter's diamond' (see Porter 1980)).
- 'Competitive analysis' frameworks, which focus on the analysis of the competitive environment, and are generally used for organizations that are significantly affected by other similar organizations with whom they compete (see for example, the 'five force' analysis of Porter 1980; or McFarlan 1984).
- 'Value-adding' frameworks that characterize an organization or organizational unit, as they play a role in the wider 'chain' of activities that are involved in providing products and services to consumers (see for example the 'value chain' analysis of Porter and Millar 1985).

- 'Classification schemes' of issues, which are considered to help identify certain aspects such as the key factors that enable 'success' in a particular area of work activities (see 'critical success factors' and the 'SWOT' analyses).
- 'Financial analyses', which concern themselves with financial ratio analyses and generally involve the use of data to analyse various aspects such as the quality of shareholder investments, risk and loan assessment, liquidity, stock turnover and sales margins.

There are many associated debates, particularly about the nature and context of strategy and the role of technology (see for example Tapscott 1998; Porter 2001; Clemons and Lang 2003). The above bullet points give a set of 'categories' of strategic construct. Any one construct or combination of constructs can be used within a process of inquiry. However, the use of constructs may guide the inquiring process, but are not themselves *the inquiry*. They are an *element* in a teleological process of inquiry. The *process* would also involve other aspects, such as the analysis of:

- The validity of the choices made about the constructs that are used within a given organizational situation.
- Observations of the organizational situation.
- The way the construct is used within a particular social situation.
- The explicit and hidden purpose of the 'strategy process'.
- How a given strategy impacts on current and future organizational processes.
- The cultural, social or political feasibility of changing organizational processes.
- How it helps to underpin the actions required by a range of intervention options.
- etc.

As can be seen, a process of strategy is not the application of a given strategic construct. Within each 'category' given above, there are a wide range of specific strategic constructs, and there is a wide-ranging view on how they should or could be used. For instance, some people might use the constructs as if the constructs themselves are 'fact', i.e. the constructs are not questioned (or questionable). Thus, the empirical observations about the context, situation or organization to which they are applied are often equally considered to be 'fact'. Treating the constructs as 'fact', or the observations that are derived from the use of the constructs as 'facts' is common, but is untenable in rigorous inquiry (e.g. in academic work). This is because rigorous (or academic) work in a practical discipline, such as IS, must be concerned to *critique the constructs in practice* with the view that they can be 'improved', 'refined', 'developed' or 'ditched' etc. They can only do this by inquiry into their 'usefulness' within the context. It would not be reasonable to assume that all practitioners always have the same concerns for the perfections of a given construct and its application, and it would, therefore, be reasonable to suggest that practitioners, too, would be keen to critique both construct and its application within a given context.

For example, the application of a specific 'life-cycle' construct can be done with a level of critique – evaluating how it is being used, why it is being used in the first place, what the results indicate and assessing the usefulness of the construct etc. In practice of course, there are various ways in which a construct might be used. It may indeed be used to determine policy, but it also might be used to substantiate an existing '*ad hoc'* decision, or to justify a particular perspective or further a political agenda, or even aggrandize the user's 'intellectual abilities' or 'greater education' etc. However, 'life-cycle' type tool and frameworks will be given a explicitly stated purpose, which is normally to 'map' some sort of trend, and to assess future possibilities in a given case, given that trend. For example, they can be applied specifically to:

• Product life cycles.
• Sector or industry sector life cycles.
• The development of organizations' 'maturity' in some way (e.g. see Figure 8.1).

Life-cycle constructs are well known and well used in strategy. The formal and explicit purpose of their use is to give insight into current and future products, services, sectors, organizations or some of its functions etc. In their application, a user can also subject the construct and its use to a greater and more in-depth level of critique. As with similar constructs, a life-cycle model is one that may be used to highlight changes in the situation that can be rationalized in order to develop greater insight into a particular set of circumstances as they affect decisions and actions. They are of course predicated upon the accuracy and validity of the 'life-cycle trend' as it is portrayed in the construct, which (i) is not necessarily 'appropriate' at all, or (ii) is not 'appropriate' in all situations (a generalizability issue), or (iii) its 'correctness' is contingent on a number of factors that can be explored at the point of application. Indeed, the 'correctness' may depend on the organizational situation or other factors. Thus, (i) there are often implicit assumptions made by the application of a 'life-cycle trend'. For example, that a product, service or industry sector will be changing, or should change, in the way the model suggests, with the associated assumptions and implications for policy, priorities and investments, and (ii) there are responsibilities that are incumbent on users of life-cycle models: to consider the relevance and 'correctness' of the particular life cycle to the peculiarities of the organizational situation. These are aspects of the inquiry for the purpose of strategic prognosis.

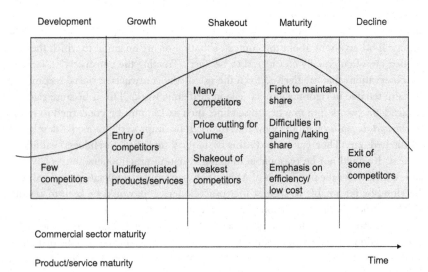

Figure 8.1 A generic 'life-cycle' model

Stages ⟶ Issues ↓	Stage 1 Initiation	Stage 2 Contagion	Stage 3 Control	Stage 4 Integration	Stage 5 Data adminis - tration	Stage 6 Maturity
Planning and controls	Lax	More lax	Formalized	Tailored	Shared data	Strategic planning
IS organizaton	Specialized	User oriented	Middle management	User teams	Integrated	Data resource Management
User awareness	Hands off	Superficial	Arbitrary	Learning	Effective	Joint user accountablity
Expenditure Level	Steady from zero base	Steep rise	Steep rise	Steady rise	Steady rise	Appropriate

Figure 8.2 A summarized 'stage-growth' model

These types of construct have been applied in many ways and to many different contexts. For example, 'life-cycle' constructs can be applied within particular sectors and organizations (public sector, private sector, big organizations, small organizations), or within sectors with higher or lower levels of inter-organizational competition, or to giving specific insights into particular organizational functions, e.g. see an extended version of the Nolan (1979) model to depict the trends and investment priorities to 'assist' with decisions about information technology investments (Figure 8.2).

Usually, there is a certain cognitive clarity and simplicity about such constructs, although sometimes they can be considered to be problematic. For example, they can be considered (i) to be too general, or (ii) to 'state the obvious', or even (iii) to be invalid, in that there is relatively weak evidence that the trend indeed 'reflects reality' in a given situation. Normally, in the process of strategy, in which they are used, there is very little done in the way of (i) linking the policy making to explicit changes in processes, or (ii) analysis of the social processes in which they are used and applied (see also Benbasat *et al.* 1984). Further, their purpose in practice can have hidden goals, e.g. to 'sell consulting services or computer technologies', rather than to inquire into particular current or future situations and possibilities.

There are some good reasons why such constructs appear to be rather simple: they are not methods or methodologies. They are simple 'thought structuring devices', which are embedded into an (often informal) inquiry (a 'strategic prognosis'); they are often required to have the purpose of *communication* between human groups of decision makers.

Thought structuring devices

Broadly speaking, a strategic construct can be considered to be a 'thought structuring device', simply because they 'exist in the mind'. Their role is limited as they do not

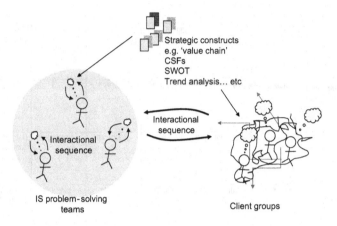

Figure 8.3 Strategic construct as a 'thought structuring device'

determine action, policy, methods or processes etc. However, they *may* play a role in some aspect of these, and the extent and role may be subjected to critique in at least three ways:

- They can be subjected to critique as a component of a discourse between people who are involved in undertaking work (e.g. formulating strategies, policies, projects).
- They can be critiqued in action to determine what and how it is perceived to have 'helped' or otherwise, by a variety of users.
- They can be subjected to critique to determine 'missing elements', ambiguities and logical flaws etc.

It is also reasonable to say that all three of these would be necessary in order to provide a reasonable evaluation of the application of one or more strategic constructs. Further, it is a responsibility of the users of such constructs not to simply use them, but to evaluate their use during their application. Such an evaluation would need to include (i) the user(s) of the strategic constructs, (ii) the process of application, and (iii) the situational characteristics of application as depicted in Figure 8.3.

If strategic constructs such as a 'stage-growth model' can be considered to be 'thought structuring devices', and a component of a method for discourse, then they can be used to help (or hinder) certain types of inquiry into current or desired situations. Because they can 'help' or 'hinder', then they must also be considered to be a 'fallible tool' (i.e. they are 'more useful' or 'less useful'). The usefulness of the strategic constructs can be subjected to evaluation and human critique in order to determine (i) the value of the use of a particular strategic construct within the specific context of purposeful work activity, and (ii) the value of the generic construct for purposeful activity of a particular type (e.g. 'strategy formulation and implementation'). The evaluation method that has the goal of assessing the value of the application of strategic constructs is itself rather difficult to implement (which may explain why it is so often ignored!).

Evaluation

In the previous discussions, we have suggested that strategic constructs can be applied in a variety of ways, and for a variety of human purposes. For example, consultants can use them because they can lend weight to justify changes, such as increasing their clients' expenditure on technology or marketing etc. A cynic might take a set of constructs (e.g. life-cycle constructs) and argue that they can be used to justify the use of more consulting services, or more technology sales etc! On the other hand, a critic might retort that it is essential to have some form of growth model, and that managers will often have some sort of plan based on an implicit stage-growth model. The critic may argue that an explicit stage-growth model can provide a level of precision, new lines of thinking, and an explicit process of communication between decision makers, in the process of planning action. A growth stage model can provide (i) an explicit thought structuring device, and (ii) a way of communicating ideas to others.

And to which our cynic might retort that decisions in organizations are never taken quite as rationally as our cynic seems to suggest!

Although it sounds rather vague and obvious, it would be true that the usefulness of any particular strategic construct is in the 'purpose to which it is applied' and, thus, gaining clarity of what the explicit and implicit purpose could be considered to be, is an essential aspect of the use of strategic constructs (a teleological question). It would be easy to see why our rhetorical cynic could conclude that a strategic construct could be simply manipulated *to appear* as if it were some sort of 'objective' or a 'scientifically developed' framework, denying the social processes: 'it shows X … thus we need to do Y, and it just so happens that we can sell you help with Y'. To an IS practitioner, the purposefulness of the social process *is as important* as the construct itself, and both the social process and the use of the construct should be elements in a given process of strategy, and the *inquiry* into a given process of strategy is a feature and an aspect of a strategic prognosis.

The cynic might also point out that in the literature on organizational strategy, there is quite a variable language used in the use and application of various constructs (for a sophisticated debate on the nature of strategy, see Wittington 1993). Our cynic might note that, in the literature, there is sometimes assumption that the constructs are seen to have been 'tested' in the past, alluding to the notion that a strategic construct is valid and verifiable as if it has been subjected to testing a hypothesis (e.g. in a chemistry laboratory, where variables have been identified and conditions controlled). Our cynic would be entirely correct to suggest that no strategic construct can be 'tested' in such a manner, since they can only be subjected to evaluation during their human use and application in uncontrolled conditions (that is to say, in organizations where the variables and the conditions cannot be controlled). Further, unlike in the 'testing' of physical phenomena (e.g. chemicals) the 'test' of the validity of a strategic construct requires the testing of 'non-physical' things (i.e. the constructs are entirely conceptual or non-physical), as are notions of 'organization' and 'processes', and these are highly dependent on how they are conceived by different human observer(s). Thus, ignoring the teleological issues in their construction and in their application, strategic constructs are open to be abused or misused. If the teleological aspects are ignored it can only be considered used in a way akin to any fad. As such, inquiry for strategic prognosis must integrate the teleological issues by including, as a component, an '*an inquiry into the purposeful use of the constructs, in a given context*: purposeful use includes the explicit and the implicit purpose that it serves within a social context.

Despite their fallibility as highlighted by our rhetorical critic and cynic, the strategic constructs may be able to be used in such a way that they can bring a sense of order in the form of a 'common language' to groups who are concerned with constructing policies with a long-term impact, and the development of projects or programmes etc. In that sense they have some form of power: strategic constructs have an extrinsic power dimension (i.e. one which is used by people in particular ways, to help them communicate and justify their thought and action) and an intrinsic one (e.g. where the strategic constructs reflect the social power or hierarchy of any decision-making process). We could say therefore, that there is a *social process* in operation in using any strategic construct, which uses the intrinsic and extrinsic power of the constructs within the particular context of the social process in which it is used. In order to evaluate the effectiveness of the strategic construct(s), the evaluation analysis cannot disconnect the strategic construct(s) from the social process (Figure 8.4).

In management and consulting, strategic constructs are widely used, and despite their 'fallibility', they allow for shared (or at least communicable) thought structures within a social process. Overly complex strategic constructs may alienate too many who are already extrinsically less wedded or able to use the strategic constructs as a tool for structuring their thinking about strategy or policy. This aspect is especially important if one of the underlying assumptions behind the application of the strategic constructs is that it is a participative process that allows the seeking of commonality and buying into a common 'mindset' of aspirations or goals, and thereby providing a foundation of agreement for action and group communication. This assumes that the purposeful application of the constructs is to enable a group process. However, as indicated, it may be that the application of the constructs may be used for other purposes (e.g. of hiding certain issues, or of furtherance of 'political' goals, aggrandizement of the importance or the skill of one social group in an attempt to dominate or influence another, or even simple things such as attempting to demonstrate competence in order to gain favour and career development etc).

If we consider that any strategic construct is a component of a teleological social process, then it is necessary to recognize this interconnection, and to try to make improvement in (for example):

- The social process itself.
- The clarity of the role that the strategic construct plays within the social process by influencing people.

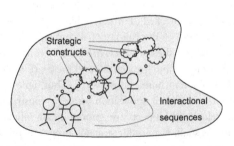

Figure 8.4 Towards the social dimensions of a process of strategy formulation

• The clarity (or otherwise) that the strategic construct plays in 'structuring thoughts'.

In planning, design, implementation, monitoring or evaluation activities that involve strategic constructs, it might be considered important to use some sort of facilitator in order to be able to 'cut through' these social and teleological dimensions. Such a role is often expected of IS practitioners of various kinds (e.g. consultants). Commonly, a facilitator is considered to be somebody who can both (i) help groups use the constructs, and (ii) help them analyse the associated social dimensions of their use. Additionally, and perhaps more importantly, a facilitator's role would be focused on helping those in such activities to question their own assumptions and social agendas, in order to bring a more robust analysis of issues, by recognizing the interconnectivity between the strategic construct and social process. In this way, it may be possible to refine the social process, rather than focusing narrowly on the justification of the strategic construct(s) (!). Further, if the application of strategic constructs in organizations is to be improved and refined, there must be some form of evaluation and monitoring activity in place, which may be able to abstract essential lessons for the improved application of a strategic process on future occasions (i.e. there needs to be a learning process that is operationalized alongside the process of inquiry for strategic prognosis).

Subjectivity

As we have noted, each of the strategic constructs are used in practice in a variety of different ways, for a variety of different purposes. It stands to reason that if a particular construct or set of constructs are used within a social process, then observing the social dimensions are as important as the construct itself! For example, a 'SWOT' analysis is a commonly known and applied strategic construct. It is a 'checklist' type construct that is sometimes used to try to summarize and communicate the strengths, weaknesses, opportunities and threats faced by an organization, an organizational unit, or even a product or product type etc. It is perhaps typical of a form of 'communication device' different groups of its users. Using a SWOT is often assumed to help to structure perceptions of a set of changes in 'the environment'. As in any of the strategic constructs, there is no inherent consideration of the intrinsic or extrinsic social and power dynamics in the *use of* the construct, nor a critique of the construct itself. As a consequence, there are some limitations and problems. For instance, sometimes it may appear that a 'strength' can also be considered a 'weakness' in a different situation or circumstance, or that one person can see an 'opportunity' and another person can see the same situation or circumstance as a 'threat', depending on their own 'mindset' or role within an organization etc. Further, language, roles, social power etc. are aspects that must be considered in the analysis of the social process. In practice, a group discussion about 'strengths', 'weaknesses', 'opportunities' and 'threats' can be undertaken for a variety of purposes (i.e. the process of undertaking an activity using SWOT is itself purposeful). The idea that a SWOT can be undertaken without consideration of the socio-political human issues and context might be considered to be a consequence of a particular ontology, e.g. that a SWOT is in some way an 'objective' tool or device, as in an experiment in the natural sciences (for a fuller debate on the 'strategic' tools and concepts, see Johnson and Scholes 1997). These observations are also true in the use of other strategic constructs, such as in a product portfolio analysis (PPA) or a PEST analysis.

Like the SWOT, PPAs and PEST analyses are widely applied. They have different explicit purposes. For example, a product portfolio analysis might be considered to have an explicit purpose of inquiring into the relative maturity of a range of products, in an attempt to obtain a mix of products that will serve a perceived longer- and shorter-term organizational need, whereas a PEST might be considered to have an explicit purpose of inquiring into the current and changing conditions in which an organization or group of processes operate. Each construct has great simplicity and the fact that they are cognitively simple, easily communicable and understandable make them ideal as 'inclusive' communication devices within a social context (i.e. their simplicity means that nobody need necessarily be 'excluded' from the discussion). They can be very helpful in developing *discussion* in formulating group thinking, especially where the intrinsic and extrinsic power dimensions are considered. Each can be used in a variety of ways, and with a variety of outcomes. If a construct was genuinely used to formulate policy and action, then its application in a particular context remains either more or less valid. In its application, and during communication within the social process, there may be themes and ideas that would not have otherwise surfaced. These might be of various types. For example, in undertaking a SWOT, there may be observations (or data) made about:

- 'Strengths', 'weaknesses', 'opportunities' or 'threats' that may not have been considered before.
- The variation of people's perspectives on the constitution of the 'strengths', 'weaknesses', 'opportunities' or 'threats'.
- How agreement on policy and priorities are being reached.
- The contribution that both the construct and the social process makes in the formulation and implementation of policy.
- The use of the construct and social process in changing human processes or human behaviour and action.
- etc.

Observations can help to make a judgement on the way the human process of policy is formulated or communicated etc.

There are many types of strategic construct, some that are used for different explicit purposes and different contexts (e.g. public sector, private sector etc.), see Johnson and Scholes (1997). In the application of them, data can be collected and considered in making assessment of their value, and in the consideration of the validity of taking action based on the judgements about their application. In all cases, in utilizing strategic constructs, there is a role that data derived from observations plays in making such judgements. Most of the above discussions are based on situations in which judgements are made from observations, which are largely qualitative in nature. Thus, they are very much open to the interpretation of the humans who are engaged in making such judgements.

Sometimes, it is possible to utilize quantitative data in developing the inquiry that can help to make judgements. In the case of applying financial ratio analyses or in using data to analyse various aspects such as shareholder investments, risk and loan assessment, liquidity, stock turnover and sales margins the data is normally quantitative.

It is, nonetheless, collected and applied both within a social process, and for both explicit and implicit purpose. Such data is sometimes considered to be 'objective' or 'factual'. Thus, the data is 'collected', and humans process it in some way, attach meaning to it, make judgement and act on those judgements (e.g. to implement a 'strategy'). This is perhaps the most common 'rationalization' of the use of quantitative data, and this is worthy of some further consideration in terms of the role it plays in the strategy process. Maybe if God had created the data, upon which strategic prognosis was based, then it might be argued that data was 'objective', and that humans subjectively attached meaning to it. However, the data is of course humanly constructed. No matter how 'objective' the data appears to be, it is constructed in a social context for a given purpose, as well as being applied for a social context. It may be only recording events, activities or transactions etc. but there is human purpose in the recording, and the process of recording may or may not be valid or adequate. Thus, in using quantitative data (financial ratio analyses, analysing shareholder investments, risk and loan assessment, liquidity, stock turnover, sales margins etc.), it is important to be able to assess the validity of the use of that data, and to relinquish the illusion that it is 'objective' or reflects 'truth' in an absolute sense. Like qualitative data, it too reflects a set of social values, and is imbued with human purposefulness, and can be used in a variety of ways. Thus, as in undertaking a SWOT or in the use of any other set of constructs, the strategy process will require an inquiring process that questions, for example:

- The purpose of the collection of the quantitative data.
- The validity and accuracy of the data.
- The way in which it is being used in a whole process of strategy.
- How it informs action or inaction.
- Its role in giving indicators that are used in a process of judgement about future policy priorities.
- The social interests of groups who are associated with the construction and use of the metrics.
- Alternative ways of viewing the policy priorities that have resulted from the use of the metrics.
- etc.

Integration

As already discussed, strategic constructs might be best considered to be a 'framework' or 'thought structuring device' of some sort, to help think and communicate ideas about the current or future design and operationalization of a set of activities (the current or future processes). Sadly perhaps, strategic constructs, principles and ideas often are used in a way that seems to isolate the operational aspects (e.g. they are used in a way that separates the operationalization (or the operationalizability) of the outputs of the strategy process). For example, from the analysis of both practice and literature, it might be observed that there is often a *schism* between those who are undertaking a sort of strategic analysis and policy construction and those who are involved in the operationalization of the projects or programmes. Logically perhaps, this does not always and necessarily cause major problems but, in practice, this schism can lead to social groups with different priorities, resulting in operational activities that do not fit the strategic intentions, or the 'strategic' view becomes of little relevance to the operational activities. Furthermore, it can result in attempts at trying to 'cover up' such differences rather than to develop a genuine dialogue about how those differences can be accommodated. The strategic constructs often tend to be used in particular ways that do not necessarily help to integrate the two together. A systemic approach to strategy must, therefore, involve inquiring activities into the integration between a number of key elements, such as:

• The problem situation, which includes the expressions of issues of concern, and the social dynamics and constraints of the situation.
• The prognosis of 'where we want to get to' by designing a project or programme (i.e. a set of operational processes).
• The designs and implementations of human processes such as projects or programmes.
• The design and implementations of the human processes involved in monitoring of the processes.
• The analysis of interventions taken as a result of monitoring.
• The evaluation that would include all of the above.

Each of these are required to be integrated together. They involve inquiring activities of sorts to help refine precision of thinking. Central to this is the need for integrating strategic constructs into the modelling of human processes. There is of course a natural linkage, which is articulated in much strategic literature. For example, Porter (1980) is perhaps a landmark academic piece that has influenced the thinking of academics and practitioners alike. His work categorizes the components of any organization, as they attempt to provide goods and services. His work is not concerned about the modelling of organizational processes, nor particularly on how each functions in an integrated way. His concern is about the creation of value and wealth. The purpose is not focused on methodologies for IS practice, nor on the practicalities of improving organizational processes in order that they meet certain purposeful human goals. Porter's contribution is at a macro level, and on the direction and need for change. Porter uses general categories to depict the sub-components, whereas systemic notions are more specific in terms of the modelling of the actual activities in practice, and the process of construction of them, and the changes to them. It seems, therefore, that there is a natural and powerful integration between the two domains (e.g. of 'strategy' and 'systems'). Porters 'primary and secondary activities' are, in the language of this text, equivalent to organizational processes, but do not contain the modelling activities using systemic constructs and ideas.

There are other parallels and natural integrations. For example, Porter's 'value chain', which implies that an organization is a component of a 'chain' of organizations that come together in order to provide services or products to end consumers. In systems terms, the same idea would be to consider the linkages of a number of subsystems in larger interrelated 'systems of purposeful action'. The history of systemic ideas and that of much of 'strategy' is perhaps a little different, although there are compatibilities and linkages. Systemic thinking is perhaps focused more strongly on operations and implementation of change, whereas strategy provides a number of constructs that

Strategic thinking

Systems thinking

Policy pot

Figure 8.5 Mixing strategy and systems

can help to identify the overall direction of change, given a particular set of social, economic and other types of circumstances. In a sense, the two domains or fields are ideal partners, because the rigour and precision of systems thinking can help to justify the processes that are involved in strategy, and may also provide methodology for implementation and change. The combination of the two may help to provide a 'tasty mixture' (Figure 8.5), which combined can underpin much of the activities involved in organizational problem solving.

The process of learning and evaluating this 'tasty mixture' is perhaps of significant importance to the future of organizations, in order that they can cope with the 'destabilizing disturbances' that affects them, and to operationalize change that integrates a teleological social process of inquiry (a strategic prognosis).

9   Intervention

Abstract

Information systems practitioners are often required to underpin their intervention actions with a precision in thinking about *how* to make intervention and, for example, how the 'implementation' of technology integrates with a range of interventions to change organizational processes. IS practitioners are required to simultaneously *inquire* into their intervention options, and also to evaluate the effectiveness of their interventions in achieving different types of outcome. Arguably, intervention starts at the earliest conceptualization of a project or change process. This is because an effective IS intervention (to change organizational processes) is possible only if appropriate role-relationships can be established with various client groups.

Introduction

If it were hypothetically possible to 'know' everything about what it was that needed changing in a given organizational situation, then the process of making changes would be relatively simple. IS practice would consist of 'getting to know what needs to change', and then 'designing and implementing organized action to change it'. It would mean that the IS practitioner could undertake the 'getting to know' bit, then to convert the resultant knowledge into action and then tell everybody concerned what to do! Simple!

In this hypothetical and unreal situation, the IS practitioner would be undertaking a role as if they were the parent of a small child teaching the child to read. They will have 'superior knowledge', and they are in some way imparting some of that 'superior knowledge'. Sometimes IS practitioners do, indeed, assume that they are taking on such a role (i.e. they assume the role for a variety of reasons), but do not have the knowledge to substantiate it. This is because knowing 'the things that need to change' and knowing 'about how to change them' is an impossibility in organizations. Such 'superior knowledge' is simply not attainable because of the relative ambiguity of organizational situations. Thus, such a role is implausible.

In most organizational situations, there are often complexities and doubts, different interpretations about what needs changing, different viewpoints and values to be considered, there are power dimensions that can influence and determine different priorities, ideas etc. There are various levels of dissonance, disaffection and disagreements. This ambiguity makes organizational problem solving far too problematic to allow for the simplistic application of a role that is akin to a parent teaching a child to read. The IS practitioners must be much more realistic with what can be achieved, how it is to be achieved and what they can do given the resources and time available, and given a set of conditions in a given situation. It also means that an IS practitioner is required to take on alternative types of role.

Whilst an IS practitioner cannot 'get to know everything', they, nonetheless, are involved in some manner, in a role in which they are bringing their thinking to bear on organizational situations, within a social context. It also means that they are obliged to take responsibility for preparing their own thinking for such a role. For example, they must be able to:

- Consider the design of new organizational processes.
- Consider resource implications for new operational activities.
- Identify problems in the monitoring and control activities of existing or future organizational processes.
- Analyse the limitations of existing organizational processes.
- Consider explicitly a range of new and alternative possibilities.
- Evaluate priorities in change and intervention options.
- Design organizational processes to change one situation into another.
- Identify and recognize the limitations of their own thinking as it relates to their own action.
- Evaluate the effectiveness of the processes of strategy and policy formulations.
- Recognize the socio-political dimensions that can act to cloud the humanly constructed operational objectives.

Gaining clarity about how to undertake these types of activities in a given situation is a form of inquiry. As such, the process of intervention is underpinned by a set of inquiring activities, where the ultimate purpose is to design and implement an organized set of actions and interventions to bring about change. Further, a process of intervention is much more than simply 'doing a set of actions'. It is concerned to make inquiry into what is or what is not possible in terms of a set of actions, and in seeking to maximize the possibilities in those actions. Since all actions are socially constrained, the IS practitioner must be concerned to make inquiry about the constraints and, where possible, would be concerned to change the social relationships (and, thus, the social constraints) in order to change possibilities involved in making suitable interventions. This chapter focuses on some of the issues and challenges that are involved in intervention actions, the underpinning inquiring activities and the social challenges that are involved.

Role-relationships

In order to prepare the mind to make an intervention in organizations, it would be reasonable to suggest that there is a process of inquiry and thinking, which the IS practitioner is *obliged* to undertake. It is the process of inquiry that is the key to preparing the thinking, and like all processes, the outcome is only as good as the process. Part of this is the ability to think carefully about: (i) the formal and informal role-relationship that they *currently have* with different client groups, and (ii) the role-relationship that they are required to have with different client groups. This is because the role-relationship can significantly influence the social processes that are involved. For example, in undertaking a particular role, it can often influence and determine:

- The social interactional sequences.
- What is and what is not possible in terms of behaviour and actions.
- What is and what is not possible during intervention and change.

It is, therefore, incumbent on the IS practitioner to establish an appropriate role-relationship. The appropriateness of a particular role-relationship is required to be subjected to inquiry. There may need to be an intervention to change the role-relationship, depending on the outcome of such an inquiry.

Since an IS practitioner must be careful to develop the correct role-relationship with client groups, it involves a dynamic inquiring process about how the relationship changes over time, and the effect of certain 'messages' a particular role-relationship gives (see Chapter 4). It is dynamic in the sense that it must be applied and considered *whilst engaging* with clients and client groups. It is an ongoing inquiring process, which is very important because it determines the possibilities about what is and what is not possible in the process of intervention, i.e. it underpins the actions and activities in intervention. This is particularly important in situations that demand that there is an appropriate level of support amongst client groups. For example, whilst an IS practitioner will often be a catalyst for change, they rarely undertake change on their own, and are sometimes involved in roles in which they are some sort of facilitator of change, arbitrating between different perspectives on change possibilities, assisting groups to come to conclusions about priorities etc. This has very important implications for the role-relationship that they develop during the process of intervention.

Without the support of the client group(s), who has the capability, power and/or authority to change things, information systems change is normally impossible. This means that the IS practitioner must rely on an effective interactional sequence in both (i) setting up the most appropriate role-relationship with client groups, and (ii) helping client groups to consider change options, their role in the change options etc. Since IS practitioners do not undertake organizational changes in isolation from their client groups, it also means that, at some point within the process of IS practice, the client group(s) will be required to take responsibility for the required change, and this again is very much dependent on the roles and interactional sequences of the IS practitioner during the process of a given project. Further, since intervention by an IS practitioner is something that depends on effective social relationships, *intervention must commence at the beginning of that social relationship, and not be considered to be something 'tacked-on' at the end!* By implication, therefore, intervention starts at the beginning of a process of organizational problem solving, not at the end as is sometimes assumed!

When a human, such as one who is purposely undertaking the role of IS practitioner, enters the presence of others, there is data gathering by way of interacting and interpreting gestures (see also Chapter 4). For example, client group(s) may note the issues of socio-economic status and consciously or subconsciously attach meaning to them, in order to seek to appraise certain attributes (e.g. competence, trustworthiness etc). In constructing a human relationship, there are many 'sign-carriers' both given and received. The 'sign-carriers' are highly functional, because they allow both parties to make judgement according to their personal experience, values, interpretations etc. The information gathering and the judgements (Figure 9.1) that are made allow

Category	Good	Medium	Poor
Trustworthiness	✓		
Competence			✓
Socio-economic status		✓	
Rapport		✓	
Role-relationship			✓
Past experience	✓		
Cultural compatibility			✓
In tune with issues	✓		
Good communicator		✓	
Copes with pressure	✓		
Etc...			

Figure 9.1 Data gathering in a social situation

relationships to develop and can influence the role-relationship and other major aspects that may become very important during the process of organizational problem solving.

These categories are representations of a subconscious process of data gathering and meaning attachment, and are constructed dynamically in the process of interaction. By engaging in a process of critical analysis of the self or of others in such a process of 'data gathering and meaning attachment', it is possible to develop learning in order to, for example:

- Gain insight into the effectiveness of the self and others in the process of interaction.
- Test the assumptions being made by the self and by others about how meaning is being constructed and used during interaction.
- Develop awareness of the difference between the basic beliefs that help to drive action and the gestures in a situation that are constructed for that situation.
- Make intervention to change aspects of all of these, in order to influence the outcome of the interactional sequence in future group situations.

In many human situations, the interaction is taken 'as given' and is not subjected to critical analysis and inquiry. However, this inquiring activity is an essential skill because, as discussed in Chapter 4, IS practice is not passive or observational: it is one that is specifically oriented to changing human affairs, and human processes. It is not possible to be able to do this without being able to understand and improve upon the self's own 'sign-carriers' that are given in social situations. Even in 'technical' work (e.g. consulting in IT, building databases), the interaction has significance to the outcome. One of the most important consequences of the early interactional sequences is in setting up the role-relationship, which can potentially determine what can and cannot be undertaken during the process of IS practice. Schein (1988) gives an insight into the role-relationships in organization development work, in which he characterizes three role-relationships: (i) the 'expert' role-relationship, (ii) the 'doctor–patient' role-relationship, and (iii) the 'process consultation' role-relationship, (see Schein 1969, 1987, 1988; see also Block 1981) (summarized in Figure 9.2).

Sometimes, in practice, roles are ignored or are seen as unimportant or irrelevant. For instance, in technical and 'expert' domains, the importance of the role-relationship can be considered irrelevant or subservient to the technical expertise given by the problem solver (e.g. in the 'expert' model of Schein (1987: 23–4)).

If a computer specialist was programming a database, then their role is one of 'expert', and is easily definable. Often the client group will have undertaken the diagnosis, and the computer specialist will offer expertise in fulfilling their perceived needs. However, there are a number of dangers in a role-relationship between client groups and IS practitioner in which the IS practitioner takes the role of expert to undertake a specific area of work defined by the client group. For instance, it assumes that:

- The problem is correctly diagnosed by the client group who assumes that the IS practitioner can be given ownership of a given 'problem', defined in a narrow or specific way.
- The IS practitioner's capabilities to provide the expertise is also correctly identified by the client; given that information systems is in a confused 'pre-paradigm' stage (see Chapter 1), it would be easy to assume that IS practice is solely the enactment of the role of 'database programmer'!
- The client is able to communicate accurately the nature of the problem and the nature of the expertise that is to be purchased to solve 'the problem'; this is much

Role-relationship	Organizational problem solver as technical problem-solver 'Expert role'	Organizational problem solver as teacher 'Doctor–patient role'	Organizational problem solver as co-learner and facilitator of learning about change 'Process consultation role'
Who solves the problem?	The organizational problem solver has primary responsibility for solving the problem	The organizational problem solver tells the client group how to solve the problem. It is the client group who does it!	The organizational problem solver provides methods; it is done as a partnership, in a joint learning process about what actions to undertake in a process
Who defines what the problem is?	The client group	The client group describes 'pain' and the organizational problem solver provides answers about causes and 'solutions'	Jointly, in a process of learning, and inquiry

Figure 9.2 'Categories' of role-relationship (after Schein 1987)

easier in 'programming a database', but much more difficult in the 'organizational problem-solving' role that is involved in IS practice.

- The potential consequences of obtaining the expertise are understood, thought through and accepted by the client group.

A key aspect of IS practice is in the capability to develop the most appropriate role-relationship with client groups. For example, it could be considered that if an IS practitioner benignly accepts a 'diagnosis' given to him by a client group, he is likely to fall into a specific role-relationship, e.g. akin to Schein's 'expert' role. If an IS practitioner accepts the 'diagnosis' of a client, they (i.e. the IS practitioner) are not undertaking the whole process of organizational problem solving. Indeed, they are likely to be acting 'under instruction' of a given client group. If this were the case, sometimes there may not be a need for an IS practitioner at all (e.g. all the client group needs is a bit of help justifying a set of prescribed changes!?!). The client group can undertake the activities themselves and, thus, their expectations of the role played by the IS practitioner is simply to support them in their own problem-solving activities. Thus, the role of an IS practitioner becomes that of a 'pair of hands', perhaps to do a bit of 'dirty work', or to be a 'glove puppet' to the paying client! In such a situation, the IS practitioner can become rather passive, bringing a narrowly defined 'expert' role to a situation, and may become relatively unimportant in the process of organizational problem solving. They can easily fall into the role of simply a 'helping hand', or to bring a narrowly defined 'expertise' to a predefined 'problem'.

In IS practice, the interactional sequence must be set up in such a way that a working relationship can be developed that is appropriate for the work in hand. Sometimes, this means making an intervention in the social processes, norms etc. (e.g. in the *modus vivendi* of a social group), in order to establish the most appropriate role-relationship. If it is a narrowly defined technical role, then the 'expert' role may be appropriate, but this role might also be considered inappropriate for undertaking IS practice. If it is deemed appropriate to undertake a technical role (e.g. to program a database), it would be entirely appropriate to take on an 'expert' role. Whilst a task such as programming a database may be considered a necessary element if improving organizational processes, the operationalization of the task with the role of 'expert' does not itself constitute 'IS practice'. Whilst an information systems practitioner may well have the necessary skills (e.g. in programming a database), by undertaking the task, it demands the undertaking of an 'expert' role; the danger is that the expectations of client groups changes, and the IS practitioner is unable to simultaneously build a role of 'process consultant' and somebody who is involved in a process of organizational problem solving. The danger for the IS practitioner is to fall into a trap in which the process of IS practice will be constrained by the role-relationship that is prescribed by certain perceptions about the constitution of 'IS practice'! Establishing the wrong role-relationship can have a huge impact in determining what is and what is not possible, in terms of undertaking of 'organizational problem solving' and developing suitable interventions.

It also might be that a client group perceives that they require something that is narrow in scope, or have expressed it in that 'narrow' way in a diagnosis report or in a 'Terms of Reference' document. However, invitations to tender (ITT) and terms of reference (TOR) documents are commonly written by groups who may have their individual doubts about the robustness of their own diagnoses. There is commonly a lack of consensus in complex organizational and human situations, even though ITT and TOR documents often provide a façade that suggests that there is! Further, many client groups do not necessarily have consensus about what is required. A consultant's 'Terms of Reference' document is a product of a human process and certain members of a client group may have doubts over its efficacy. It is often created in a social-political environment, dominated by self-interest and power politics. Some members of a client group may feel threatened and, thus, they may be using strategy documents or terms of reference documents for the purpose of defending against an impending and threatening change. If an IS practitioner accepts the 'diagnosis' given by such groups, in such situations, there are some significant dangers in undertaking activities that are not based on *suitable inquiring activities*. It is common that a client group will have a set of expectations of an IS practitioner: to be able to provide answers and solutions. They may often couch the requirements in technical language, or specify the role of the IS practitioner as if they were to provide narrow technical expertise (see Figure 9.3).

Any interactional sequence between human groups can be consciously influenced, and sometimes controlled, by its members. In practice, the interactional sequences between IS practitioners and client groups that are directed by the IS practitioner, may need to change the expectations of the client group(s), because it is they who are going to undertake the actions necessary for change. For example, in consulting, a 'Terms of Reference' document is often reflective of a client group's view of what a 'problem' is and, thus, what they perceive their needs to be with to the role of the IS practitioner. Sometimes, there is a need to challenge such a document, because such a document

Role-relationship	Organizational problem solver as technical problem solver	Organizational problem solver as teacher	Organizational problem solver as co-learner and facilitator of learning about change
	'Expert role'	'Doctor–patient role'	'Process consultation'
Boundaries of task	Boundaries of tasks are highly specific, and generally very clearly specified.	Fairly specific, but with flexibility, depending on the diagnosis	Potentially very wide, muddly and complex. Boundaries are negotiated by the interactions between organizational problem solver(s) and client group(s)
Diagnosis	Done by client group. Assumes client group is correct and tells others what to do.	Done by organizational problem solver, but assumes that the client group reveals sufficient information!	Although the organizational problem solver drives the diagnostics, it is done in the context of joint negotiation

Figure 9.3 Boundaries of tasks of assumed role-relationships

can (i) prescribe a 'problem' that might be some sort of 'symptom', (ii) be quite a 'political' document, derived from a high-conflict situation, and, most importantly, (iii) act to push the IS practitioner into a particular role-relationship (e.g. to provide narrow expertise as in Schein's 'expert role') and, thus, assuming that the diagnosis that has been undertaken by the client group is valid. The process of challenging such a document may be done via an interactional sequence, and be done in such a way that it can help to set up the appropriate role-relationships for the undertaking of the task in hand.

There are good reasons why IS practitioners, and client groups, commonly fail to acknowledge the interactive sequences and the role they play in determining the subsequent activities. For instance, typically in the natural science-based disciplines (e.g. engineering, medicine) there are tools, techniques and methods that are commonly seen as independent of the user of them. That is to say, as long as the user of the tools has the knowledge and experience of using the tools, then the application of the tools will be the same, regardless of who uses them, with the same results. Therefore, a consultant taking the expert role is often mistakenly taken as somebody who applies tools, techniques and/or methods that are independent of their user and, therefore, the interactive sequences and role-relationships are seen as irrelevant and are ignored (see also Argyris 1980). In that sense, the influence of the roles that are played out in an interactive sequence are denied as an influence on the manner in which the tools, techniques or methods are applied. However, since IS practice deals with human organizations, with their complexities and ambiguities, analysable from different perspectives and value sets, it is not possible to 'mechanize' the application of tools, techniques, methods etc. As will be seen in Part IV, there is *always* a gap between the method as constructed and the actions in practice. As a result, it is generally not possible to fulfil the 'expert' role in quite the same way as it is in the natural science-based disciplines and in other practical domains, (e.g. engineering, medicine, computer programming). Indeed, it would take a huge leap of faith if the IS practitioner left the diagnosis of the 'problem' to (for example) the client group. Rather, there must be an alternative role-relationship between client group and IS practitioner, which is much more collaborative in nature than is commonly the case in the 'expert' role.

Process models

In starting a discussion about intervention in bringing about organizational change, and the intervention process, it is perhaps appropriate to postulate on the things that are possible to change in an organizational situation. One way of thinking about this is to consider the integrated content of a given organizational process (see Chapters 4 and 6), for example, the 'elements' that make a process transformation occur (e.g. actions, tasks, information, behaviours, norms, beliefs, skills, control structures, monitoring processes and metrics, organizational hierarchy, power). If any one of these changes within a process, there can often be a fundamental change in the operation of that process.

Whilst models of a given process may be able to give insight into the likely effects of changes in the elements of a given organizational process, the models will always be imperfect. For example, if a new large-scale computer application is to be installed as part of a process of organizational problem solving (e.g. an 'ERP'), then it will be changing a number of elements of one or more organizational processes. Typically, for example, a computer will be designed to assist in communication and information tasks within a process, or to help to monitor a process. It will have effect on the tasks that need to be undertaken, and may challenge certain aspects of power, organizational hierarchy (sometimes technology implementation can result in the de-layering of organizations, for example). It may affect skills (by making certain tasks more 'systematic', which commonly would often result in 'deskilling'). In this example, we have abstracted certain core elements of what might change within a process resulting from a computer installation. In this case (i) communications, (ii) power and organizational control structures, and (iii) skills. These are 'generalizable abstractions' about what is likely to be changed in a given hypothetical situation, and there may be other abstractions that could have been made. This has been done without a model of a given process in practice. These 'generalizable abstractions' can help in future organizational problem-solving activities, and can help to develop precision in the thinking about areas that are required for change in any given situation. For example, it is possible to think about such 'generalized abstractions' in order to help structure inquiry into future interventions. That is to say, the 'generalized abstractions' can indicate the areas that might be required to make intervention, and might include (for example):

- attitudes of people
- knowledge and skills of people
- activities and tasks that people undertake
- communication between people
- information
- power that makes human societal structures operate in particular ways
- control to try to align activities to purpose
- the enabling technologies
- etc.

IS practice often includes attempting to change some or all of these simultaneously. Indeed, it is not possible to change the information, or the enabling ICT, without changing many of these other aspects of a given organizational process, or sets of processes. Since such aspects of organizational processes may require to be changed simultaneously and in conjunction with each other, intervention to improve processes must include suitable interactional sequences with client groups that span such aspects. It is the inquiry into organizational processes that gives insight into the specifics of what needs to change and, thus, how to structure a series of interactional sequences, activities and actions etc. that are required to instigate change.

If an IS practitioner has been able to construct conceptually, and in sufficient detail, and (broadly) gained agreement about an organizational process, then this can be used to structure the thinking about areas that might require change and 'improvement' in practice. That is to say, the model may help to identify areas of a 'real world' process that are considered 'inadequate' in some way. This situation assumes that the model is sufficiently adequate to give insight into one or more changes, and that it has helped to highlight or demonstrate a 'reality' that is 'inadequate' in some way, i.e. the model has guided the thinking process into highlighting specific change requirements.

It also might not be inconceivable that the model might be inadequate in some way. Thus, there is a requirement to consider the adequacies of the model, whilst simultaneously consider the adequacies of the 'real world' that it helps to reveal. Thus, there must be a form of inquiry into both the model and the 'reality' that it presents, which are simultaneously evaluated. In this way, a process model acts as a way to structure inquiry into (i) 'reality', and (ii) the refinement of the model. This is an iterative process, in which client groups and IS practitioners can engage in how to undertake 'improvement' and what constitutes 'improvement' in a given situation. This inquiry is the basis for developing potential actions and activities aimed at 'improvement'.

It would be unrealistic that one model could adequately describe an organizational process in an absolute sense. To suggest that there was only one model for a given process in 'reality', is akin to suggesting that one model can adequately describe a range of viewpoints and interpretations about the elements and the functions of an organizational process. However, it *is* realistic to suggest that, through a process of modelling, and engaging client groups, it is possible to develop insights, ideas and precision about issues, current inadequacies and future possibilities for an organizational process or sets of processes. As such, it *is* realistic that models of process can provide a basis for discussion, learning and thinking regarding one or more organizational processes.

The above discussion suggests that there are a number of key issues when attempting to bridge the gap between the *conceptual modelling of processes* and the pragmatics of undertaking action to improve or change *processes in practice* (i.e. intervention). For example:

- The conceptual model is unlikely to be 'correct' in an absolute sense, but it can be continually improved in a process of learning and inquiry.
- The conceptual model can help to give insight into areas of potential improvement in a problematic organizational situation.
- The conceptual model can be used to explicitly discuss issues with client groups, and thereby give them insights into organizational processes that they may not have otherwise considered.

Comparisons

At some level, the conceptual models are used in a learning process, in order to refine thinking about both the models and about practical organizational processes. Therefore, purposeful application of the models is to provide learning. Unfortunately, this is not always how modelling is perceived, or how models are perceived to be used. For example:

- They are often seen as 'reality', i.e. that there is no difference between the models and reality, thus denying the opportunity to explore the difference.
- They are often used to purposefully 'specify' (e.g. as a technical specification), rather than as a learning or rhetorical device (for 'learning' see Kawalek, 1996).

Indeed, a model can never outline *all* the essential characteristics of an organizational process in practice, but it can be of relevance in order to develop an engaged debate with enhancements made to: (i) the model, and/or (ii) 'reality'. In other words, the

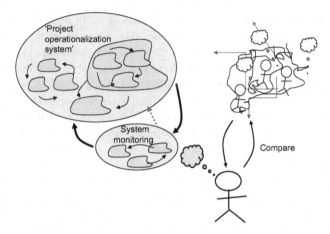

Figure 9.4 The process of comparison models with 'reality'

models can provide a basis for intervention and change. Further, the intervention and change is a process of engaged social interaction between IS practitioner(s) and client groups (see also Schein 1993a, 1993b), in a process of exploration, where the models are used implicitly or explicitly and are compared with the 'real' situation as depicted in Figure 9.4.

The process of comparison can be undertaken in a very explicit manner, by taking each element or subsystem, and thinking about how it is operationalized in practice (if at all!). For example, if we take a conceptual model, and break it into different elements, each can be explored by relating it to the 'real world' situation. This might be considered to be an iterative learning process of 'relating to and comparing', and it is a process that is illustrated in Figure 9.5.

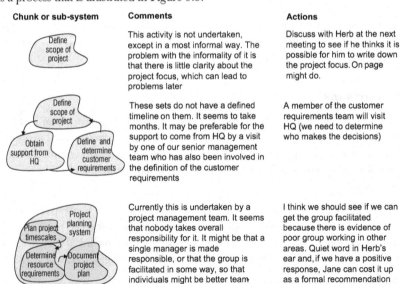

Figure 9.5 Determining the requirements for action from models

Intervention as a 'learning process'

The ideas presented in this chapter assume that intervention is a teleological process with the formal purpose to (i) bring clarity to the thinking of the IS practitioner, and (ii) assist in engaging the client groups into the consideration of change. Since it is the various client groups that ultimately make the changes happen, not the IS practitioner, it is necessary to be able to communicate ideas in order to instigate change. Indeed, it is often impossible for an IS practitioner to undertake changing anything in organizations, without gaining a form of support for change from a variety of client group(s). This 'support' implies the development of trust as well as a social support (e.g. a power and political form of support). In an ideal situation, it would be good if this was support that had consensus, but this, too, is virtually impossible in many organizational situations. Nonetheless, it is essential that the IS practitioner helps client group(s) recognize the need for change and undertakes actions of various sorts, in order to change a situation. In that sense, the process of intervention might be considered to be a learning process on the part of the IS practitioner(s), operationalized through their inquiring activities and, for the client group(s), operationalized as part of the same process of inquiry (see Figure 9.6).

If it were considered that IS practice was essentially a learning process, then it is perhaps important to think carefully about what is being learned and how it is to be achieved. Client groups, for instance, may be focusing in on learning about:

- Issues concerning their organizational processes.
- Alternative ways of viewing a situation.
- Designing new processes.
- The integration of organizational processes.
- How to make changes to improve processes.
- Alternative ways of undertaking activities.
- Designing policies and strategies.
- Their own actions and the way they are contributing to change.
- Designing and implementing processes that operationalize particular policies and strategies.
- etc.

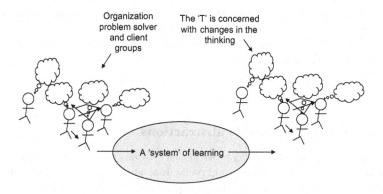

Figure 9.6 Intervention as a process of learning

Perhaps obviously, client groups would not consider doing things that are not in their interests. For example, in certain potential 'reorganizations', it may mean that one set of people will need to change the way they work, or change their attitudes, or change their roles etc.; or sometimes it may result in 'deskilling' or loss of jobs. By modelling the processes, the IS practitioner should be able to gain insight into such potential areas of difficulty and, in a learning process, may be able to facilitate the inquiry into finding new 'socially acceptable' alternatives. However, invariably this is not easy, nor always possible, and often the learning process must recognize the limitations or feasibility of change that is broadly based on seeking consensus and 'agreed action'.

Thus, if the process of intervention is considered to be a process of learning, as outlined, there may be some observations that are worthy of consideration. For example:

- As in any learning process, there are various levels of willingness on the part of the learners to embrace new ideas.
- In learning, there is always a power relationship that can exert pressure on a human learner. For instance, a university holds significant power because it can confer a degree, or choose not to if a learner does not prove themselves an 'adequate' learner in some way. In organizational change situations, although there is not the same pressure, there must be a form of pressure because without it there is less likelihood that the process will help people to learn.
- An IS practitioner will be a learner, but also must be able to play a role as facilitator in the learning of others.

In any human learning process there are roles and relationships that are involved. Also, as in any learning there are constructs and concepts, the application of them, and learning derived from the critical evaluation of the application of them. Thus, there are some potential changes that might occur as part of the 'transformational' aspects of a learning process. For example, there might be learning about:

- The concepts and constructs.
- How concepts and constructs could be applied in a given situation.
- The strengths and weaknesses of a rationale for using particular constructs and methods.
- Some aspect of the situation from the application of concepts and constructs.
- The methods for applying the concepts and constructs.
- The results of applying the constructs and concepts in the way specified, and in the particular situation.
- The imperatives for action.
- etc.

Generating generalizable abstractions

During the process of undertaking such learning activities, it may be possible to discover new knowledge about the process and methods of intervention, and also to abstract insights into particular situations, the appropriateness of concepts, techniques, tools, methods etc. This type of knowledge generation from the process of 'doing' a range of activities associated with the interventions during a problem-solving process, can instigate new ideas, and meet the goals of researchers as well as practitioner (e.g. (A), (B), (C) and (D), as discussed in Chapter 2). Thus, any set of learners (e.g. IS practitioners and client groups) can simultaneously be 'solving problems', as well as distilling the experiences and abstracting the lessons in doing so for generating new knowledge ((D)). Thus, learning in the intervention process need not only be concerned with the immediacies of IS practice or 'solving problems in organizations' or 'managing change'. Rather, they can be focused on generating abstractions and knowledge about how it can be done! This is of course a concern and challenge for methodology and epistemology. It also may provide a basis for certain research types that are relevant to the field of practice in IS, e.g. how to operationalize 'mode 2' research (see Gibbons *et al.* 1994; Tranfield and Starkey 1998; Etzkowitz and Leydesdorff 2000; Gibbons 2000; Starkey and Madan 2001; Harvey *et al.* 2002; Maclean *et al.* 2002; Maclean and MacIntosh 2002).

As might be expected of a systemic approach, use of the constructs, the method of application and the situational characteristics in which they are applied, are all closely interconnected. However, in IS practice, the interest is in the outcomes or the actions taken that result from the learning process and, thus, the process of learning is sometimes forgotten. By including groups (e.g. academics) who have the primary concern of generating learning and knowledge, when organized in a particular way, it might be possible to generate significant human knowledge, which might serve future organizational change and intervention activities.

10 Evaluation

Abstract

If the information systems practice is not evaluated, it is not possible to know whether it has been worth the effort. It also can result in an inability to abstract learning into future policies, procedures, processes and methods. In practice, evaluation has taken a secondary role. Sometimes, it is often not undertaken at all; or it is undertaken half-heartedly, because of the immediacy, imperatives and challenges of practice; or it is undertaken badly, because there is a poor conceptualization of some key characteristics of the process of evaluation, e.g. what it is that is being evaluated, how to undertake the evaluation, and confusion as to the purpose (e.g. is it for learning, or for control of project etc.). This chapter will discuss the characteristics of a process of evaluation as it is relevant to information systems practice.

Introduction

One of the major challenges faced by organizations is in judging the success of change initiatives. In practice, the judgements that are made are often intuitive and implicit, and are insufficient as a basis for learning for future change initiatives. The judgements are often undertaken in an *ad hoc* manner based on informal and implicit personal interpretations and experiences of events and issues. Often this is done without reference to (for example): (i) the roles and relationships that are involved in a change project or process, or (ii) the teleological considerations (e.g. the *purpose* in the judgement).

There are many reasons why it is important that evaluation is required in IS practice. Whilst there is learning for the IS practitioners involved in a given project, their experience is not necessarily internalized, verified or analysed. Often the learning and knowledge gets lost and future projects, initiatives and change processes cannot make use of the knowledge gained from past projects. It is, perhaps, little wonder that organizations often seem to make similar mistakes, because there is little appreciation of the need to generate knowledge derived from the experience of practice. This can only be done with effective evaluation, which can abstract lessons in a particular way so that it is reusable and generalizable for future IS practitioners. This is indeed one of the roles of research in the field of IS.

Unfortunately it is common to find that, in IS practice, evaluation is generally done in an 'intuitive and implicit' manner, possibly because of the difficulties in thinking through the methodological issues in undertaking an explicit evaluation process. Furthermore, often in practice, the process of a project, or the changes in human organizations that result from the project, is evaluated by a person or group who are involved in, or closely associated with making the changes! In such circumstances, such evaluation degenerates into (i) a justification of actions taken, (ii) a political weapon (e.g. to justify career progression), and/or (iii) a social defence. It is quite simple to see that in such circumstances, such judgements are completely inadequate because the process of evaluation of change is teleologically incompatible with the process of change: if one individual is involved in both, then it implies that they may be judging themselves! This in itself may not inherently be problematic, but in organizations, in which there are power groupings, and judgements over individuals' performance, it is unusual to find individuals able or willing to develop a robust critique, in which their own 'failings' might emerge. This is a situation that is completely inadequate, given the failings in IS as outlined in Chapter 2. Project designers, managers, funders etc., must be able to recognize the need for evaluation, which can move beyond a monitoring function (see Chapter 7), but which concerns itself to generate learning.

It seems quite shocking that there are commonly sizeable changes that occur in organizations, with sizable budgets, with little consideration about evaluation of the change. How is it possible to know with reasonable certainty that an IS process, and the change in organization that results, can achieve the assumed benefits? Often the evaluation of change is complex and challenging because the changes themselves are complex and challenging. For example, on implementing a new Enterprise Resource Planning (ERP) computer application, which affects changes and integrates many groups, departments and activities, it becomes very complex to evaluate the change. It can result in 'efficiencies' being claimed, but sometimes these are rather unsubstantiated or unverifiable. How is it possible to substantiate and verify the process of change, and the performance of IS practitioners, in such complex change activities?

Perhaps it is much easier to apply monitoring or control mechanisms during the process of change, e.g. via the establishment of a steering group or planning group. It is also much easier to apply rigorous controls on project targets, deadlines, steps, stages, dates etc. Such control mechanisms can help the process of the change. However, these do not evaluate the change to give some way of assessing how benefits have accrued. Or where they do, there is commonly the type of teleological incompatibility as outlined in the previous paragraph. For example, the planning group is given the task of evaluating their own project, with the inevitable outcome that the evaluation is uncritical and simply a form of 'justification' of action!

There are potentially many explanations of why the evaluation of change is sometimes weak or not done at all. For instance, conceptually, there is little clarity about the difference between monitoring and control, and that of evaluation. Sometimes they are seen as the same thing! Further, the methodological issues that are involved in undertaking an evaluation of change are rather ambiguous and tricky. It is the purpose of this chapter to explore evaluation in broad methodological terms. It is an essential element of IS practice because, in practice, it is essential to be able to gain insight into both:

• the *changes in organization* (e.g. new processes, activities, technologies, information, metrics, coordination, communication etc.) and

- the *project or process*, the actions and activities involved in making the changes to organizations (e.g. methods used, principles of method, assumptions, approaches, techniques, interventions, interactional sequences etc.).

Evaluation teams

In IS practice, there is often a project management process and one or more people (commonly a 'team' of sorts) involved in the activities of assessing the progress and determining policies and actions during an organizational problem-solving process. However, there are some common mistakes that result in some potential problems. For example:

- Such a group is often set up by a client group, who are required to justify expenditure on the processes involved in IS practice. It means that sometimes there is a conflict of purpose, which is teleologically incompatible with an effective method of evaluation, because (i) critique is commonly and mistakenly assumed to be criticism, and (ii) criticism (and therefore 'critique') cannot be made public because it might question the judgements made about the need for the change initiative in the first place.
- Often the people who are undertaking the tasks involved in the project also form the monitoring or evaluation team, making their roles teleologically incompatible.
- There is often a lack clarity of the meaning of 'monitoring' and that of 'evaluation' and, thus, there is often a lack of clarity about the goals and activities that are involved.
- The group who perform 'project monitoring' may fail to consider carefully enough the metrics or criteria, or cannot agree or clarify what they are or what they should be. Thus, the metrics or criteria may reflect hidden agendas and implicit purpose etc. These are situations that can result in them being unable to work effectively or failing to ensure quality in the organizational problem-solving process.
- The purpose is unclear. For example, is it to 'control' the activities of the IS practitioner, or is it learn from experience?
- The group is unable to take control action because those who are undertaking organizational problem-solving activities will not allow it, and may cover up activities that might be perceived to be 'failing'.

These points can help to explain many failings in various projects that aim at organizational problem solving and improvement (see also Lippitt and Lippitt 1978). It can also help explain why there is often scope for unethical and incompetent behaviour, especially in the provision of consultancy services (see for example O'Shea and Madigan 1999; Ashford 1999; Pinault 2000). If there is confusion about monitoring and evaluation processes, the processes themselves are open and ripe for abuse.

It seems that the organization of the process of evaluation of IS practice may itself need organizing conceptually. This is particularly important for change initiatives that are high value and high-risk investments, or are complex in structure and purpose (e.g. many IS projects).

Systems constructs in evaluation

If it were possible to design an evaluation process, which would act to help make judgement on whether or not a certain organizational problem-solving activity could be considered to be 'successful' or otherwise, then it might be easily conceived that there could be a number of alternative ways in which it could be done. Perhaps a useful starting point might be to consider that the project, or IS problem-solving process, itself has transformational qualities. Since it is intended to change some things within an organization, then it is reasonable to consider the possibilities of modelling it as a transformational system, and apply the conceptual constructs as outlined in Chapter 6. For example, it might involve making some sort inquiry into the transformations that have been made by the explicit and hidden actions and activities of the IS practitioners. We could depict this using one of the core systems constructs, e.g. input and output (Figure 10.1).

In Figure 10.1, the process of organizational problem solving is considered to have transformative characteristics, and is purposeful and, thus, is sketched in an outline process model. In taking this approach, there are some significant challenges. For example, since (Si) and (Sii) will always be perceptions, which (i) change over time, and (ii) cannot outline all aspects of a complex and messy situation, they cannot be considered to be 'absolute'. How would they be characterized, given the difficulties in outlining the different situations? Such an approach would assume that situations (Si) and (Sii) can easily be considered 'absolute' or frozen (e.g. as in an output of a 'diagnosis', but assuming that it is devoid of interpretation by an observer, complex and unchanging). However, rather than seeing (Si) and (Sii) as absolute, it is possible to see them both as being the subject of inquiry by an evaluator of an organizational problem-solving process. Seen in this manner, evaluation is primarily an inquiring process focused on inquiring into situations and the changes (formal and explicit with purpose, as well as informal, emergent and implicit in purpose).

Structuring the nature of evaluation in these terms would necessitate consideration of what features and characteristics of both situations, (Si) and (Sii), would be

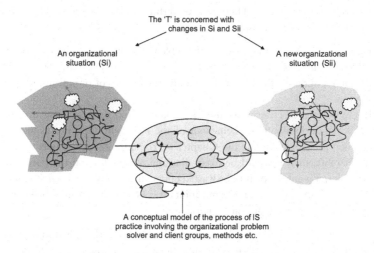

The 'T' is concerned with changes in Si and Sii

An organizational situation (Si)

A new organizational situation (Sii)

A conceptual model of the process of IS practice involving the organizational problem solver and client groups, methods etc.

Figure 10.1 A model of transformation applied to 'problem-solving' process

subjected to inquiry in an evaluation process. There are of course many features and characteristics that could be selected. For example:

*   The perceptions of the various issues, concerns, anxieties etc. of those connected to the situations (Si and Sii).
*   The perceptions and clarity of purpose of organizational processes at Si and Sii.
*   Perceptions about the way organizational processes are structured and organized at Si and Sii.
*   Perceptions about the way in which the monitoring of the processes takes place and its implicit and explicit effect on the processes at Si and Sii.
*   The perceptions of strategic priorities and policies in situations Si and Sii.
*   The way these different perceptions are arrived at (i.e. the perceptions of the evaluators, the IS practitioners, client groups etc.).
*   etc.

In undertaking an inquiry of this sort, there are some dangers and pitfalls. For example, in undertaking such an inquiry, quantitative metrics or qualitative criteria could be utilized, in order to inquire into the what the core characteristics of (Si) and (Sii) could be considered to be and, thus, derive (i) what the differences are between (Si) and (Sii), (ii) evaluate whether the changes between (Si) and (Sii) are attributable to the actions and activities of the IS practitioner; and (iii) evaluate whether Sii can be considered 'better' than Si.[1]

Whilst there is a certain conceptual simplicity in this 'transformational' view of IS practice, there are some obvious difficulties in attempting to achieve this in practice. For example, the 'metrics' or 'criteria' that are used to inquire into the input situation (Si) and the output situation (Sii) are difficult to operationalize to ensure the effective outcome. For instance, taking a rather extreme example, if the metric or criterion was 'profitability' in both (Si) and (Sii), then there is the assumption that it is possible to isolate the variable 'profitability' at point (Si) and also isolate the 'profitability' at point (Sii), and that if profitability (Sii>Si), and that the change in profitability is in some way attributable to the project and interventions of the IS practitioner, then 'success', otherwise 'failure'(!) There may be certain challenges and problematic issues associated with this. For example:

*   How can the change in state be attributable to the process of change? The metric or criteria are often influenced by other factors, in addition and over and above the interventions of the IS practitioner and the process of organizational problem solving.
*   If the metrics or criteria are used in isolation, and they are known, then they can serve to dominate the behaviour of the IS practitioner (in this instance the decision makers as outlined in Chapter 6). For instance, if the only criteria was profitability, then it would be likely that any other effort on the part of the IS practitioner would appear to be wasted effort; thus, the process activities (i.e. what goes on in the process of organizational problem solving) may become target driven to the extent that other criteria are ignored.

If the metrics or criteria are inappropriately defined and applied in a process of evaluation, then those who are undertaking the task of IS practice may feel pressured by the metrics (which act to make judgement on their actions), and may influence their behaviour in order to 'pander' to the metrics, or attempt to demonstrate that the metrics show 'success' by altering the metrics or criteria.

In this latter example, the criteria are taken in isolation and, thus, form a 'performance goal' of some sort and, thus, act to alter the behaviour of an IS practitioner during the organizational problem-solving process. It is tempting to see the process of evaluation as 'criteria driven' in this manner, but this can have highly undesirable consequences. Rather, an evaluation must be able to focus inquiry on: (i) the situations (Si) and (Sii), and the relationship that these each have with (ii) the transformative actions of the organizational problem-solving process. In order to achieve it, there must be suitable inquiring methods. These sometimes may required an evaluator to be in close proximity to the situations, and using observational methods, but it is also reasonable to suggest that effective inquiry can be implemented by a very focused set of activities including personal interviews and focus groups. Furthermore, the evaluator must be able to avoid being seen as a monitor; rather, the purpose must be clear, i.e. it is for learning and, thus, the inquiring process cannot be seen to be simply 'applying criteria'.

Evaluation of process change

Fundamental to the inquiry into the process and explicit and implicit outcomes of IS practice must be the change to organizational processes, and the monitoring and control activities involved with them. Thus, the evaluation inquiry must be able to consider various models of any given process. For example, it is an inquiry that involves:

*   The rhetorical use of models in order to gain insight into changes in the situations (Si and Sii).
*   The clarity of purpose of processes, and the purposeful behaviour and actions of humans within the process in Si and Sii.
*   The efficiency and effectiveness of the transformational qualities of a process in Si and Sii.
*   The perceptions of the beneficiaries of the process in Si and Sii.
*   The appropriateness of the characteristics of the processes (e.g. level of 'systematicness') in Si and Sii.
*   The efficiency and effectiveness of the information and communications within the processes in Si and Sii.
*   The control structures within the processes in Si and Sii.
*   The emergent outcomes of the operation of the process in Si and Sii.
*   The decision making, values and associated assumptions that affect the process in Si and Sii.
*   etc.

These follow the characteristics as outlined in Chapter 6. However, an evaluation would be concerned to attribute the actions involved in the IS practice to the changes in certain organizational processes at Si..Sii. Evaluation is also concerned with the appropriateness of the control and monitoring processes, and the intended and unintended effect that they have on the organizational processes. This is depicted in Figure 10.2.

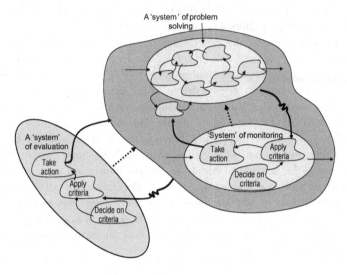

Figure 10.2 Towards a systems model of evaluation

As in a process of monitoring, it is inevitable that an evaluation will be selective of certain 'real world' issues, events, activities, behaviours, attitudes etc. An evaluation will encompass the effectiveness of the monitoring on the processes, and it will have long-term consequences for current or future processes. In many ways, it can be considered to have a structure much like the monitoring process. However, its purpose is fundamentally different. Its purpose is not to monitor and control the process of IS practice, but to inquire into the effectiveness of an organizational problem-solving process, i.e. a monitoring process is designed to influence behaviour and to act as a check on events, actions etc., whereas a process of evaluation involves *learning* about key aspects of practice, and will include inquiry into elements such as:

- The evaluation of the methods used by the IS practitioners.
- The effectiveness of their 'mindset' including motives for being there in the first place.
- Their ability to undertake effective diagnosis, model purposeful processes etc.
- The appropriateness of implementing suitable monitoring activities.
- Their roles and relationships with client groups.
- Their interactional sequences with client groups.
- The rationale for their interventions.
- The constraints on action in a given situation.
- etc.

Indeed, from the undertaking of evaluation, it is possible to generate new knowledge about the problem-solving process itself! It can provide some generalizable abstractions about (for example) (i) the methods, techniques, tools, methodologies, and (ii) the use of methods in a given situation.

Evaluation at different time intervals

If a process of evaluation were to be designed and applied to a problem-solving process, then it could be required to be undertaken at different time intervals during the process (see Jayaratna 1994). We will term this time 0 (t_0), time 1 (t_1), time 2 (t_2) etc., up to time n, (t_n), as depicted in Figure 10.3.

If it were conceptually possible to undertake evaluation at three or more different time intervals, as depicted in Figure 10.3, then it seems reasonable that the process of evaluating organizational problem solving can include a range of things. For example, it might involve the evaluation of such things as the:

- Situation as it changes over time.
- Changes in the problem-solving methods employed by the problem solver.
- Development of the interactional sequences of the IS practitioner.
- Devolving group dynamics of the IS practitioners.
- Changes in perceptions of a situation.
- Development of the implicit or explicit models used in the process of problem solving.
- Metrics or criteria in applying judgement about processes.
- Actions of the problem solver(s) and the rationale for the action(s).
- Purposeful interventions of the problem solver(s).
- Emergent outcomes of the problem-solving process.
- etc.

It may also involve the evaluation of all such aspects at the different time intervals, or the integration of such aspects over time. Central to this is the evaluation of the IS practitioners themselves as an integrated component of the problem-solving process, and simultaneously to inquire into the evaluators own inquiring process (i.e. the 'thinking about thinking' principle in Chapter 3). It is the appropriate organization of evaluation methods and teams that will bring benefit to IS practice in the future. Evaluation is not some sort of 'add-on'. It is centrally important to the development of the discipline.

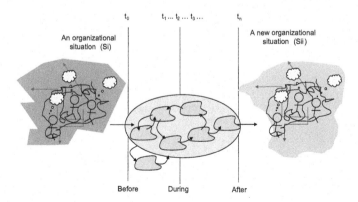

Figure 10.3 Towards a process of evaluation

Part IV

Whither inquiring activities?

This part discusses the possible implications of our rethink about the discipline and practice of information systems. It does this in two chapters.

First, a case study is developed, which applies some of the core principles and ideas that are discussed in Parts II and III of the book. The case demonstrates the approach taken by an IS team in their application of certain principles that have been outlined. The consulting team in this case was two consultants working for an independent consulting company in the US. The consulting company works in an advisory only, i.e. it does not have own proprietary technology applications. This makes it 'independent' of any technology application that is used in the course of 'organizational problem solving'. In a sense, the work of these consultants made a useful case study because they were not tied to a particular set of consulting products, service, or technologies. They were not 'solution providers' who ignored (i) the complexities of defining a given 'problem', and (ii) the process issues and complexities in 'organizational problem solving'.

Second, certain conclusions are drawn about current practices, and the potential for change in the discipline of information systems. In particular, it questions the potential for the discipline to grow into the 'de facto' discipline for organizational problem solving, in which technology is an enabler. The increasing power, reach and accessibility of technology suggests that organizations are able to continue to innovate, and this means that policies, procedures and processes are required to be subjected to change and continuous 'improvement'. But this is not done by oversimplifying the nature of 'improvement' or how to achieve it. There are certain barriers, not least in the way the discipline of information systems is commonly perceived, commonly taught and commonly researched.

11 Case study

Organizational problem solving in Morrígan Engineering LLC[1]

Abstract

This case is based in a medium-sized manufacturing engineering organization, which was part of a larger corporate group of companies. The corporate group had been expanding rapidly through a series of acquisitions since the 1980s and 1990s. Morrígan was one of the original companies in the group. It had been built on supplying engineering components, largely to the automotive industry. However, recent developments had meant that they were supplying to other sectors. Demand for large batch manufacturing was considered to be decreasing, which brought with it a diversification in product, type of manufacture, customers etc. Morrígan had been highly profitable in the past but, in recent years, it was considered to be suffering due to increased competition from imported supplies. It also was under increasing pressure at a corporate level to increase shareholder returns from its acquisitions. Within the wider group, there were about a dozen different companies, trading under different names, and including a number of manufacturers, and a distribution and logistics company that served to deliver to a variety of customers (manufacturers, maintenance garages, parts stockists and retailers). The case provides a set of interesting challenges for an IS team, armed with technical and 'organizational problem-solving' methods, knowledge and skills.

Introduction

The case that follows outlines the process of information systems practice by two consultants, called Richard Hewlett and Lesley Edmonds.[2] These two consultants and their project were selected for inclusion in the book, because they were largely undertaking IS work in a way that was informed by the methods outlined in this text. Indeed, the methods and ideas in this text originated a component of a training course in a consulting academy in the US. These two consultants had been on this programme and had worked together on a variety of projects which operationalized them. They also are colleagues of the author, having worked on projects together. As such, they have familiarity with the methods and principles that are outlined in this book. Therefore, their approach was one of 'organizational problem solving', which considered information and technology to be a key modern-day area or source of 'organizational improvement'. Further, because their consulting organization had no proprietary technology, it meant that they were not searching for 'solutions' from any one technology type or supplier. As such, their view of the 'information systems' work involved much more than information and technology, which, in effect, took their place alongside other problem-solving actions, activities and interventions, undertaken as part of an IS 'problem-solving' process.

In this case, the project was termed an 'INSPIRE project'. INSPIRE was coined to describe the project from the acronym '**IN**novation **S**ystem for **P**erformance **I**mprovement and **RE**organization'. In one sense, the term 'INSPIRE' is really only a label, or descriptor, which aims to capture the imagination of, for example, IS practitioners and client groups. However, following the use of the term in several projects, INSPIRE was formally defined to refer to *the use of the inquiring activities to help to structure the thinking to guide intervention actions in practice*. Of course, it would be naive to imply that the inquiring activities would or could be used mechanistically to guide human action. But it *is* reasonable that the underpinning principles, and the structure of inquiry, can influence and affect a particular process and approach taken by a group of IS practitioners. In that sense, the principles are usable in a variety of ways, and usable in a variety of contexts. The case is only one such instance. As will be seen in the case, client groups came together in order that they might engage with some of the same inquiring activities. In each instance, the degree to which the inquiring activities were used to guide the process, the 'interpretation' of them in a given context, their usefulness, shortcomings and value, were subjected to evaluation. This is essentially part of ongoing research, of which this is one case. The observations and selection of material for inclusion in this book is done in order to demonstrate the way a set of consultants have operated as organizational problem solvers in information systems, and in a way that linked the resultant 'thinking and action' together.

As will be seen in the case material, the principles of inquiry are not used prescriptively or via a rigid structure but are, nonetheless, used to guide the process in a variety of actions and activities in practice. There are no clear-cut stages during their use. Rather, they are used in a way that is integrated into a process of 'organizational problem solving' in a way that is 'implicit'. The principles as outlined in Parts II and III of this book are more 'infused' into the 'problem-solving' actions in practice. As such, their use is much more than following a number of steps in a rigid form. This is probably true of any practice-based set of ideas and principles that are required to be used in human contexts and in human 'systems'. For example, much of the process is determined by unfolding events and actions, and responses result, in part, by the demands and needs of various client groups. As such the principles are integrated into these unfolding events and actions, by the interactions of the consulting team.

This case followed a number of cases, in which some of the principles outlined in this book, were being formulated and developed. The case organization is not considered to be particularly leading edge. It is perhaps quite typical of the kind of consulting that occurs in the smaller organization sector. Indeed, in some ways, Morrígan was quite old-fashioned and problematic. However, the process and method that underpinned much of the practice of IS was seen to be the key focus of interest. Indeed, the case study is presented as if looking through the 'lens' of the principles of the organizational problem-solving methods and ideas, and how they can be integrated into IS practice. Perhaps the most interesting challenges to change agents, such as IS specialists, are the rather old organizations, and transforming them. It is the process and method that is the primary focus in this chapter.

The author took no part in this case, except as a passive observer. Indeed, when the bulk of the project was undertaken, there was no intention that it might appear in a book! However, the case was one that was to be included in research and, thus, has been used for research purposes. The two consultants kindly worked with the author in a post-hoc analysis of the process of organizational problem solving, to relate the key events of the development of the case, in order to prepare it for insertion into this book. The reason why this was done was, in part, to maintain the perceptions of the consultants in the text. There is of course a certain complexity in this undertaking. For example, in a series of interactions, the consultants were rationalizing, in a post-hoc way, a set of actions and events, and this is interpreted and expressed by the author!

The purpose of the case is to demonstrate the process of organizational problem solving in a particular context. The case (as outlined) can only ever be a 'snippet' of the unfolding events. In order to give a coherence, the presentation of the case has resulted in a certain licence being taken, to present the case in a way that it demonstrates the process. At the time of writing, the contract is still ongoing and the consultants remain engaged in the process of organizational problem solving with the case organization. The contract has since expanded to incorporate the whole group of companies, although most of what follows is focused on only one company of the group. The scenarios have been carefully selected, in order to (i) demonstrate the application of some of the inquiring activities, and/or (ii) highlight some key outcome relating to the application of the inquiring activities, and/or (iii) are considered a turning point in the development of the case. These are preceded by a note of welcome by the consultants themselves. Direct quotations are italicized. Although the case presented is one that is undertaken by external consultants, the process issues and the use of the inquiring activities might be similar, if undertaken by any practicing manager or IS practitioner.

A note of welcome

Hello, we are Richard and Lesley ... we have been leading this project with Morrígan Engineers. Hopefully we will give you a feel for our approach in operating in the exciting world of Information Systems. We are writing these words together. Forgive any typo's!

In the Morrígan case, Lesley has been taking the role of lead consultant. Between us, we have quite a few years operating in the IS world. Lesley has a computer science degree and an MBA. She is British, from Manchester. She supports Oldham Athletic soccer club (sad eh?). Richard has an undergraduate degree majoring in Management, a teaching qualification, and is currently working on a PhD. He is American, from Arkansas. He's into any and every sport.

We have worked together on a number of projects. Morrígan is our fourth project working together. It is our opinion that so many organizations are requiring IS skills, and so many organization do not quite manage to integrate IS with adequate organizational change, and thus realize the innovation potential of their technology and information. Most acknowledge the need to employ specialists with organizational change skills, but then go on to employ out and out techies, or consultants out to sell them a specific product. We feel strongly that this results in seeing technology as an end-goal, rather than seeing technology as just part of the task. Actually, most of our time is spent in changing organizational processes, helping people to do things differently, including '... using or applying computers ...'.

But it's much more than that. We see it as trying to help organizations to grow and change, to find ways to solve a range of problems ... these things might be quite wide in range and scope. For instance, changing processes, tasks, procedures, etc., often require changes in other areas, e.g. in HR policies. Changes in processes often require challenging certain assumptions about how such processes are monitored and controlled. Changing processes that cross organizational boundaries, or integrate in a 'joined-up' manner, within a given organization, will always carry a lot of complexity. Sometimes there is substantial technical complexity. Always there is organizational complexity. Changing processes will always be politically loaded, often requiring careful consideration of power groupings. What we must do, is to find ways to 'improve' performance, and that means being sensitive and realistic about what we can and cannot achieve in a given situation. Often, (but not always), it involves technology, because technology is so very pervasive nowadays. It gives huge opportunities that our clients often are oblivious to.

Most of all, our work is about deep, high quality thinking ... This has been a key aspect of our work since we studied together at a consulting academy. We both realized at more or less the same time, that to undertake consulting and organizational problem-solving, we needed to work hard on understanding the self ... this job involves thinking about the knowledge you have, and the knowledge you don't have (and the knowledge that you need to acquire, in a given consulting assignment). It also requires that you are willing and able to be a good learner. If you think in these terms, you can start to plug the gaps, set your own agenda's regarding acquiring knowledge, and putting yourself in control. IS is not about 'hiding behind the technology that you know about'.

If you do that, it is likely that you can end up trying to impose on a client, something that you have knowledge about, rather than thinking more widely about the 'problems' and the varied paths that exist in the course of 'problem-solving'. We hope that you enjoy reading about what we do, and how we do it. We hope you find it useful, even if you do things differently! Best Wishes!

Lesley and Richard.

Intervention commences – the invitation to tender

The following is taken from the tender document. It is included here to demonstrate the 'thinking' of the internal client group, and how the consultants were able to change this thinking during the process of their work. This constituted an intervention of sorts, which started, as Lesley points out in the discourse, at the earliest possible point, even before the project had formally commenced.

Project Title: Optimizing MORRÍGAN Manufacture
processes using Six Sigma and e-business
Published by: MORRÍGAN Engineers LLC
Publication date: 04-Jan
Application Deadline:
Notice Deadline Date: 14-Feb
Notice Deadline time: 16:00
Notice Type: Tender
Has Documents: No

Outline

MORRÍGAN Engineers LLC is seeking a provider or providers who will undertake to enter into a contract to provide all or part of our lean manufacturing solutions. This will conform to the lean manufacturing principles of Six Sigma and e-business.

The vision of the MORRÍGAN Engineers LLC senior management is to enhance the processes of MORRÍGAN, and to continue to strive for the highest quality and most advanced products, in the engineering arena. In order to achieve this, continued improvement is required, and the use of advanced information processing systems into key areas of work processes. Thus we are seeking a supplier who will provide guidance and resource, in order to implement lean principles in conjunction with the development of e-business applications to support value chain processing.

- one provider tendering on all aspects of the performance monitoring solution.
- one provider tendering on only one aspect of our performance monitoring solution

Joint bids from two or more providers would be acceptable.

This will be a staged programme, starting with the precision tools manufacture in Ohio. This is one of our 12 manufacturing units. It is the intention that the precision tool manufacture will lead our wider goal and vision of system integration of manufacture, whereby there will be seamless integration of a number of back end service functions, with integration into customer systems. Currently, each plant have different systems based on MRP II. The precision tool manufacture operates a Kanban production process. The rapid acquisition of companies in the MORRÍGAN group has resulted in the need for integration and rationalization. In order to support our vision of being at the forefront in our sector, the MORRÍGAN senior management team is looking for:

- Improvement in manufacturing capability with reduced overhead. We envisage that this will be attained by continued application of lean principles;

- The integration of an e-business computer application, which will be capable of integrating our processes with existing and future suppliers and customers;
- The integration of the e-business application to integrate internal functions, and thus in the long term, becoming a backbone to our future enterprise resource planning application.
- A change programme, which will bring about the on-going improvement in performance, which in the long term will support our strategic vision of becoming a public limited company.

We will welcome tenders from the following:

- one provider tendering on all aspects of the performance monitoring solution.
- one provider tendering on only one aspect of our performance monitoring solution

Joint bids from two or more providers would be acceptable.

About MORRÍGAN

MORRÍGAN is a precision engineering company, traditionally supplying metal based engineered products to, for example, the automotive and aircraft industries. MORRÍGAN was established in the 1940's, when the then Welsh owner, Dick Morrígan, recognized the opportunity to manufacturer parts for military vehicles. During the 1950's and 1960's, the plant diversified into a range of peace time engineering, supplying parts to the automotive and aircraft industries. This work expanded and MORRÍGAN established two further plants. One in Detroit, and another in Michigan.

During the 1970's, the original Ohio plant underwent a diversification programme, and the management of that time changed the mass production of engineered items, to become a more flexible production unit. Thus the range of engineered goods could be increased with the same basic production techniques, to service the need of a wider range of customers. Detroit and Michigan followed this approach by the late 1970's. It meant that Morrígan could service the demands of many potential customers, and were not tied to the ups and downs of single customers.

By the 1990's, it was recognized that MORRÍGAN remained small in the sector. This was a strength because it could adapt to markets and new product launches quickly. But it also meant that it was having to compete with much larger corporates for the same markets. Thus it was decided to positively seek to consolidate via a series of mergers and acquisitions, culminating in the current situation whereby MORRÍGAN is now looking for the integration of functions and services across a group of companies. The group currently employs around 480 full time employees. It also has a growing number of staff on short term contracts. The Ohio plant remains the head office, and provides support functions, and currently employs 109 full time staff.

There has been some concern about the rising relative cost of manufacture, and consideration has been given to the outsourcing of some or part of the production. However, the policy to date has been to concentrate on quality, combined with lean manufacture. This has put MORRÍGAN in a market leading position, close to its customers. This project is an extension of existing strategies, by taking the lean principles, and applying them across value chain activities and group integration.

Scope of tender

The integrated technology systems will be used to manage the conformance to agreed targets. The process of implementing lean and technology driven processes will be headed by Chance MacIntire, whose role in the organization is CFO. The consulting team will work under and report to Mr MacIntire. An agreed action plan and project will be agreed between Mr MacIntire and the successful consulting team.

Type of procedure

Open – Purchaser invites tenders from all interested parties.

Language or languages in which tenders or requests to participate can be drawn up
English

Time limits and timings

- Time-limit for receipt of completed tenders Date 14/02, Time 14:00.
- We aim to notify providers of the initial shortlist by Date : 19/03.
- Providers who are shortlisted will be invited to present their proposals in person on Date : 1/04

MORRÍGAN LLC does not bind itself to accept the lowest or any offer.

The invitation to tender (ITT) document from the client organization, was sent to a number of potential suppliers, and included a number of well-known consulting companies. In addition to the above, it was accompanied by brochures that talked of 'a new era' for the company, supported by a 'new ambitious management structure' and the exciting prospects for the company of becoming a global corporate and 'investments required for supporting the ambitious changes' that were taking place. Within the documentation, there was a summary of the requirements that were perceived to be needed in terms of actions by the consulting teams. For example:

- 'to oversee the modernization via lean principles'
- 'to oversee the implementation of an e-business technology infrastructure to integrate functions across the group'.

It was decided to respond to the invitation to tender in such a way that might open up the opportunity to challenge these perceived requirements. This was because it was felt that the terms of reference (TOR) assumed that there would be a narrow role, which focused on (i) lean and (ii) e-business, whereas the consultants concerned recognized that change in the organization might involve moving beyond these confines. An IS consulting team was formed for the project, made up of three members with what were perceived to be complementary skills. One had a technology background with nearly twenty years experience of software development projects (Lesley); the second also had nearly twenty years experience largely in organization development, finance and business (Richard). Both of these individuals were full-time consultants. The third was to oversee quality and process, and would take no part in the process of consultancy except as evaluator and adviser (Chris). This case study was, in part, taken from the documented notes made by Chris.

These were discussed by the team, which precipitated a carefully worded tender document, which argued that the team could bring 'an innovative method (i) for bring[ing] about change, which could link organizational processes to modernization and the application of information technology ... (ii) enabling knowledge sharing of user groups ... [and to] instigate learning as part of the post implementation evaluation activities'.

The team made a range of inquiries prior to the tendering meeting. By using a number of telephone conversations, they were able to gain insights such as (i) which consulting company had been involved in Morrigan and, from personal contact there, (ii) the issues that were perceived at the corporate level, about the issues, 'problems' and failings of recent projects, and (iii) a sense of what was driving the senior management team to seek new consultants. They were even able to find out that it was a senior manager (François Lacoste) who had been the primary mover in the writing of the tender document and the TOR for the current project. The team felt strongly they had the capability to precipitate new innovations and change and, therefore, constructed a tender.

Diagnosis commences

Having written the tender and attended the interviews, Lesley and Richard were hired by Morrigan commencing in May of that year. Lesley said that Rich made a few stupid jokes in the interview. Lesley gave them lots to think about by saying that the method to be adopted would involve '*Think Tanks*' – more of that later. They were interviewed by the CEO, the CFO (chief financial officer), someone from HR, and a data processing manager. Both Lesley and Richard were a bit surprised by winning the contract. Here is a brief dialogue from the post-hoc analysis.

'We thought they might go for a team from a very well known corporate consulting company ... When we reflected upon it, we had emphasized the relationship, and partnership side of things ... a long term thing, not the implementation of technology. I think they liked that, although that was not really in the tender' said Richard. 'Sometimes it is a good thing to challenge the invitation to tender document a bit. In a sense, by challenging the tender, we were challenging the perceptions of those who had written it. We had consciously decided to seek a long term relationship, and had tried to get that over in our tender document and interview'.

'Intervention starts at the beginning, not at the end!!' added Lesley.

'What do you mean?' Richard asked.

'Well, we engaged them and challenged them from the word go. Intervention is not a stage in a process. It's an ongoing thing … , an interactional sequence', replied Lesley.

'Don't give me all that intellectual stuff. The CFO was flirting with you … that's what got us over the line!! Ha! Consulting in information systems is a human process!' laughed Richard.

Indeed, as soon as the contract had been drawn up, the CFO (a guy called Chance) rang. But it was not a phone call to chat up Lesley. He was already badgering the 'INPSIRE team' about the implementation of an ERP package. Apparently, they had spent quite a bit of time evaluating SAP R/3, which Chance had mentioned only in passing at the interview. Chance said on the phone to Lesley, 'we need you to get this damn thing over here and working for us'. That was the first Lesley and Richard had heard of their involvement in a SAP application. Lesley and Richard found out later that Chance and the data processing manager were all for going for SAP. Despite the wording of the tender document, it was obvious that Chance and the data processing manager saw Lesley and Richard as a resource to help them justify and subsequently implement SAP, 'a means to increase efficiency, perfect to drive a lean initiative', Chance had said. Lesley and Richard quickly realized that SAP was a sub-agenda in the tender document, and wondered why it was not mentioned explicitly. Lesley had used SAP R/3 to a limited extent, having been involved in an implementation three years earlier. She knew SAP sufficiently well to know the extent of the commitment it was to implement it, 'it's certainly not the kind of thing you undertake on a whim, I just don't know how much they have looked into it, and how much they understand the implications … but we should keep an open mind on it', she said.

Actually, this gave both Lesley and Richard a bit of an anxiety attack. Were they going to have to oversee a project to implement SAP? Were they hired on the very same principles that they argued against, i.e. that they were not IT implementers, they were organizational problem solvers. 'They could get better people than us two to do that!' Richard commented with irony in his voice.

Lesley was reassuring. 'Don't worry about it, you're getting agitated because you don't know what expectations they have of us. It's that role–relationship thing again. We need to make sure they see that we are great with the technology, but are going to drive our work from an organization development perspective. Let's just see what they bring up when we see them.'

'… that's why working in teams is a good idea in this game, you have each other to help get over these anxiety attacks!' said Richard.

About a week later, Lesley and Richard popped down to see Bob Wright. He was on the sales side, and Chance had said that Bob would 'give a first glance at the operation'. Lesley and Richard saw it as an opportunity to commence their diagnosis phase. Chance saw it as a tour of the factory.

Bob's problem

Whilst waiting in the rather plush reception area, Lesley noticed a diagram of the organization structure, with photographs on it. She took some notes. This was the start of an inquiry for diagnosis. The management of the company consisted of a board of directors with a typically functional management team – sales, marketing, production, purchasing, design etc. After a few minutes, in popped a young woman called Anthea, who introduced herself as ' working for Chance in accounts'. Apparently, Chance had been called to a meeting, had to and send his apologies. The small office block where the managers and office functions were based was a short walk across the street from the main production shops. 'Bet the street is a 'barrier'', whispered Lesley. 'So, how long have you been at MORRÍGAN Anthea?' asked Richard, '... err, about nine months, still a newbie!' came the reply. Lesley and Richard continued the inquiry for diagnosis by engaging Anthea. It turned out that the Ohio plant was largely a medium-sized factory, with two production lines, stores, maintenance and warehousing. Anthea pointed out of the window at a number of shabby buildings. The computing facilities in the main office were for the payroll, general ledger, purchase ledger and sales ledger. She appeared to be highly competent and very organized. She said she was using an old proprietary package to handle these functions. She referred to the 'new system' but the conversation was interrupted by a fifty-something-year-old man, a bit harassed, who introduced himself as Paul, 'Bob Wright's right hand man, so to speak', he said. As Lesley and Richard walked with Paul towards the sales office, he introduced two product design engineers who sat at some large computer screens in an adjacent office. The office was clean and organized. The engineers looked a bit bored and sleepy. Again, Lesley and Richard engaged with them to develop the inquiry. It appeared that once a design was agreed with the customer, the bill of materials was generated by the design software, 'by exporting it to an .rtf file'.

'That means the design office software is not integrated into the manufacturing and scheduling', Lesley muttered quietly. 'How the hell do you know that?' Rich asked her. 'Rtf is a text format, no database uses a text format, it's because they have legacy applications that don't really talk to each other'. ' Oooh very clever!' Richard replied sarcastically. 'Yes I know, I come from the cultured side of the pond' Lesley and Richard have a relationship whereby they are always poking fun at each other! Lesley continued, 'I bet that is why they are thinking in terms of an ERP ... long overdue I think. I feel like I'm going back in time in this place.'

Paul took Lesley and Richard to the sales manager, Bob Wright. Bob had responsibility for a group of products that all had heat treatment. Locally they were all known as 'hot' products because they used the furnace facilities. Bob was looking flustered; he was on the phone and signalled for them to take a seat. There were a number of tatty chairs nearby and Paul pulled a few over. Whilst waiting, the inquiry continued, by observing the office. Paper was piled high, drawings, documents, order sheets etc., all over the place.

Bob proved to be quite friendly; indeed, he was very keen to be helpful. The main problem seemed to be 'pressure of work', and time. The phone rang constantly and there were numerous interruptions. These were mostly from people wanting to know, or reporting on, the progress of items in various orders; there were documents, engineering drawings and manuals everywhere. But Bob seemed to know where to put his hands on them in successive phone calls. Lesley and Richard soon formed a picture of a busy, non-stop manager who was at the heart of the day-to-day relationship between the company and its customers. For example, Bob would receive a telephone enquiry about a particular job from a customer, contact somebody in the commercial or production side of the business about its status or progress and then get back to the customer with answers or reassurances.

Paul had popped out to get some coffee, and Bob was on the phone again. Richard said to Lesley, 'This is exactly what Mintzberg wrote about years ago ... Bob is a message switcher and boundary spanner. ... Much work at unrelenting pace.' After Bob put the phone down, he put this analysis of the position to Bob, who (sort of) agreed. 'Yes, it's all to do with information is this job and that's the biggest problem. Finding out what is going on around you and being sure that what someone is telling you is accurate.' The validity of this statement was about to be demonstrated!

The phone rang (again) and Bob greeted an old customer contact in a cheery and good-humoured way. The enquiry was about a job that had been promised for that day. Bob's good humour was the result of the fact that he was able to confirm that the work was ready 'and would be despatched today'. Bob winked at Lesley and Richard as he said this to the customer on the phone. Rich muttered to Lesley, 'He fancies you too!' Bob continued on the phone, 'It went through the forge this morning and I've got a note here from commercial section that a wagon will be collecting the stuff at 2.00 pm this afternoon. Should be with you down at Rouge before 4.30, OK?'

Bob put the phone down contentedly. He paused, looked at Lesley and Richard in a blank sort of way. And then said, 'Do you mind, sorry, I just have one last call to make, then I'm all yours'. He picked up the phone again. It was apparent that he had decided that he'd better check on that wagon. He phoned the manager in the commercial section who was responsible for the despatch and billing. A wagon was ordered, but because it had been short notice he'd had to go to a more expensive small haulier. 'Well that will eat into things a bit, but not to worry, it's good job and I promised them for today'. He looked at Lesley and Richard, 'important client', and winked again.

Sensing a lull in proceedings Richard asked Bob to tell him more about the nature of the ordering process and how it fitted into the other departments in the company. He did this in the form of a sketch, which showed the routes and interactions between different departments (see Figure 11.1). He included the agencies outside the organization who might be involved in the setting up of a job as well. Obtaining information from departments such as commercial or production was, he said, crucial to dealing with customers about whether a job could be done, at what cost and about the progress of work in hand. '... but they tried to integrate our systems together, and it failed ... I dunno, it's just too complex'. He was about to expand on the problems in this process when one of the buyers, George Walker, came in. George, as turned out, was a great friend of Bob's and settled down with a coffee. George observed casually that there had been a real fuss in one of the shops as he was coming over because one of the forges was out of action. 'Tripped this morning at half eight and they've been wrestling with it ever since', he added.

Bob exploded. 'What? Bloody hell! Why didn't someone tell me?' His eyes were wide and his face was red. 'They never said anything about it this morning and I only saw Barry at 10.00.'

'Calm it, Bob', said George. 'Since when was production your concern? You'll be taking over the accounts department next.'

Bob wasn't listening. He was already on the telephone to the forge shops. 'Is this right, that the forge has been down since before 9 o'clock?' 'That stuff for Rouge never went through then?' 'Why didn't you let me know?' 'When I saw Barry he gave no indication that there was a problem' 'Of course, it's important, I've got a wagon coming at 2.00 and the customer has been promised them. I spoke to them this morning. If I'd known I could have got round it, now we are going to look really stupid. And we are going to have to pay off the wagon aren't we!'

'mmm! A source of problems in the supply chain problem eh?' whispered Richard to Lesley. Lesley was busy scribbling on a sheet of paper.

Bob slammed the phone down. 'There you are, that's what I mean about information being a problem. Nobody will give you an honest answer in this place when something goes wrong. God knows this'll be the death of me … systems, we have no effin' system … I'm so pissed'. 'Hello, is that Rouge, it's Bob from Morrigan Engineers here … it's about your order. We seem to be having some transport problems and its looks like being Monday now. Yes, I know I said earlier 2 o'clock but …'

On the way out, Lesley handed a scribbled bit of paper to Richard:

Q's for you and for our diagnosis …
- In what ways might computerization help Bob's problem?
- What sort of 'system' might be introduced, and how would it work in practice?
- Where might a database for this system be located, and who would centrally be responsible for it? What are the key information flows?
- Will computerization ensure that Bob always gets the right answer about what is happening in other departments?
- What sort of problem do we have here? Is it …
  - o   technical?
  - o   systems?
  - o   behavioural?
- Can computerization be introduced and applied to the existing process, or does some form of new set of work need to be implemented?

Richard clipped this together with Bob's diagram (Figure 11.1). 'What do you think about Bob's little diagram?'

Lesley replied, 'Well, it tells us nothing in many ways, but it does tell us Bob's view of his little world. His view is based on his background, and its twenty years out of date'.

WillDo

Chance had set up a meeting with the data processing manager, so after the meeting with Bob, Lesley and Richard were taken by Anthea to the data processing department, and they met with the manager called William Newton. Anthea had told them that William was known by the nickname 'WillDo' because he kept saying 'Will do! WillDo gave Lesley and Richard a very brief insight into his department.

In the brief meeting, Lesley and Richard were struck by the number of references WillDo made to both SAP and OOPs (object-oriented programming). Richard thought that WillDo was out to impress, and wanted to show off his knowledge. It was either that or WillDo genuinely believed that the company desperately needed SAP, and all

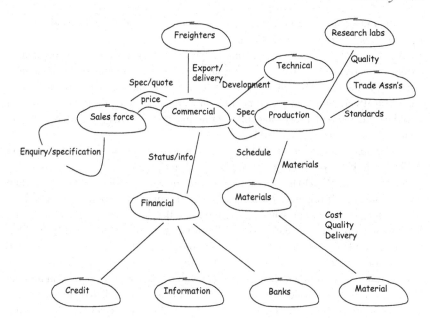

Figure 11.1 Bob's view

proprietary stuff would be built on an OOPs platform, 'such as Dolphin SmallTalk'. ' but what we are stuck with is a range of patched applications, Access applications, with Visual Basic ... We have a server running Windows server and another running Apache, MYSQL and a client-based piece of software called Navicat to query some of the bigger databases. We also use PhP as a way of building our web applications.'

Later:

'We have a number of data processing applications, invoicing, accounts receivable, ledger management, a whole load of manufacture planning applications, stock control and the like. But it needs rationalization and some of the legacy applications need to be updated, and put onto an integrated platform. My predecessor started the implementation of an ERP, but moved jobs, and the whole thing seemed to collapse. I need to get that moving again, but some members of senior management don't see the reasons why ... I think you guys might help to see the benefits. Being outsiders they'll listen to you'.

'Why do you think SmallTalk might be used?' ask Richard.

'Because it is object oriented, development can be very quick', WillDo replied.

'But it can be a bit hellish to learn', said Lesley.

'Yes, I know that, but when you get over that, the development time will be cut massively'. said WillDo.

'Well I can't disagree with that ... it is very powerful once you know how to use it', said Lesley. 'Can you give me a print of the object structure, with methods. I'd like to have a look at it'.

'Will do'. said WillDo.

Later:

'It looks like a typical, small and a significantly outdated department to me', Richard commented afterwards. 'It's got a load of old stuff, with a few bits of new stuff, all jumbled together. I don't really know much about the ins and outs of 'OOPs'. Do you think he's right?' asked Richard.

'No, absolutely not. Not in my opinion anyway! … Well, maybe I am jumping to a conclusion here, but I got the impression that he was thinking about Dolphin to develop some of the standard DP stuff … to move from a relational database architecture to a pure OOPs environment would be a big investment in time and learning, you just would not do it in data processing applications, maybe that is not quite what he had in mind … I'm not sure …', replied Lesley.

'To be honest, I can see where WillDo is coming from. I'd probably be thinking in similar terms if I was in his shoes', said Richard later on.

'mmm, maybe WillDo had a point about some of the rapid development of certain applications, which might sit on the outside of the main data processing functions. But much more important would be to rationalize the data processing functions, and SAP would definitely do that. SAP are more focused on the smaller organizations nowadays, I'll have to find out a bit more about what they are doing … What I find strange also is that they have two different server types. I guess it a case of legacies, histories and different people being in charge with their own ideas … he said nothing of a minicomputer, I should have asked … We'll have a lot of work to do to understand the various applications. But I have a strange gut feel that this is all far off the mark. We need more time with WillDo.'

'Yeah, and there is no way the board are going to agree to much investment, I just cannot see it. They are seeing this stuff as a lead weight … that's why they are so backward. I know Chance is keen, but in the cold light of day??' said Richard.

'What about the open source stuff? I am sure I read about something called 'Sequoia' ERP somewhere, I'll look into that too … Have you got your recorder on? I'm going to lose track of stuff to do' said Lesley.

'Seq wot?' said Richard. 'lol! You're just such a girly swot Lesley'.

Politics, policy and differing perspectives

About two weeks later, Lesley and Richard attended a project planning meeting. Thus far, the project had not really been defined beyond the presentation at the tendering interviews. Lesley and Richard were to meet the group CEO in order to finalize contractual details. This was to be held in a new building adjacent to the main Morrígan factory. The new building was quite impressive, and on the smoked glass doors was emblazoned 'Morrígan Group Head Quarters'. This meeting was held with Chance (CFO), William (data processing manager), Alan (CEO) and Deardrie (HR). Alan had asked Bob Wright and somebody called François Lacoste to attend, who was introduced as group general manager, 'Alan's right-hand man', Bob whispered to Richard. Alan chaired the meeting, and commenced by announcing that the following day was his seventy-second birthday. Despite the introductory bonhomie, this was to prove quite a tricky meeting. Suddenly, and without warning, some of the political agendas surfaced, with questions being raised about the scope of the project, which had important implications for the role–relationships. Both Lesley and Richard recounted how anxious they had got when François talked about them helping him to rationalize by the implementation of 'lean principles'. After the meeting, Lesley and Richard decided that Chance and William were advocating the implementation of an ERP, specifically SAP r/3. Alan and François were looking for a project to improve production, focused on lean manufacturing. Bob was interested only in avoiding technology altogether, and keeping his safe haven in the interface between production and sales. And Lesley and Richard were advocating a wholesale 'organizational problem-solving process'. Here are some dialogues taken from the meeting.

FRANÇOIS 'You are asking to do things that are not in the invitation to tender document'.

RICHARD 'We can implement efficiency drives, but that is likely to be only a partial answer'.

Later:

FRANÇOIS 'The SAP project is not on the agenda; there is no need to consider it in this meeting'.

CHANCE 'We need Lesley and Richard to do a full evaluation [of SAP], including costs, and the realization of benefits for the whole group'.

Later:

CHANCE 'In this day and age, any company like us will have an ERP, and we are desperately falling behind. We are acting like a group of different companies; integration is a key concern for us.'

WILLIAM 'SAP will provide an engine to realize a number of streamlining opportunities.'

Later:

FRANÇOIS 'This is likely to overrun; we need to take account of this ... it is obvious that a proper scope to this project is not developed yet."

LESLEY 'Well let us rehash our ideas a bit, and we'll come back in a week or so with a few proposals about how to move forward, based on what we have seen so far'.

It became apparent, that François had not thought it necessary for any further work on an ERP project, 'it is well known that it will not achieve what it promises'. Lesley and Richard were to given one week to 'poke around', and then propose an end-to-end project plan 'to achieve lean objectives'.

Afterwards:

'That was a terrible meeting', Richard said.

'Yes, but the outcome was good.' Lesley added, 'Basically, they have given us licence to define the project ... basically because they had not really got to grips with what they wanted from us! We need to seize the chance ... we need to get a programmer with XML skills, some Java script. Also, we need the UDM [universal data model].'

'What are you plotting now?'

'I'm thinking of a Java-based ERP, hosted on a third party, running on something like FireBird, or MySQL. I need you to do the "poking around" and I'm going to mock something up to give them an idea about what might be achieved.'

That week, both Lesley and Richard worked all hours towards (i) understanding, as far as possible, the situation being faced by Morrígan, and (ii) putting a presentation together, 'which will open their eyes, they are fighting like cat and dog, and missing the real opportunities' said Lesley. 'we need to make it a learning experience for them, not just a presentation.'

Alan made a special announcement to all staff by email that they would see two new consultants 'around the place', and asked staff to be co-operative and open. Lesley and Richard were delighted with that. 'It means that they have given us licence, and we can set our roles ... this is going to be like a process consultation, not an expert piece, although they are still thinking in terms of "expert mode". It'll be better if we avoid being their glove puppet', said Lesley. Towards the end of the week, they had a call from Chance explaining that the meeting would have to be put off, as he and Alan have had to go to Chicago 'its one of the companies, we need to restructure the debt, we'll be away for a few days, then we'll get together again'. In actual fact, the meeting did not take place for some weeks.

Inquiry for diagnosis – continued

In his PhD work, Richard had been looking at the power and politics in managing projects. Lesley picked up some of his notes: 'I often find that organizations are in a much more chaotic state than the people in them like to admit. Thus, when you are dealing with the formalities, e.g. tendering, project management, you have to play by the rules, and go along with their lie (i.e. that their organization, and/or their managers are organized, in control, rational etc). But what a load of nonsense! It's never like that in practice. Organizations are simply not that rational, but so many Management ideas are based on the assumption that they are! Including project management methods. There are always complexities, contradictions, ambivalences etc., and most decisions are made in a very serendipitous way. It's funny that we call them 'organizations' actually. Maybe we should call them disorganizations really! But this lie thing, puts us into some tricky situations. In our 'going along with the lie' (which we have to, because the rest of the world does), means that in reality things like the tender document sometimes appear to commit us to stuff that simply will not work - because it assumes that the client organization is rational. Take Morrígan for instance. How could we implement a new manufacturing 'system' amongst the chaos that we were finding? Before doing anything, we need to change the way people work, and change the way people think about their work. It's not as easy as 'implementing a new computer application'. The textbooks in IS don't say any of this. They just say it all much too simplistically ... all you do is to get a bit of software, and implement it! They say stuff like, 'do a feasibility study, do systems analysis, design databases, changeover, and then do some post-implementation reviews'. Good grief! Some of that stuff might be useful it does not reflect the realities of working in the contradictory contexts of organizations.'

Richard set up a number of interviews with people from Morrígan. He set himself up in a room, and put a note on the door, 'the INSPIRE HQ'. He was observing everyday events, analysing the meaning of what people said and did and was bouncing ideas off Lesley to try to keep analysing his interpretation of all observations. Richard's strength was in his communication skills. Everyone likes Richard. Within a few days, Richard had made friends all over the place. He went to lunch with lots of different people, went to bars after work with Morrígan staff. He even got Chance and Deardrie to agree, in principle, to get key managers into a room for a day or so 'for some management training'. Unfortunately, this was not going to take place immediately. In the meantime, Lesley busied herself with some of the technical details, 'we need to sort this ERP skeleton out. We've got to give them options, and we need to show them what's involved. I'm going do a mock-up for them, using the OFBIZ shell software, and stuff it on a Tomcat.'

'A Tomcat?'

Lesley ignored Richard's bemused question.

'For a mock-up, a simple Apache server will be fine. These people have never properly even seen an ERP, it's only a buzzword to them. I need them to see one in operation, then we can get into a proper discussion about the possibilities.'

She had got a programmer to help her, from another project that her consulting company was running. In the event, she did not need the programmer too much. The implementation of OFBIZ was more straightforward than she thought. 'I had not realized it, but the implementation of the back-end database is already done, it's on something called Derby, but it can be changed to MySQL, PostgreSQL or Firebird or something a bit more robust. But for a mock-up, Derby will be fine. I've put it all on a Java Server'. She showed Richard the ERP engine, which linked to a virtual shop. 'I have not worked my way through it all, it'll take some time, but I'll be able to show what its capable of, and what's involved in terms of risk, commitment, cost etc. I don't intend to recommend this, certainly not at this stage, but to use it to discuss how an ERP works, to talk about value chain issues associated with it, and to make our meeting into a learning process for them ... Now it's on a server, they can muck about with it to try to understand its power and the opportunities'.

Lesley took Richard through the application. The ERP included the usual things: invoicing and order processing, linked to the sales ledger, purchase ledger, general ledger. These linked to modules that analysed general accounts, taxation modules. The application had customer handling, materials and workflow, inventory management, bill of materials, manufacture resource planning, catalogue management etc., linked to a virtual shop.

'Wow, you did this in a week?'

'Yep. It's all more or less pre-coded. So I didn't do too much, really. Basically, I have implemented it on the server. The tricky bit will be the meeting! But it's easy, it really is!'

'Could this work to integrate the whole group of companies?'

'Well we need to be careful here. I don't want to appear as if I am selling them a piece of kit; this is going to be used to demonstrate certain things. But yes, it will work, although I will need to look at the capabilities of the back-end databases.'

Richard stared in amazement, 'You got a whole ERP working in a week? From scratch?' He was often amazed by the things Lesley did.

After a while he said, 'The thing that I need to do is to have a look at the integration between companies in the group – are they suppliers to each other? And what we can and cannot consolidate within the group – then I need to look at how other outside companies could integrate with Morrígan. You know, Morrígan have a retail side, they sell to maintenance shops all over the place. This virtual shop could be perfect. This is big, really big.'

Richard became very excited at the opportunities that this was opening up in his mind. Richard's efforts were suddenly oriented towards understanding some of the issues in the wider group. He discovered other ERP-type initiatives that Bob had referred to in their meetings, 'classic mistake, dealing with complex technology and the expense of effective organizational change. There is no way people like Bob could have bought into it. This explains why Morrígan look so ancient … they have tried to modernize, but failed, and it has set them back years.'

'Of course, that might explain the politics. François is frightened of yet another disaster, he knows modernization is required, but is avoiding technology', said Lesley.

'… ah, the cost of failure eh?'

'Yes, and he doesn't trust technology, so he's gone for the relative safe haven of Six Sigma – and he's right to an extent. Six Sigma could really benefit Morrígan. It will bring lots of rationalization and efficiency to this dinosaur. Chance is right, too, in his own way. SAP r/3 has huge power and could transform this business. Alongside "lean" there could be a revolution here. It needs a bit of revolution too!'

Lesley and Richard armed themselves for the meeting. They never claimed that they knew enough. Nor would they have claimed to have done enough 'diagnosis' to *make* intervention or any effective and realistic changes. But they had done enough to bring the management team behind them at the meeting. They discussed a process of organizational problem solving, how Six Sigma principles could be incorporated, the ERP and virtual shop; they discussed a planned process to bring about change. François was not entirely happy about moving beyond the specification in the invitation to tender but, by the end of the meeting, there was real enthusiasm shown. Lesley and Richard had also got agreement to do some management development workshops that were going to be entitled 'Improving organization' workshops.

'Yeah it was pretty good today, we just need to get Alan and François in a bar. That will cement our relationship I think', suggested Lesley.

Lesley believes in alcohol. Not that she drinks much of it. But she believes that you get to a deeper level of understanding of people when you've been drinking with them 'it's part of building an effective interactional sequence'. Richard just likes drinking.

Modelling processes by 'ThinkTanks'

A core component of the first 'Improving organization' event was to instigate a process where managers would model the organizational processes that they were familiar with, and to outline failings in the 'real world' processes in practice, derived from the discussions within the small 'innovation teams' (called 'ThinkTanks'). These ThinkTanks were geared specifically towards becoming 'organizational problem solvers' of sorts. It meant giving the members of the ThinkTanks methods, concepts and tools, in a learning process, in order that they could undertake such things as 'diagnosis', 'modelling processes', 'identifying road-blocks', 'identifying possible changes' etc. However, this was tricky because there were substantial politics standing in the way. That is one of the functions of the methods – to help groups 'work together' to clarify perceptions of 'problems' and to work towards some way of solving perceived 'problems'. By doing this, the INSPIRE team were able to develop a dialogue that provided in-depth accounts of the organizational processes, their 'problems', issues, challenges etc. It was designed to enable selected managers to engage with the 'organizational problem-solving' principles, to harness individuals' implicit knowledge of processes, and provided Richard and Lesley great insight into the 'problematic' situation and context. Indeed, during these discussions, the failed ERP implementation was referenced many times, and became the primary subject of one of the ThinkTanks.

The ThinkTanks were using a form of process model as a form of language and a set of constructs to underpin the language. These were derived from systems ideas, and were presented as a set of constructs in an attempt to make them easy to access and to use (e.g. 'transformation', 'input–output', 'purpose', 'measures of performance', 'clients', 'designers', 'efficiency', 'effectiveness', 'control' etc.). During this phase, the managers were also encouraged to consider certain more generic inquiring activities and principles (e.g. examining the relationship between their perceptions of 'problems' and 'symptoms', the application of critical reflections on assertions being made, inquiring into the basis of observations made etc.). Simultaneously, the ThinkTanks were encouraged to analyse their own group process, the strengths and weaknesses of individuals in the group, actions, roles etc. Each ThinkTank represented a social process of sorts, in which the explicit objective was to consider and justify their perceptions of: (i) 'problematic issues' and processes within the organization, (ii) the designs of processes that might 'help' in some way, (iii) their own thinking and justifying it to other members of a given ThinkTank, and (iv) other members' thinking with a view that it might be critiqued in a 'constructive manner'. The learning, thinking and communication was intended to inspire new ideas, by providing a 'new' language of sorts, to encourage dialogue and communication about an individual manager's own 'lived experience' of organizational processes. This centred on ThinkTank members' personal perceptions of organizational processes, their frustrations, anxieties, stories, 'problems' etc. of operational issues. As such, one of the most important goals was perceived to be to 'tap into' the latent knowledge of the managers about the functionality and 'dis-functionality' of organizational processes. The ThinkTanks were the generators of an inquiring activity. As the ThinkTanks matured, it was considered possible to introduce new concepts in order to deepen the inquiring activities. However, the constructs had to be carefully introduced so that they were used in order to clarify emergent issues and ideas within the sets; it was a consciously designed goal that the ThinkTanks 'pulled' the application of a variety of constructs. The constructs themselves were not considered the central goal of the discussions. Rather, it was the organizational issues and processes that were of central concern, and the constructs were used as an enabler of sorts. The constructs only helped in the inquiring activities by providing a language and a legitimacy to discuss issues that were previously hidden or suppressed.

To achieve this, the ThinkTanks were facilitated, in order to assist the set to access various constructs. Lesley and Richard had pulled in three consultants from their consulting company who were familiar with facilitating groups. For the purpose of the 'Improving organization' event, the facilitators were called 'ThinkTank Advisers'. The ThinkTank facilitation was concerned with how the constructs were being used and the related social process in which they were used (i.e. they can be used as a power weapon in a social process, or to purposely obscure the issues in hand etc.). ThinkTank advisers were to 'monitor' the discourse to keep it focused, to stimulate discussions, help to identify flawed arguments and assertions, help groups to evaluate each other's contributions, help overcome some of the power or ego issues that were perceived to have the potential to inhibit a genuine discourse etc.

Towards the end of a two-day workshop, the teams were organized into 'online ThinkTanks' with the view that discourse could be undertaken (partially) online. This was because some of the participants were geographically dispersed in different Morrígan companies. A technology platform was set up that could guarantee confidentiality amongst small teams, could store documents and had synchronous and asynchronous discussion areas, and could integrate videos and sketches (e.g. set members' drawings of models of organizational processes etc.). The INSPIRE team considered that confidentiality was essential because it was assumed that there could be some sensitive issues that could arise from the critical reflections and the explorations of 'lived experience'. The online facility was to help with the future communication lines between the INSPIRE team, ThinkTank Advisers and the members of the ThinkTanks.

There was lots of learning that ensued. For example, William (the data processing manager) was in a ThinkTank that was discussing the process models of his own processes. Thus, the ThinkTank had discussed how to model a process that transformed 'bad information' to 'good information'. This of course necessitated the ThinkTank to explore a definition of both of these, and fortunately the ThinkTank had such knowledge within its ranks! 'Good information must be "timely", "relevant", "accurate", "complete", "cost-effective" etc.', explained William. One of the most enlightening moments occurred in discussion where the facilitator questioned the assumptions of the members of the ThinkTank. How easy would it be to transform 'bad information' to 'good information'? The group recognized the flaw in their assumptions: these characteristics of 'good information' were indeed reasonable, but the ThinkTank discussion was attempting to model the transformation in information, not the transformations involved in a grouping of work activities (i.e. an organizational process). The ThinkTank recognized that its discussions were at the wrong starting point! It was not the information that needed to be transformed. It was the organizational process in which the information is used that is the correct starting point. It was a moment of real enlightenment for the ThinkTank members, because *they had discovered it themselves*, and resulted in significant inspiration. It was also recognized as a breakthrough by the INSPIRE team. There was a group of managers who were suddenly exploring ERP technology as it integrated with the organizational processes, using a set of constructs to guide them. This set went much further, e.g. exploring the purposefulness of the ERP in terms of serving processes: (i) to coordinate or control actions in fulfilling the purpose of a given model of an organizational process, or (ii) to monitor a given process, in order to 'know' whether a given process is working or not. It was a significant ThinkTank because it was going to help to drive the changes necessary, associated with the technology.

Although this was serendipitous and fortunate, this was a breakthrough that the INSPIRE team wanted to exploit. The ThinkTank had recognized the value of the models of organizational processes and the monitoring processes determined the function of the ERP. Aspects such as the dynamics, changeability, the degree of repetition or the level of mechanization of a given process, determined how the ERP was to be used. The original assumptions of the ERP implementation team were being challenged, within a constructive learning process in this ThinkTank. Models of organizational processes were drawn, and redrawn, and models of how it was to be monitored and controlled were also drawn and redrawn. Indeed, anomalies and missing elements were identified. Suddenly, there was interest in Lesley's mock-up. Since it was server based, it was accessible to each member, and since it was a mock-up, each could relate it to their own experience and interest. The technology per se was not of interest except in a secondary sort of way. It was the organizational process definitions, and the relationship that the technology had in enabling certain options. Questions about the way the ERP could be set up were raised, as well as failings in the earlier ERP project. On reflection, it appeared that there had been overly strict demarcation lines between the ERP implementation team and its 'users', whereas the 'ThinkTank'-type idea could be a way to overcome such barriers.

In this way, the ongoing discussions, both in the two-day workshop and subsequently, provided results that were startling. This was because the learning process had enabled a discourse by which internal managers could (i) evaluate the way the ERP could be applied, and (ii) how it could be 'optimized', 'improved' or 'changed' in some way or, indeed, ditched – as it related to the operation of given organizational processes, expressed as sketches of teleological process models. The INSPIRE project had provided a forum for an engaged discourse about organizational processes and the role that the ERP might play in them. The ThinkTank concluded that the methods applied by the previous ERP implementers had also 'started in the wrong place', i.e. they had started with technology and with information, but not on the vagaries of the organizational processes. The conclusions were that the ERP (as was) could not be applied effectively except in the most obvious or simple areas of work (i.e. where there was little ambiguity in the organizational process, its purpose, how it achieved its objectives etc.). Further, it attempted to make changes in work practices that were either not possible, or which shoehorned people like Bob into working in a way that was uncomfortable. The e-learning platform recorded some of these discussions, 'they took their experience of another organization, and imposed it on us', 'we don't work as machines in this company', 'they never really tried to understand how we do things 'round here', 'lots of things changed ... but nothing changed'. Another emergent outcome of this was that the ThinkTank realized that the effectiveness of the ERP can only be judged using models of organizational processes. An ERP cannot be evaluated without having clarity of the process models, and the inquiry into the ambiguities and complexities inherent in the processes in practice. These were not the consultants' findings, these were the findings of the ThinkTank.

This is an example of one ThinkTank that subsequently became the key group to drive in change. But it was only one ThinkTank. All the ThinkTanks had the potential to shoulder the responsibility for change and, thus, the managers themselves were 'in control' of change, rather than feeling that they were victims of it. This was a learning process for engaging with client groups, and a focus on 'organizational problem solving'. Each ThinkTank were drawing and redrawing models, openly discussing a range of 'problems' and 'situations', and it proved a very rich source for change. Richard recorded many of the diagrams by taking photographs of them. Voice recorders were also used to a limited extent. There were many points made on the e-learning platform, and the ThinkTank Advisers relayed back a whole load of material. The first 'improving organization' event was considered a big success. It was seen as significant by the INSPIRE team because it was learning and pedagogy that had provided a structure of sorts for attempting the process of change, including the 'optimization' process. The INSPIRE team knew that they had to act quickly on this success and, in particular, link it to group-wide opportunities and challenges, and the group-wide strategic direction.

Monitoring processes

Lesley and Richard sat down and analysed some of the outcomes. They drew pictures about issues of concern, problematic areas. They identified a number of areas across the organization that were particularly 'problematic' in one way or another. In undertaking this, Lesley found some of the notes of one of the ThinkTank members. They read as follows:

'... Remember, we are always dealing with

(i)   our perceptions of a given situation,
(ii)   the basis of our perceptions,
(iii) the observations and interpretations involved in building those perceptions

(... maybe (ii) and (iii) are the same thing?),

(iv)   We need to communicate with each other and with others about those perceptions;
(v)   Doing this sort of stuff is not easy, it takes quite a bit of bottle at times. It is difficult. You need to work hard on your intellectual skills, you need to 'think about the way you are thinking, all the time'.
(vi)   You need quite an armoury in this job ... think of our methodology as an armoury. It can guide and help, by structuring your activities, actions and tasks; most of all it deepens your thinking, so that you know about what you do and don't know'.

During this discussion, they noticed some immediate areas of concern drawing upon their particular interpretations of issues, events and perceptions. During the work undertaken in the 'improving organization' workshops, the ThinkTanks undertook the modelling of organizational processes. It was far different from the way the textbooks in IS commonly describe process modelling. This is because the textbooks in IS tend to see process modelling as a way of specifying the role of a computer in a computerized process. This is of course important, but it misses many of the more social, behavioural and managerial issues, whereas the 'teleological process modelling' can be used as a language to analyse how transformation is achieved (or not achieved). It also avoids the temptation to 'automate' or to see processes in a rather mechanistic way. The main goals of the 'improving organization' event were to: (i) undertake a diagnosis, (ii) start the ball rolling in helping the client groups to start seeing 'problematic issues' and taking responsibility for organizational change, and (iii) establish a social context for change, particularly to help managers take control and responsibility for change. As part of this the INSPIRE team had started to introduce some basic 'teleological process modelling' ideas. The principle of this is essentially an inquiry into (i) how 'transformation' works in a given area of organization, (ii) how transformation could work in the future in a given area of organization, and (iii) the purposefulness of the activities of a given area of organization. This helped the ThinkTank members to engage in questioning 'how things work now' and 'how things could work in the future'. In other words, the ThinkTanks could integrate their 'implicit' or 'hidden' knowledge to express the way processes 'transform' or fail to 'transform'; they could bring in events, contentious issues, hidden outcomes, hidden and explicit control structures and measures of performance – and a whole load of other aspects of processes. And what is more important is that they themselves are encouraged to recognize what needs to change, what could change, and what to do to make change happen. The point from Lesley and Richard's perspective was that it enabled the ThinkTanks to consider the way technology might be used as the 'what could change' thing, in the organizational processes.

Lesley had been explaining this to Deardrie, 'In our experience, the failures are the result of people not really using them. It is often not a technical reason why they fail. It is an organizational reason. Sometimes people just do not see the reason for change. It is often seen as resistance. But in our experience, it is not resistance. It is more to do with understanding, knowledge and learning. People need to see the reason for change before they can change their actions.'

Later, Lesley started thinking out loud in conversation with Richard, 'in fact, the "improving organization" sessions are an instance of INSPIRE, because there is a definite use of the inquiring activities. That is to say, we are helping people to access the systems constructs, in a social learning process. This is not to say that there is some "objective truth" in any of this ... we should call the process of operating a ThinkTank, the "inquiry to explore the intersubjectivity of members". In this case, the subject of intersubjectivity is organizational processes.'

'Why is it, Lesley, that you think in a completely different way to any normal human being? I'd hate to go to England. You are all just such bores. In fact, I think you are infiltrating my mind too ... Nowadays, I find myself finding it completely unbelievable to think of information or computers, without understanding the organizational processes – and this means developing inquiry into the organizational processes – including the nuances, different interpretations, ambiguities, structures, intended and unintended outcomes etc etc. And this also means consideration of the informal and formal aspects of processes. Not just the formal stuff or the stuff that we assume should happen, and not analyse what actually does happen! I'm turning into some sort of weirdo, just like you!'

'Gosh, that's quite a soliloquy, Richard, you need to get that into your PhD!'

'Don't worry, it's on my voice recorder, lol! I tape everything nowadays!'

Lesley and Richard spent some time trying to verify their ideas about the processes and how they were being monitored within Morrigan. They were very aware of the fact that one of the things that must be done, in all situations, is to monitor whether a given process is working or not. One of the most important questions in doing so will be 'what criteria do I use to judge whether an organizational process is "working"'. Another is to consider the roles of a computer in helping to monitor processes in some way. Richard again recorded their conversation, 'Look at how the ThinkTanks depicted the monitoring of the furnace process. This is largely a non-human process, but they identified problems in the quality, what was the guy's name, the young one?'

'Peter?'

'Yes, him. He understands, look', Richard pointed to some of the messy notes as follows:

> Any given organizational process must be monitored.
>
> The monitoring process and the thing that is being monitored will have a relationship, like the furnace is measured on heat.
> So too must a human process.

'I think he has got the basic gist', replied Lesley, 'but in a human process, the actual information and the criteria, and the perceptions of the information being used and perceptions of the criteria being applied, are as important as each other. I don't think he's got there yet. Look at this …', Lesley pointed to some more of Peter's notes.

> … a process of monitoring might be computerized, but the human process of judgement is not!
>
> The computers can only assist in the judging process!

'Actually, he's also linked the quality issues to the heat of the furnace. Look at this.'

Peter had written a lot of points about quality, monitoring and control. This area of quality was an area that Richard had been concerned about after his 'poking around'. Richard made a point of popping to see Peter because it looked like there were some areas of potential. Richard felt that Peter might be able to look at a number of areas for improving quality. Peter explained that he'd been thinking about a number of areas of concern, which had come from his ThinkTank's 'diagnosis'. One of the areas was in the production of the hot products. 'We are having quite a few quality issues … coincidentally we are having a few problems with the heat in the furnace, it's been jumpy recently. But my boss says it's nothing to do with it.' Richard explored this. From the discussion, it seemed that Peter might have a point. So it was agreed that he would collect some data. When Richard returned to discuss it with Lesley, she said 'regression. We need a regression model but, more importantly, we need Peter to collect the right data, and make sure it is accurate. He needs to understand how to collect the right data, he'll only understand the possibilities if he plays with a regression model.'

'OK, where will we get a regression model?'

'We can knock one up on a spreadsheet that he can play with'.

A few days later Lesley had put a regression model onto a spreadsheet, so it was nice and easy for Peter to play with. 'It's only linear regression, but I think that's all he needs … I'll go and see him to see if he will use it.'

Peter had used spreadsheets at school. But since then, had avoided them (by his own admission). However, within half an hour, Peter was using the model that was created by Lesley. And they discussed what data to collect and how. It was a classic bit of prototyping, and a classic bit of learning. Within a week, Peter was fiddling with his spreadsheets as if they had just been invented. He also was trying other data in the model. Several weeks passed before Richard bumped into Peter, who said, 'I want to show you something.' He had decided that the fluctuations of the heat in the furnace were nothing to do with the quality problems, 'I now think it is the variation in the thickness of the sheet metal.' He showed Richard an enhanced form of the original spreadsheet, full of data. He demonstrated the correlation between both the furnace heat, the thickness of the sheet metal, and the number of faults in particular batches. Peter was quite excited by his discovery! So was Richard, for completely different reasons. Peter went on to develop a range of simple spreadsheet applications in the factory (e.g. an 'economic order quantity' model). A few weeks later, Lesley and Richard discussed Peter again.

'You know it's quite remarkable what Peter is doing. He suddenly is doing stuff that he'd never thought he would be doing, you know what I think Lesley, it's the power of learning ... he's excited, trying stuff out, it's as if he's been liberated or something'.

'You can see something in his eyes, he's switched on all of a sudden', said Lesley.

'But, you know, he has not grasped that much of what he's doing is applying quants in monitoring processes', Richard commented.

'What do you mean?' asked Lesley.

'Well, his EOQ model is part of the monitoring process, which monitors stock levels ... his regression model is a monitoring process, monitoring aspects of the production process ...', said Richard.

'OK, I think I know what you mean', Lesley didn't sound too sure.

'Mmm! But this is my question ... is there merit in helping Peter to see it too?'

'I dunno, I guess we should discuss it with him. Will he get it?'

'Well, we've both been amazed at what he's done so far. You never know what he'll do next!'

When Richard engaged Peter on the nature of monitoring as a teleological process, Peter did not seem to take anything Richard said on-board. He seemed disinterested. But a week or so later, he came to Richard and said, 'Yeah, I know what you were saying. I just realized it in the bath last night. The tap was dripping, and I was counting the regularity of the drips and imagining that they were irregular. Then I realized it. In my models I am doing the counting, but I am not doing anything about the data. I am not turning the knob on the tap. I am just watching it drip. I need to turn the knobs.'

Peter had realized something quite important to him. Several months later he enrolled himself onto a course at the local university in computer science and cybernetics. He is slowly taking responsibility in Morrígan, for 'turning the knobs'. Recently he said to Richard, 'I love statistics but I hate statistics'. He meant, he loves their potential, but hates the way they commonly fail to link the data to action in practice.

Strategic prognosis

In the process of organizational problem solving in Morrígan, Lesley and Richard had discussed their own views on whether technology could be considered a 'strategic' issue, weapon and/or plan. Here are some quotations taken from Richard's voice recorder.

'Well, if it is going to make changes to operations in quite a radical way, then it must be "important". And if it does that, then it will end up sucking investment. In that sense it has a "strategic" importance', remarked Richard.

'It's funny isn't it … it seems "strategic" is "good" and not strategic is "bad"', Lesley replied.

Richard laughed. 'Yeah, you're right. Ultimately, and in whatever context, technology must demonstrate benefits to operations. It would be easy to go and computerize, say, the stock control area, or tighten the accounts receivable area … so it's really operational, but these are centrally "important"'.

'I guess these types of things are simply taken as given nowadays. They were revolutionary twenty or so years ago. Just like ERP is becoming today. It's suddenly got to be something that is "taken as given" nowadays. Funny how Morrígan have never really managed to get to grips with it. But they have lots of the bits, just not joined them up!'

'So is an ERP strategic?' Richard was in his 'PhD mode'.

'I don't really know. I suppose it depends on what you mean by "strategic".'

'Mmm! If we take strategic to mean "gives competitive advantage in the sector"?'

'Technology can easily be copied and replicated nowadays, being non-proprietary. Take the ERP demo that I put together …. But on the other hand, if one company in a sector improves operations, they are more likely to improve their position in the sector', Lesley replied.

'Well, I think technology is a strategic issue in Morrígan. There is an urgent need to integrate back-office functions across the group, and not in only one factory, and the integration of functions across value chain activities … broadly speaking, integrating the "system"' of suppliers and customers into the operations', concluded Richard.

A bit later in the project, Lesley and Richard were in a chance meeting with Chance (!) and discussed a number of action points. '… let me add another', he suggested. 'We will get some SAP consultants to do a preliminary study into the ERP, you two will oversee and evaluate their work … as independents you understand … I can get a preliminary piece done, to give us an idea of its benefits, how much it will cost and so on.' Lesley and Richard looked at each other as if to say, 'He's still on about implementing SAP!' … 'OK', said Lesley, seizing the chance, ' but Chance, we need to do two things in conjunction with this. Firstly, we need to integrate the large customer databases into the manufacture scheduling immediately, it's just not working as it should be, and its causing operational problems in production, we need to look at it … and, secondly, we'll go across to the other main plants in the group, to look at the feasibility integrating areas of the back office functions'. 'OK', said Chance, 'I'll ring up the ERP consultants, I play golf with one of them, I know him quite well, and get them to give us a proposal'.

Later, Lesley said, 'I knew it. Chance is so fickle. His mates at the golf club are wheedling their way in'.

'Well let's see what they propose', said Richard.

Lesley and Richard needed to act quickly to get an insight into a range of different possibilities. In part, they needed to inquire into the other companies of the group. The reason why Lesley made her intervention in the way she did was that they both perceived that there needed to be an 'integration study' that they could be happy with. The 'problem' of integration of customer data, had been discussed both between themselves, and also in one of the ThinkTanks, 'Look at the production planning processes that the ThinkTank's came up with … there is no integration with customer data on sales. They have their own models, but I think if they could analyse usage trend of various product lines by directly linking to customers' databases it might be better data; it also might lock supplier and customer together more tightly across the value chain.'

This comment was based on one of the ThinkTanks that discussed weaknesses in the anticipation of orders, or 'what's coming', with the knock-on effect on the production scheduling. This had been an ongoing problem as Morrigan was, in part, a jobbing shop, which required rapid retooling as different orders were fulfilled. Richard had commented that, 'They should be making the stuff before the order comes in … at least the standard stuff.' The ThinkTank had identified that, 'The lead times are much too long on some products', 'They'll be losing customers, they will be going elsewhere soon', and even discussed the resultant pressures 'Bob is trying to paper over the cracks, but it'll kill him'. Lesley had some ideas about an approach to the technology. She had said (rather flippantly), 'Initially, I suggest we get hold of customers' databases, we'll probably just RTP them down, and then write a bit of code to analyse the trends and stuff. I can do that in a day or two, I've done it before with SAS. It will be fairly basic at first, just to test it out. The tricky bit will follow, that is, to help the production planning group to take account of it. Well, we'll see'. She did not fail to recognize the potential issues involved in liaising with customers, 'Each one will be different, there are potentially loads of issues, not least security and data integrity issues. We'll need to get an analyst to work full-time on it for a while, but let's just get a feel for the possibilities at first.'

At the same time, it was immediately obvious that this work was integrated into the strategic vision.

'… you know, Morrigan have been doing quite well, especially given the lack of a strategic vision',

'… Alan is of an age where it's becoming less important to him'.

'… but to be fair, the takeovers and mergers have worked so far?'

'… to a point, so far the integration is not really bringing substantial benefit. I think it could be like a pack of cards job, it could collapse'.

'… yes, this is a major piece of work. Not just in terms of technology, but in terms of organizational processes, products, group integration, markets and so on. Morrigan are a fairly small group relatively speaking, and will be increasingly under pressure because there were some far bigger players who were likely to undercut based on cost advantage.'

In Morrigan's case, Lesley and Richard knew that they had to act fast, to seize on the opportunity to help to provide an effective overview of the possibilities, focused around bringing changes to both (i) 'back-room' services, in order that shared services across the group of Morrigan companies. It was perceived that this might bring about overall cost reduction, and hopefully improve effectiveness of key operations, and (ii) to integrate the work activities of Morrigan with both its suppliers and customers. They also had to do an evaluation of the proposals that some SAP consultants were going to come up with. It meant working really fast, and being very proactive. Thus, often they brought in other consultants from their parent company. There was one young consultant called Wendy. Lesley and Richard had been impressed by her. She'd been doing a lot of work with SAP recently in a bottled gas production, supplies and logistics group of companies called 'LGS' ('Liquid Gas Supplies'). It had been her job to optimize an ERP, 'to make better use of its functionality'. Part of her work was to evaluate the ERP application and how it had been implemented. Here is a snippet of her conclusions in her report as it related to LGS.

- In our opinion, the ERP team have been excellent at implementing technology, but have missed some areas concerning the integration of the technology into business processes;
- The ERP team have little understanding that the ERP is being used to monitor other operational organizational processes;
- Where it seems to be being used as a monitoring device, it is not used with discretion, nor with any analysis of the outcomes of its application (e.g. the resultant behaviours of operatives);
- The ERP team have no conception to use any other methods by which monitoring can be applied to organizational processes, and thus have no way of knowing the effectiveness of the applications of the technology and the alternatives that could be used;
- There are many processes which could be considered to be 'out of control' and where simple data collection and/or new reports could be constructed simply (e.g. on absenteeism). The examples given in the body of the report, demonstrate the improved use of the ERP in many areas;
- Although there seems to have been a lot of 'strategy' in the ERP application, there are huge gaps. For example, there is little linkage between the grand statements of strategic goals and ideas, but little in the way of the operational changes to processes that are required;
- The integration between supplier side data, particularly in the logistics area, has not been considered. This is potentially a major area of cost saving, and will require a changed relationship with suppliers, but based on last year's figures, will be able to yield at least 240 of saved 'down time' of key equipment;
- The financials and associated procedures are not Sarbannes-Oxley compliant, and for an organization of this sort, this is an immediate issue of concern;
- The claimed 14% profit ratio, which is currently calculated by the ERP is based on certain assumptions about sales ratio's to fixed cost. We think this is giving a false impression because it is dependent on sales forecasts, not 'actuals'. Our analysis suggests that it is more realistic that it will be approximately 6.5%. This is a major flaw in the construction of the accounts;
- The metrics used in the collection of efficiency data of the factory is being used for dual (and ambiguous) purpose, e.g. it is dangerously affecting performance in the factory. It was recognized that these are important metrics for the purpose of reporting to shareholders, but it should not be

used to apply pressure to individual managers, who are already alienated from senior management;

- There remain problems in value chain integration, and bottlenecks are evident and require attention;

- The senior management are not working in and integrated way with the operational staff. Largely the operational managers have been with LGS for many years, and the senior management have been put into place by the new corporate. Not only does this create natural divisions, but the senior management group are not sufficiently acting as a team;

- The dominant assumption in the ERP implementation has been that the implementation can give efficiency benefits. However, this has been done at heavy expense, and has in some areas resulted in a detriment of effectiveness;

- The senior managers are using the ERP to deal with their own pressures and anxieties arising from the pressure that they are under for performance improvement. The danger is that the manipulation of data is giving an indication of improvement but this is not substantiated in practice;

- There are a lot of examples of data from the ERP that is being downloaded into spreadsheets, and sometimes uploaded again. This is a practice which is sometimes inevitable, but there is strong evidence to suggest that the scope of the ERP has been limited for a variety of reasons;

- The integration of the work practices of managers and the ERP has been limited. The consultants *[i.e. the current project team of which Wendy was a member]* considered that one of the explanations of this was the continued lack of ownership for the ERP by middle management. They have not been integrated into the project teams involved in its application;

- The ERP is not integrating with the stated strategic objectives of moving from reliance on a small number of customers, to a global supply of gases to smaller customers. There is little web based support for this, and sales cannot be made via the web. Monitoring of distribution networks is not undertaken, which would be a necessary pre-requisite for such an initiative, nor are there suitable stock, pricing and ordering processes integrated into the ERP for this purpose;

- There continued to be discrepancies in stock data, and actuals, and procedures are required to be tightened and appropriate monitoring activities applied;

- Although basic sales data is available, there might be opportunity to analyse further the discrepancies and differences in supplies to the health sector. The data in the ERP is showing huge variation, but there is very little done in terms of explanation for these trends;

- Data on the sales team performance is non-existent in the ERP as it stands at the moment;

- There remains a 'silo' mentality in the organization. Generally speaking, the sales teams are given a rather lot of criticism, which is probably largely unwarranted. There is poor communication between production and sales;

- The ERP has replaced much paperwork, but there is evidence that (i) the manual processes are being undertaken alongside the ERP, and that (ii) trust in the ERP is still lacking. The facilities of the ERP has not been exploited in many areas;
- The ERP has been most effective in sales purchases and the linkage through to invoicing, which is practically all quite seamless now, but the integration into the operations, CRM, HR and purchasing, has some way to go;
- Integration with the corporate group ERP is still underdeveloped, despite this to have been a core reason for implementing the ERP in the first place.

Lesley asked Wendy and Richard to spend several weeks in the companies of the other parts of the group. 'We need a thorough analysis of three main things: the supply–customer relationships that do or could exist between the companies of the group; we need to understand where there might be benefits to the sharing of certain backroom services and functions; and then, also, we need a proper understanding of the customer-side sales functions.'

'Oh, a small job!' Richard remarked sarcastically.

'I know, it's a mini diagnosis of sorts.'

Wendy didn't know Lesley very well when she said, 'This is already in existence, it's in the report of the ERP consultants.'

'No, I don't want to use that, it will be full of technology push stuff. I want to be sure. It's like when you go to a doctor. The doctor does his own checks and stuff, I think we need our own checks, not somebody else's.'

Richard said, 'I think we might need some help to do it properly, this could take weeks'.

'Yes, you are completely right. I will see if I can get a bit more out of Alan to fund it. I need to see him anyway, I think we need to try to get a handle on the strategic priorities that he sees, and to make sure that our work fits it in some way', replied Lesley.

Whilst Richard was away, she asked another consultant to help her with the 'strategy stuff'. Richard's temporary replacement was an Irishman called Tommy. He was extremely gregarious, and a maverick. He had huge experience of financial accounting, and described himself as 'a systems-based accountant'. Lesley felt his skills, experience and knowledge would complement hers in the 'strategy phase'. Lesley and Tommy made appointments with a number of people who they felt could help them to understand the various perceptions of the 'strategy of Morrigan'. That is, to establish perceptions of the key policy priorities as perceived by various individuals, and how these were integrated into practical operational changes, actions, tasks and processes. She wanted to understand the flaws, assumptions or contradictions that might exist. Lesley did not focus on the senior management group in isolation. She wanted to get the perspectives of other people, how strategy was constructed, and how its messages were 'translated' and operationalized. She said, 'I want to see the process of the strategy, not just bland statements, policy statements … I want to understand the system of strategy.' Tommy was to analyse the profitability of both the Ohio plant and the other companies of the group. This was the first time Lesley had undertaken this type of inquiry in this way, 'The objective, as I see it, is to know about the strategy of Morrígan so that we can integrate our own work into it.' It was focused on 'what the strategy is now, in practice. For the time being I want to avoid the temptation of jumping to conclusions about what it should be before I have a clarity about what it is now.'

In all, she met with sixteen individuals and Tommy joined her for the final four. He had been busy with a financial audit. Lesley had said, 'I will not fall into the "representative sample" thing, I will stop when I have sufficient understanding.' But she felt as if she was getting nowhere and, thus, asked Tommy to stop his work on the audit to help her. So together they started exploring the process of strategy. For example, they explored what the current priorities were. Generally, the message from the senior management group about expansion through acquisition, quality of service and client satisfaction were recounted by all. 'But this is not "strategy", its propaganda', complained Tommy, 'is all this corporate stuff has its place, and it might even be necessary, but it's not much more than that.' Lesley found Tommy's somewhat controversial views quite refreshing. She mulled over the statement for some time. 'If it's not "strategy", what is the "strategy"?' In the post-hoc reflections, she described the gnawing of Tommy's words to be like 'toothache'.

One of the interviewees was William, the data processing manager. They asked him to outline the current strategy of Morrígan. As with the others, as Tommy put it, he '… poured out the propaganda'. He was asked about how these strategies helped to prioritize his work, particularly the resources he was using for the maintenance and development of various applications. William gave some general statements about how one application was 'more important than another', rationalizing it against the previous statements. He also was asked about the IT strategy, what it was, how did it come into being. William's eyes lit up. 'Yes, we have one!' (He sounded relieved.) 'I'll go and get it.' He went off. After about ten minutes he returned, 'Sorry, I couldn't find it, but here it is.' He sounded delighted, and handed a forty or so page report, which was obviously fairly old as the paper had yellowed a little. It had been written six years previously by the consulting company who had attempted to implement the ERP application. Afterwards, Lesley and Tommy discussed this.

'I don't believe it, God be damned', Tommy exclaimed.

'What do you mean?' asked Lesley.

'How could he think of the strategy as a document!'

'Yes', Lesley agreed, rather amused.

'And an unread, tatty old document at this!' Tommy was flicking through it. He continued, 'And you know, this is why he thinks this is strategy'.

'Why?'

'… it's because it legitimizes his spend on IT, and it justifies more spend on ERP. And you know what I think'.

'No, what?'

'… he wants to install an ERP because it just might help his career. He thinks with that experience, he'll get a better job'.

Lesley felt quite shocked by this statement, and again it gnawed at her. Tommy saw a quizzical look appear on Lesley's face.

'Well, people often hide their real purpose – they hide it and then call it "strategy". It's a joke, don't you see it Lesley. It's human. This is not your rational world of technology.'

Lesley was slightly affronted by Tommy's directness. After a moment or two she tried to summarize their findings in a rational sort of way, 'So we seem to have found that there are quite a lot of policy directives and initiatives that are understood and, to a limited extent, acted upon. But they tended to be very general, and in many respects there are actions and tasks undertaken in practice which contradict these general company statements.'

'Thank Christ for that', said Tommy.

'What do you mean?' asked Lesley.

'Well, if you think about it, if everyone followed these directives, the whole place would collapse. There has to be leeway in the system, because these simple "strategy statements" are not constructed using any thinking skills; the purpose of them is hidden and dressed up in legitimating a set of actions ... They are only partially appropriate at best. The system is a good one, because it has slack in it. If the slack was not there, the place would fall to pieces. Senior management see their job as imposing strategy, but blame the slack for perceived failures, but in reality, the "strategy" is flawed in the first place.'

Lesley was a dumbstruck (for a change). She was realizing that her technical training, her information systems experience and her MBA had not helped her to see the merit in seeing the world of strategy in the way that Tommy was seeing it. It gnawed at her even more. A few days later, she scribbled her ideas down as follows:

Although there appears to be substantial effort put into 'strategy' at corporate HQ, there is very little inquiry undertaken in practice, hence it cannot progress from being primarily a set of general, and rather obvious statements;

What 'strategy' there is, seems to be fuelled by simplistic assumptions about '... increasing shareholder value ...', and '... the next takeover acquisition';

Attempts to make efficiency gains seem to be considered to be 'strategy';

The integration of the ERP with operations across the corporate group, so far have been negligible ... there was an opportunity lost here because there was too much overlap in functions, services and processes. There needs to be something (maybe a 'strategy' of sorts) should provide guidance in the process, it needs to be costed, with proper risk assessment ... and other stuff;

Outsourcing of key services to the corporate group has not been considered;

Due to recent takeovers, the corporate group were temporarily raising shareholder value and expectations, but until there was some sort of integration of operations, the corporate group was only ever a '... a group of companies ...'

which would not be able to bring about cost or competitive advantages to any of its company entities. It is very unsteady in the long term ...

The corporate group level management team are hugely knowledgeable and experienced, but they are not *genuinely* involved as a group in a strategic prognosis, their process is lacking somewhat. This is a social group process thing I think.

Perhaps 'Strategy' should be considered to be 'general statements' (with 'propaganda'), but also 'help' in achieving it in a number of targeted areas (does this mean that 'strategy' is basically a 'learning system'?)

Until some of the corporate level management failings can be addressed, there will be limitations on what can be achieved ... we will need to engage the senior management group somehow.

Keep calm!

We have to work really fast. We were battling on a number of fronts simultaneously. One of the big battles was with the naivety of some of the key managers in MORRÍGAN. It's a funny feeling when you feel as if you are battling with your own client. They think you should be doing as you are told! But if you did that, there would be disaster, and then they'd blame you! Lol! Scary!

Lesley decided to talk to Alan, and ask his opinion on providing some workshops in 'strategy' for the senior management group. She had on her mind that the group process was lacking. She also had in mind that they might formulate the depth and the 'learning system' of strategy implementation using the ThinkTank type learning process. Politically this was a dangerous position to be in because it was tantamount to telling the power brokers that they could not do their job! But it was perceived as necessary. The appropriate interactional sequences would have to be carefully constructed in order to enable the consequent interventions. Unfortunately, Alan had fallen ill and, thus, the meeting was a long time coming (nearly two weeks). Even more unfortunately, Alan then asked that François step in, as he had such a backlog of work to do. François instructed his secretary to tell Lesley that 'She had one hour, and one hour only.' It appeared a daunting task, and being succinct in the arguments being presented was considered essential, as well as clarity about what the team wanted to do. It was essential that the INSPIRE team needed to help the corporate managers to undertake a learning process – a process of strategic prognosis – in order to progress their work. Here are some snippets of the dialogues of the meeting, as recounted by Lesley.

FRANÇOIS 'What the hell has this got to do with the lean project?'

Later:

FRANÇOIS 'You cannot come and tell us how to do our job'.
LESLEY 'We're not. I am only suggesting that improvements in the process [of strategy] will, in the long run, be highly beneficial to you all.'

Later:

LESLEY 'Many of the opportunities of the new technologies and processes [she avoided using the 'ERP' to François] stem from the integration of operations between different parts of the corporate group. At the moment each company is operating as if it has no connection with the other companies in the group – look at how HR functions are not integrated, despite the SHRI [the "strategic HR initiative", which was essentially an integration project that had been going on for two years].'

Later:

FRANÇOIS 'I thought you were being paid to do what you were told.'
LESLEY 'You don't need glove puppets – you have enough of those'.

Lesley came out of the meeting quite dejected. She felt that she had hit brick walls. She felt that François was rude and would not listen. Strangely, later that day, she had an email asking her and Richard to attend an evening meal in a famous local restaurant with Alan 'and some other close associates'. Lesley thought that this might be François taking his revenge on her for not being a glove puppet. She thought that she and Richard would be sacked!

To her surprise, the meal was quite a turning point. Alan was quite drunk, as were the 'close associates' (including François). Not much business was discussed, but after an initial awkward stage, the evening progressed amicably with quite a lot of jokes. Alan was 'quite charming'. And François revealed his human side. Lesley later described him as 'a little arrogant, but quite witty'. Later in the evening, François muttered to Lesley, 'You know, I like your style Lesley, you have the nerve to tell me that we're wrong. Drop me an email tomorrow and tell me what you want to do with us!' Lesley later confided to Richard, 'You know, he was flirting really. Sometimes it helps being a woman'.

In the following weeks, a 'strategy event' called 'Putting our values into action' was planned. Tommy laughed when he heard the title. The purpose was to make interventions (i) to help the senior managers to develop targeted policy priorities, which were to include operational details, costs and risks action points, and (ii) the managers were to clarify their role as aiding people at all levels to both question and simultaneously access the key policy priorities. The 'Putting our values into action' event was to be designed as a learning process, structured in a number of ways:

1   It would include a selected set of constructs from an 'organizational problem-solving' process – diagnosis, modelling processes, monitoring. These would be introduced just enough to be 'usable'.
2   There would be a substantial amount of time dedicated to a strategic prognosis.

Neither 1 nor 2 were to be designed as a set of theoretical constructs. It was going to be highly applied, where constructs might be 'pulled in' to help undertake the task of (i) choosing priority areas, (ii) exploring dimensions and options, and (iii) identifying the structure of processes that would need to be undertaken to achieve given outcomes.

3   Each of these would lead to intervention options. These would be introduced as an attempt to help people engage with and interpret strategy policies, within

their own domain of work. This included where there were specific projects to undertake change.

4   As with the 'Improving organization' event, the process would involve small teams (ThinkTanks), in which various areas of 'strategy' at the corporate level were to be discussed.

5   There were twenty-two managers involved, and they were organized into seven ThinkTank groups over a two-day period. It was essential that representatives from each of the companies of the Morrígan group were involved, as a key objective was integration between the companies of the group.

6   In the sessions, a range of strategic constructs were carefully introduced; implications for policy priorities and potential actions were all critiqued in the ThinkTanks, facilitated by a number of 'ThinkTank Advisers'. The goal of the ThinkTanks were not to define policy, but to make inquiry into a range of possibilities, and to link the inquiry to 'actions for change', with an analysis of both feasibility and desirability of those actions. By setting up the ThinkTanks in this way, it was possible to interconnect different priorities, goals and requirements, and also to challenge assumptions in the process.

7   The findings of Richard and Wendy would be slowly integrated into the discussions, without being imposed on any ThinkTank. The ThinkTanks would consider the findings of Richard and Wendy, and integrate them into their own (implicit) knowledge and experience. Similarly, the findings of Tommy, from his financial audit would be integrated into the discussions.

8   As is common in the use of ThinkTanks, and the INSPIRE process, individuals would be encouraged to 'think about the way they were thinking', to gain trust in the group processes, and to express what they feel within the safe haven of the ThinkTanks.

Some major policy changes were discussed, although two days was insufficient to make any changes to any operations in practice. Thus, it was agreed to take the essential areas of policy and, over a period (initially three months), to review the progress and the actions taken. All the reviews and the actions were to be posted on an internal intranet, which itself was a strategic initiative that emerged from the discussions. The INSPIRE team were to assist in the setting up of an internal 'university of sorts', and a web-based learning environment for all employees of the group. The strategy group themselves were to be the 'guinea pigs' for it! Lesley implemented Moodle for the purpose, contracted a supplier to host the software, and it was ready within one week, with discussion boards, forums and places to store documents, some shared, others available only for certain groups or individuals.

Outcomes

Lesley and her team regarded learning and inquiry to be central to their own activities. Their methods were guided (in part) by the principles outlined in Part III of this book. They also used the same principles to govern how intervention was to be undertaken by client groups. Intervention by an IS practitioner must enable client groups to undertake change, as far as possible. One way of achieving this is to use ThinkTanks, which help a learning process and pushes responsibility for change onto the client groups. It is of course not the only way to undertake IS practice and IS change.

Lesley and her team broke the rules. They antagonized certain senior managers. They cajoled and fought to move people at various levels. Their only tools were methodology, their skills, human experience and knowledge. They were not willing to accept being 'boxed into' technical roles, or have predefined expectations of roles imposed on them by those around them. In order to break away, they had to seize opportunities when they came along, and work hard to interact at an appropriate level, to challenge 'as-given' assumptions of their roles and relationships to others. They were required to be clear thinkers, good learners and apply effective inquiry. Their methods were not prescriptive (e.g. as in a recipe). Rather, the methods were implicit in their actions, activities and attitudes. Technology skills and knowledge was essential, integrated into a process of organizational problem solving, and the inquiring activities that were required during the process. Technology was considered an intervention in organizational processes and change, and was integrated into interventions that concerned other aspects of processes such as people's attitudes, roles, skills, knowledge, tasks, power dimensions, control structures. They attempted to undertake their work by engaging various client groups and to develop effective interactional sequences, communication and learning activities.

Intervention started as soon as they put pen to paper and wrote their tender document. In that sense, intervention is an interactional sequence with people, and the interactional sequence must be carefully considered at all times. Most fundamental is the ability to critique the self, and to be able to undertake 'thinking about thinking', particularly to lose the ego that sometimes clouds precision in thinking. The project in Morrigan is ongoing, and there have been huge changes achieved thus far. These are a summarized set taken from a recent report from Chris (the evaluator of the process), which resulted directly from the 'Putting our values into action' event.

- A new ThinkTank was formed reconsider the integration of processes across the group to seek operational and cost advantages. This used Richard and Wendy's work, but was to identify priority areas and oversee the interventions, and the process of change. The first of these would be to rehash the project that had been ongoing to create a common HR function, with common HR policies and procedures. This was to be closely followed by integrating various logistics activities.

- A retail channel with support processes, procedures and information would be the priorities of a new ThinkTank. This would target business-to-consumer (B2C) sales channels for all products of the group. It was to be web based, so that retail vendors, maintenance garages and other customer groups could easily access the site. A set of processes were redeveloped to handle such things as logistics, returns, integrated into invoicing and accounts etc.

- The above was an essential component in the implementation of group-wide ERP applications. There was a new ThinkTank to oversee it. To date, this is ongoing and is being implemented on database architectures based on the UDM (Universal Data Model), and hosted on a third-party Apache server. The use of SAP r/3 was rejected by the ThinkTank on cost grounds.

- A Sarbanes-Oxley ThinkTank was created to inquire into compliance issues across the group.

- The centralized financial controls on certain operations were to be investigated, with alternative control mechanisms considered, in order to 'encourage accountability, but avoid operational blockages from the over-stringent controls. This would be the focus of another ThinkTank.

- A ThinkTank would be set up to consider outsourcing and alternative governance options, and how this might operationalize itself 'to reduce bureaucracy, cost and better control of service levels'. A tentative proposal would be a goal, and this would have impact on the way the ERP in the different companies of the group could be set up.

After the 'Putting our values into action' event, one of the senior managers approached the INSPIRE team and told them that he'd never thought of strategy as a learning process before. He added that prior to this event, he was 'in the pockets of the strategy theories', that his 'MBA had given him lots of problems'. He continued, 'Thinking of SWOTs as a "thought structuring device"' was something he'd never heard of before but it 'explained a "black box"' that he'd been struggling with for some time and never realized it. Another of the mangers said 'I thought you'd be talking about computers and stuff. How come you know more about strategy than any of the textbooks?' Yet another commented on how certain managers 'had been energized', and added 'It's the energy, more than the ideas, that has been such a revelation.' These comments themselves both surprised and elated Lesley. She never considered herself to be an 'expert' in this area. All those associated with the INSPIRE team knew at that point that they had the support and trust of the management at the highest level. Nonetheless, Lesley was keen to cement their relationship with a social event, 'We'll be like bosom buddies after a good piss-up with them', she said.

With these successes, the INSPIRE team started to make many interventions, some of which were concerned directly with the computer technology applications. Other interventions were less directly concerned with information and technology. For example, one powerful member of the Morrígan management team went through a process of mentoring. This manager had an MBA, but was considered to completely misunderstand how his everyday actions were being perceived by others; Lesley wanted to get him mentored because 'he's a control freak, he thinks he's Henry Ford'. Whilst his behaviour did not have immediate impact on the ERP application, it was having an effect on various organizational processes, creating antagonisms and communication problems.

To date there have been many changes that are directly attributable to Lesley and her team.

- The centralization of the HR function was undertaken, providing the group with one entity, with common HR policies, processes, functions, payroll activities (which were outsourced).

- The logistics company was basically dissolved and its function was outsourced.

- The ERP is now in place and integrates the whole group of companies onto one generic database. Whilst there is only one database, the different companies have their own views of their data.

- The 'virtual shop' is operational both on a B2C basis and also to handle B2B (business-to-business) transactions.

- There is a new centralized CRM team, who liaise with the customers for the whole group, not a single company of the group. There are modules that have been added to the ERP, and the data structure has remained unaltered for this application because of the flexibility of the UDM.
- New training schemes are now in existence for helping new or existing managers become 'organizational problem solvers'.
- The data processing department staff have undergone retraining in 'organizational problem solving', and they are currently putting many of their legacy applications onto the ERP. Lesley worked with WillDo to provide him with new skills and methods.
- A new ThinkTank exists that is primarily focused on overcoming supply chain problems for the whole group. Its work is still ongoing.
- New long-term contracts with suppliers (e.g. maintenance, parts) have been renegotiated, and the ERP has been extended to link to suppliers' databases, and the invoices are to be electronic rather than paper based.
- Lots of new information and new reports were developed. This time, the ERP team was not determining the data from 'interviews with users', but internal managers were directly involved in the process of determining their own perceived needs either through their membership of various ThinkTanks, or by simply feeling that they had the right to ask!
- Some of the decision making had been centralized in order to maintain financial control. One of the process changes that was recommended by a ThinkTank, was to decentralize such decisions. Control over financial expenditure was proposed in a different way, i.e. to be maintained by additional data to be added to the ERP databases, in order that information about maintenance contracts could be monitored centrally, but decisions taken locally. A ThinkTank was charged with estimating efficiency and effectiveness gains, demonstrating that the changes were workable in practice, and outlining the processes and activities to make the change happen, including a half-day workshop for those staff charged with increased decision-making responsibilities.
- The internal company 'university' idea continued to be developed, and several online courses now exist on an outsourced Moodle site, which continues to serve the various ThinkTanks, and also as a store of documents, sometimes (but erroneously perhaps), termed 'the company knowledge base'.
- A reorganization of the production areas has meant that smaller batch work could be accommodated alongside the large production activities. This meant that there was a 'jobbing shop' production area to serve smaller quantities and that the retooling overhead could be avoided. Alongside this, there has been a development of a 'small-order logistics' process introduced – basically a set of processes integrated into the ERP to handle small quantities. Three plants in the group have implemented this.
- Initially, there were persistent 'problems' and 'issues' with the ERP. For example, there continued to be discrepancies between the data held on the ERP and the actuals. At first a ThinkTank to look at this in the inventory areas was set up. Processes were tightened, and the ThinkTank continued its work with a slightly different focus – it became focused on data quality problems.

Continued problems and issues are 'part of the territory' in information systems practice. The INSPIRE team now has only a passive role in the changes that are being undertaken. However, it must always be the intention of a given problem-solving process to enable self-sufficiency and independence. There are many 'problems' still in existence. The 'organizational problem-solving' process will never eradicate 'problems', because the process is only a goal, not an outcome.

12 Concluding remarks

Abstract

There has been much discussed and argued since the opening sentences, which asserted that the discipline of information systems is required to change. The book has attempted to outline why change is required; it has outlined problems in practice, in curricula design, and in research. It has argued that the discipline needs to become much more focused on organizational problem solving, in which technology plays a key role in the ongoing innovation in human organizational processes. It has provided a set of inquiring activities that might help to guide IS practice and organizational problem solving. They are of course limited and without doubt can be adapted, enhanced or changed. Nonetheless, their integration into information systems practices might be considered by some to be a significant shift in emphasis in the discipline and in practice. This chapter hypothesizes around some of the implications of such a shift.

Introduction

It could be argued that organizational change tends to be largely determined by unfolding events, pressures of context, and determined by reactions to events and circumstances. It might be that human organizations are entities that evolve, and as such cannot be 'designed' in an absolute sense.

If we hypothetically assume that conscious and purposive action to change things for the 'better' was in the hands of the Gods, or in some other entity, or simply at the mercy of subconscious human actions, then there might be a case for simply 'throwing in the towel' and not worrying too much about poor quality organizations that cannot function to serve human needs. There would be no point in writing or reading this book. There would be no point to the discipline or the practice of information systems.

It would be extremely pessimistic to think that human organization is 'beyond design' or that change can only occur as result of the perceived imperatives and pressures of a given organizational situation at a given moment in time. It would be a very pessimistic conclusion about the fate of humankind, if it was assumed that conscious or designed change in organizations was impossible, or that humans cannot bring it upon themselves to make explicit and conscious thinking and actions that are more than simple reactions to events. Rather, a more optimistic viewpoint might be that conscious change *is* possible although, as in many aspects of human affairs, it is problematic and difficult. It is often challenging and frustrating. It is precisely because it is problematic, that humans grumble and complain, but find themselves unable to act.

Why is it that we (i.e. humankind), moan, worry and become angry about the aspects of human organization that we think are 'inadequate' in some way; but why is it that, in all this grumbling and complaining, at the same time there is often such a poverty, a dearth in methodological guidance to bring about organizational change. Could it be that information systems is at the cusp of the 'design' of organizations? Could it be that IS is a key or even a de facto discipline of organizational problem solving?

Preparing the mind

In this book, it has been considered that improvement of the process of IS practice can be based on improved inquiring activities. The inquiring activities given in Part III, and the way they were interpreted and used (as discussed in this part) are certainly not 'the only way', nor 'the best way'. A practical discipline such as IS must be able to undertake an evaluation of them, and consider certain key areas of inquiry, for example:

- How to make judgements about what needs improving and changing.
- Consider the role that information and technology has in enabling human processes, and new ways of achieving humanly constructed purpose.
- Understand the constraints on human situations and actions in undertaking change.

Perhaps most importantly, the problem might be considered to be a challenge of the way humans can learn to organize themselves and to organize their minds. In preparing the mind, it is necessary to have a well-developed set of conceptual structures and guiding principles that can help. The operational or organizational *process* is an essential construct because it is this that IS practitioners are concerned with, e.g. to *purposely* create, change, optimize, develop, make better, improve etc. In actual fact, any change programme in organizations, any policy change, any strategy, any marketing plan, any implementation of technology will be completely useless unless they make one or more processes work, or make them work 'better'. Yet there lies a big challenge: how could we or how should we develop our understanding about organizational processes? Given the failure rates of IT change programmes in organizations, and the huge importance that organizations play in our society, and to humankind in general, perhaps it is worthy of some time and effort thinking about *organizational processes*, and the effects that the IT is having on them. Perhaps it is time to think more carefully about their structure, their serendipity, ambiguities in purpose, their social and political dimensions, outcomes etc.

But constructs themselves are insufficient to transform or improve organizations. It requires coordinated human action. And this sort of action is underpinned by a relevant discipline that promotes methods, methodologies, techniques, ideas, frameworks, principles, actions, ethics etc. It seems obvious after our discussion in this book that IS as a discipline requires continued effort and precision of thinking in order to improve the management of human processes in practice.

Yet, after the discussions in the book of the failings in the discipline of IS, it remains that the IS discipline is probably well placed to undergo a quiet revolution, in order that it can become one of the most important disciplines to lead and promote the transformational change in organizations. It would be a healthy revolution if information systems matured into a core discipline for organizational change, underpinned by methods that might be considered to be 'systems by which humans can innovate', or 'innovation systems'.

Knowledge generation

It has been argued in this book that IS as a discipline, as it currently stands, is not adequately providing (i) precision of thinking, (ii) constructs that aid the precision of thinking, or even (iii) a 'science' that is sufficiently robust to give guidance in practice. The discipline suffers from huge chasms that divide theory and practice, reflecting the social demarcation lines between academics themselves, and between academics and practitioners. In particular, IS is required to search for ways to break down certain 'brick walls', e.g. (i) between theory and practice, (ii) between 'engineering' of application development and organization development, and (iii) between epistemological stances etc. Yet this begs some important and perhaps some blunt questions. Are universities, as key purveyors and contributors to the discipline, demanding or promoting research that can help in practice? (See also Hambrick 1994; Guport and Sporn 1999; Huff and Huff 2001; Lambert Review 2003.) Are they giving our future IS practitioners the skills that they require for the undertaking of their future responsibilities? There have been lots of papers written on the evaluation of inquiring methods and approaches used by academic researchers, but, relatively, rather little attention given to the evaluation of the inquiring activities that practitioners require, during the course of their practice (see Chapter 11).

Critics might argue that there are huge resources are allocated to universities, and currently they have rather few answers to the continual expressions of frustration that come from practitioner communities, who demand relevance, guidance and precision of thinking. They might argue that there is a crisis in our universities, and until politicians, university and disciplinary leaders have a radical rethink, they and their products (e.g. their methods, ideas, books, papers, students etc.), may increasingly be considered irrelevant to societal needs. If a radical rethink were to be undertaken, there may be certain consideration given to the following:

(i)   Perhaps if researchers were to be given skills in organizational problem solving, they could simultaneously undertake research whilst involved in changing organizations! They could attempt (A), (B), (C) and (D) perhaps? (See Chapter 2.) Universities might be able to organize themselves, to break away from their bureaucratic structures and public sector cultures, to incentivize their academics to engage with practice to generate wealth through innovation.

(ii) Similarly, if IS practitioners were given the skills to undertake inquiry (a traditional skill of the 'researcher') they, too ,could simultaneously undertake (D), and (A), (B) and (C). This would be a radical new emphasis in the curricula provision in the discipline, which promotes inquiring pedagogy, epistemological considerations, and how that inquiry informs action.

(iii) The 'body of knowledge' in the discipline of information systems might be better generated from the everyday activities of *undertaking* IS practice. This is based on an assumption that knowledge is not generated solely from academic institutions: it cannot be generated by *observing* practice. It must be generated from *undertaking* practice, combining suitable inquiring skills, methods, methodologies and constructs, embedded into the undertaking.

The ambivalence in the 'body of knowledge' in information systems may be rooted in the policies, processes and behaviours of researchers and their institutions: are they avoiding tackling these big questions, and settling for the comforts of traditional research paradigms and approaches? After all, is it not easier to undertake research that observes aspects of practice, and conform to (A), (B) and (C) and ignore or espouse (D)?

In cooking, knowledge is not generated from observing the cooks. It is not possible to generate knowledge of cooking by sending the cooks a questionnaire, and then analysing the results! In cooking, knowledge is generated from the cooks themselves, in practice, learning and reflecting on their own practice, devising new recipes, new principles, testing new ideas. How can the IS discipline generate knowledge based on the publishing and promotion of research that merely *observes* practice from a distance? How can good new knowledge be simply a matter of sending out another survey? Surely this observation alone is a good enough reason for a rethink of the dominant assumptions in knowledge generating activities? How can it be that the IS discipline continues to ignore the need to demolish the brick wall that sits between theory and practice?

Inquiry as a teleological process

As has been seen by the discourse presented in this text, the primary objective of IS practice is to justify and evaluate human action, in complex and changing human situations. This involves the use of constructs embedded within a series of inquiring activities. This type of inquiry has similarities as well as differences with the dominant orthodoxies in 'research'. In most academic inquiry (research) the objective is commonly to develop generalizable 'theory'. For example, the process would commonly be to induce 'generalizable theory' from data and observations. However, the inquiring activities involved in IS practice is rather different. Its objective is to justify methodologies, techniques, conceptual ideas or tools, in ensuring that intervention is based on a process of critically analysing human situations and options for change. In doing this, it is concerned to apply and evaluate a range of guiding conceptual structures and schemas and, thus, aiming to provide clarity of thinking (as far as is possible). 'Generalizable theory' is a *potential* outcome, rather than being of primary purpose. As has been discussed, this fundamental difference in purpose has implications for preferred inquiring methods, use and role of data, as well as the role of theory.

Since IS practice requires coping in practical problem-solving situations, there is no single preferred or underpinning 'science' (see, for example, Ackoff 1962, 1978; Churchman 1979; Argyris 1980). Problem solving requires the utilization of methods in the undertaking of 'solving problems', informed by a number of disciplines (e.g. from mathematics, sociology, psychology, engineering etc.). Therefore, IS practice does not prescribe a specific type of approach (e.g. quantitative, qualitative, inductive, deductive, longitudinal, experimental etc.). Rather it is focused on the selection, justification and application of appropriate methods, in the context of the particular problem-solving process. Epistemological considerations are part of that process of 'selection, justification and application'.

This has some important implications for the skills of the IS practitioner. For instance, an IS practitioner needs to have a sufficiently interdisciplinary educational background, to appreciate the appropriateness of specific approaches to the organizational problem solving process. Furthermore, the IS practitioner will not be specialist enough in all areas, and will be required to explore shortfalls in knowledge, experience and methods etc. for specific problem-solving situations. Therefore, complementing specialist skills, the IS practitioner is required to develop and apply conceptual, critical, reflective and communication skills (rather than narrow 'specialist' skills).

These broader human skills will involve methodology. If methodology was ignored in IS practice, the accounts of the organizational problem-solving process and activities would be expected to be anecdotal accounts of 'what happened' in the situation (i.e. there is little critical development of methodology). Therefore, by exploring the methodological issues and concepts, the IS practitioner will be able to develop the critical depth to their account. As such, methodology has a particular importance in IS practice. In IS practice, the justification and explicit reference to both espoused method, and methods in action is an essential aspect of the 'thinking about thinking in action' as discussed in Chapter 3. Exploring this is an essential feature of methodology in practical disciplines such as information systems.

Close

The processes involved in IS practice, are important in shaping organizations and institutions. The everyday decisions and actions that an IS practitioner takes can have important consequences for organizations, and for the society that relies on those organizations. It remains incumbent on those shouldering the responsibility to prepare their mind for the undertaking of it. An IS practitioner will be required to develop methodological thinking skills analogous to that of the master chef and, as discussed in this text, it is a creative, human intellectual activity. It requires dynamic, innovative thinking, applying and critiquing a range of abstractions, and moving them into 'real world' situations. It requires conceptual skills, expression and flamboyance. It requires creativity, critique, communication, innovation, precision, discipline. It also involves rigour, ethics, experience, enthusiasm. It requires wrapping knowledge of technology into a creative, innovative and exciting process of organizational problem solving. It requires a new breed of information systems practitioners who are guided by a (de facto) discipline of 'organizational problem solving'.

Notes

Foreword

1   In Chapter 2 of this book, we will discuss both 'IT' and 'IS' and their relationship in some detail. For the purpose of this foreword, the reader might simply consider the field of 'IT' to be concerned with technology and its development, whereas the field of 'IS' is concerned with the development of organizational systems in which IT is an enabler.
2   There is some debate about whether IS is a discipline at all! In this book, I will use the term 'discipline' to mean 'that which informs practice', i.e. the 'science', 'knowledge', 'methods', 'learning activities' etc. In much the same way as the 'discipline' of, for example, 'medicine' informs the practice of a doctor, the 'discipline of Information Systems' would be expected to inform the IS practitioner.
3   In this text, the term 'organizational problem solving' is used to mean a *method* of developing organizations that includes, as a component, the application of technology. The principles of the method of 'organizational problem solving' are discussed in Parts II and III, and are demonstrated in application in Part IV.
4   I use inverted commas here to indicate that 'improvement' is ambiguous, and achieving 'improvement' is problematic. I use the term 'improvement' to mean a goal that is not attainable (in an absolute sense) because there are often variable interpretations about what 'improvement' is taken to be in a given organizational situation.

1 Emergence

1   How 'improvement' is judged is problematic, and the process of judging 'improvement' is an aspect of the information systems discipline that is often ignored or taken 'as given'.

2 Failings

1   See Ciborra 1997.
2   For conjecture on the changing nature of application development and development methods, see Avison and Fitzgerald (2003).
3   That is to say, beyond the application (and usually the introduction) of data flow diagrams, system flowcharts, or role and activity diagrams to depict aspects of an organizational process. There is very little behavioural focus on organizational processes, teleology, control structures, monitoring methods or the complexities in changing them.

3 Ontology

1   Here, the term 'making sense of' and 'pattern finding' are used as if they are the same thing.

2 This is not to argue that the same assumptions can be made about the nature of inquiry within the two domains, i.e. medicine and information systems.

3 In this book, I use the word 'process' or 'organizational process' to refer to the 'real world' set of human activities that 'come together' in order to achieve purposeful human goals. We will use the word 'systems' to be a set of conceptual constructs and principles, to help to structure inquiry into processes.

4 Vaihinger (1911) presented a philosophy of 'as if', based on the idea that a given linguistic construct, such as a metaphor, or model, structures the mind into a set of 'what if' scenarios. It also structures the 'what if something else'! Kelly's (1955) work on personal construct psychology shows similarities with Vaihinger's 'as if' philosophy.

4 Methodology

1 For want of a better term, we will call these people 'client groups' and assume that they are not homogenous in their goals, ideas, perspectives, anxieties and frustrations etc. Often in current IS practice, the word 'users' is used. Such a term makes the assumption that an IS specialist will be implementing technology (it assumes an outcome of the process of organizational problem solving). It also may allude to a particular role-relationship that is old-fashioned for a new age of IS practice. So, instead, the term 'client groups' is used in this book.

2 This, however, is often not necessarily the purpose of inquiry in practice, even though it is sometimes assumed that it is! For example, an inquiry can be undertaken because it is considered that it gives credibility, in a politically loaded organizational situation.

8 Strategy

1 As discussed, a component of a 'strategic prognosis' is an inquiry into the nature of the inquiry as it purports to serve a number of different purposeful human goals.

10 Evaluation

1 There are some methods that are already in existence that are related to this, e.g. critical success factors (see Bullen and Rockart 1981). These and other constructs do not, in themselves, integrate with teleological process models, but probably have the potential to do so.

11 Case study

1 For confidentiality purposes, the organization name has been changed.
2 For confidentiality purposes, the names have been changed.

Bibliography

Abrahamson, E. and Eisenman, M. (2001) Why Management Scholars Must Intervene Strategically in the Management Knowledge Market, *Human Relations*, 54(1), 67–76.

Ackoff, R. L. (1962) *Scientific Method: Optimising Applied Research Decisions*, Wiley, New York.

Ackoff, R. L. (1978) *The Art of Problem Solving, Accompanied by Ackoff's Fables*, Wiley, New York.

Allport, G. W. (1968) The Historical Background of Modern Social Psychology, in Lindzey, G. and Aronson, E. (eds) *The Handbook of Social Psychology*, Second Edition, Vol. 1, Addison-Wesley, Reading, MA.

Alt, R. and Fleisch, E. (2000) Business Networking Systems: Characteristics and Lessons Learned, *International Journal of Electronic Commerce*, 5(2), 7–27.

Alter, S. (2002) *Information Systems: The Foundation of E-Business*, Fourth Edition, Prentice Hall, Upper Saddle River, NJ.

Altheide, D. L. and Johnson, J. M. (1994) Criteria for Assessing Interpretive Validity in Qualitative Research, in Denzin, N. K. and Lincoln, Y. S. (eds) *Handbook of Qualitative Research*, Sage, London.

Alvesson, M. and Deetz, S. A. (2000) *Doing Critical Management Research*, Sage, London.

Alvesson, M. and Skoldberg, K. (2000) *Reflexive Methodology, New Vistas for Qualitative Research*, Sage, London.

Alvesson, M. and Wilmott, H. (1996) *Making Sense of Management: A Critical Introduction*, Sage, London.

Argyris, C. (1980) *Inner Contradictions of Rigorous Research*, Academic Press, London.

Argyris, C. (1990) *Overcoming Organizational Defenses, Facilitating Organizational Learning*, Allyn & Bacon, Boston, MA.

Ash, J. S., Gorman, P. N., Seshadri, V. and Hersh, W. R. (2004) Computerized Physician Order Entry in U.S. Hospitals: Results of a 2002 Survey, *Journal of the American Medical Information Association*, 11, 95–9.

Ashby, W. R. (1973) Some Peculiarities of Complex Systems, *Cybernetic Medicine*, 9(2): 1–7.

Ashford, M. (1999) *Con-Tricks: The Shadowy World of Management Consulting and How to Make It Work for You*, Simon & Schuster, New York.

Avison, D. E. and Fitzgerald, G. (2003) Where Now for Development Methodologies? *Communications of the ACM*, 46(1), 78–82.

Barker, T. and Frolick, M. N. (2003) ERP Implementation Failure: A Case Study, *Information Systems Management*, 20(4), 43–9.

Baskerville, R. and Myers, M. (2002) Information Systems as a Reference Discipline, *MIS Quarterly*, 26(1), 1–14.

Bateson, G. (1948) Metalogue: Why do Things Get in a Muddle?, in Bateson, G. (ed.) *Steps to An Ecology of Mind*, University of Chicago Press, Chicago, IL.

Bateson, G. (1972) *Steps to An Ecology of Mind*, University of Chicago Press, Chicago, IL.

Beck, U. (1992) *Risk Society: Towards a New Modernity*, Sage Publications, London.

Beck, U. (1994) The Reinvention of Politics: Towards a Theory of Reflexive Modernization, in Beck, U., Giddens, A. and Lash, S. (eds) *Reflexive Modernization*, Polity Press, Cambridge.

Beck, U. (2000a) *What Is Globalization?*, Polity Press, Cambridge.

Beck, U. (2000b) *The Brave New World of Work*, Polity Press, Cambridge.

Beer, S. (1967) *Cybernetics and Management*, Second Edition, English Universities Press, London.

Beer, S. (1979) *The Heart of the Enterprise*, Wiley, Chichester.

Beer, S. (1985) *Diagnosing the System of Organization*, Wiley, Chichester.

Benbasat, I., Dexter, A. S., Drury, D. H. and Goldstein, R. C. (1984) A Critique of the Stage Hypothesis: Theory and Empirical Evidence, *Communications of the ACM*, 27, 476–85.

Benbasat, I. and Zmud, R. W. (1999) Empirical Research in Information Systems: The Practice of Relevance, *MIS Quarterley*, 32(1), 3–16.

Benbasat, I. and Zmud, R. W. (2003) The Identity Crisis Within the IS Discipline: Defining and Communicating the Discipline's Core Properties, *MIS Quarterly*, 27, 183–94.

Bizwizzz (2007), www.bizwizzz.com, accessed 4 April 2007.

Blaikie, N. (1993) *Approaches to Social Enquiry*, Polity Press, Cambridge.

Block, P. (1981) *Flawless Consulting: A Guide to Getting Your Expertise Used*, Pfeiffer, San Francisco, CA.

Blumer, H. (1962) Society in Symbolic Interaction, in Rose, A. (ed.) *Human Behaviour and Social Processes*, Rouledge & Kegan Paul, London.

Bocij, P., Chaffey, P., Greasley, A. and Hickie, S. (1999) *Business Information Systems, Technology, Development and Management*, Pitman Publishing, London.

Bocij, P., Chaffey., D., Greasley, A. and Hickie, S. (2006) *Business Information Systems, Technology, Development and Management for the E-Business*, Third Edition, Prentice Hall, Harlow.

Bolton, M. J. and Stolcis, G. B. (2003) Ties that do not Blind: Musings on the Specious Relevance of Academic Research, *Public Administration Review*, 63(5), 626–30.

Booch, G. (1999) *Object-Oriented Analysis and Design with Applications*, Third Edition, Addison-Wesley, Harlow.

Boulding, K. E. (1956) General Systems Theory: the Skeleton of Science, *Management Science*, 2(3), 197–208.

Braverman, H. (1974) *Labour and Monopoly Capital*, Monthly Review Press, New York.

Brooks, F. P. (1975) *The Mythical Man Month*, Addison-Wesley, Reading, MA.

Brooks, F. P. (1987) No Silver Bullet: Essence and Accidents of Software Engineering, *Computer*, 20(4), 20–19.

Bruner, J. (1990) *Acts of Meaning*, Harvard University Press, Cambridge, MA.

Bryman, A. and Bell, E. (2003) *Business Research Methods*, Oxford University Press, Oxford.

Bullen, C. V. and Rockart, F. (1981) *A Primer on Critical Success Factors*, Center for Information Systems Research, Massachusettes Institute of Technology, 69, June, Online at https://dspace.mit.edu/bitstream/1721.1/2010/1/SWP-1297-08770929-CISR-085.pdf, accessed 12 June 2006.

Burrell, G. and Morgan, G. (1979) *Sociological Paradigms and Organizational Analysis*, Heinemann, London.

Chaffey, D. and Wood, S. (2005) *Business Information Management, Improving Performance using Information Systems*, Prentice Hall, Harlow,.

CHAOS (1995) *The Standish Group Report*, www.projectsmart.co.uk/Docs/Chaos_Report.pdf, accessed 12 June 2006.

Chaudhry, B., Wang, J., Wu. S., Maglione, M., Mojica, W., Roth, E., Morton, S. and Shekelle, P. G. (2006) Systematic Review: Impact of Health Information Technology on Quality, Efficiency and Costs of Medical Care, *Annals of Internal Medicine*, 144(10), www.anals.com, accessed 25 April 2006.

Checkland, P. (1981) *Systems Thinking Systems Practice*, Wiley, Chichester.

Checkland, P. (2002) Thirty Years in the Systems Movement: Disappointments I Have Known, and a Way Forward, *Systemist*, 24(2), 99–111.

Checkland, P. and Scholes, J. (1990) *Soft Systems Methodology in Action*, Wiley, Chichester.

Chen, W. and Hirschheim, R. (2004) A Paradigmatic and Methodological Examination of Information Systems Research from 1991 to 2001, *Information Systems Journal*, 14(3), 197–235.

Chua, W. F. (1986) Radical Developments in Accounting Thought, *The Accounting Review*, LXI(4), 601–32.

Churchman, C. W. (1968) *The Systems Approach*, Dell Publishing, New York.

Churchman, C. West (1971) *The Design of Inquiring Systems, Basic Concepts of Systems and Organization*, Basic Books, New York.

Churchman, C. W. (1979) *The Systems Approach and Its Enemies*, Basic Books, New York.

Churchman, C. W. (1982) *Thought and Wisdom*, Intersystems, Seaside, CA.

Ciborra, C. U. (1997) Crisis and Foundations: An Inquiry Into the Nature and Limits of Models and Methods in the IS Discipline, *5th European Conference on Information Systems*, Cork.

Clemons, E. K. and Lang, K. R. (2003) The Decoupling of Value Creation from Revenue: A Strategic Analysis of the Markets for Pure Information Goods, *Information Technology and Management*, 4(2–3), 259–87.

Coad, P. and Yourdon, E. (1991) *Object Oriented Analysis*, Prentice Hall, Englewood Cliffs, NJ.

Comte, A. (1851) *System of Positive Polity*, Vols 1–4, L. Mathias, Paris.

Conference Board Survey (2001) *ERP Trends*, Research Report No. R-1292-01-RR, http://www.conference-board.org. accessed 12 July 2006.

Curtis, G. and Cobham, D. (2002) *Business Information Systems, Analysis, Design and Practice*, Fourth Edition, Prentice Hall, Harlow.

Cutts, G. (1991) *Structured Systems and Design Methodology*, Second Edition, Blackwell Scientific, London.

Davenport, T. H. and Markus, M. L. (1999) Rigor vs. Relevance Revisited: Response to Benbasat and Zmud, *MIS Quarterly*, 23(1), 19–23.

De Marco, T. (1978) Structured Analysis and Systems Specification, Yourdon Press, New York.

Dehning, B. and Richardson, V. J. (2001) Returns on Investments in Information Technology: A Research Synthesis, *Social Science Research Network*, http://ssrn.com, accessed October 2006.

Denzin, N. and Lincoln, Y. (1994) *Handbook of Qualitative Research*, Sage, Thousand Oaks, CA.

Drummond, H. (2005) What We Never Have, We Never Miss? Decision Error and the Risks of Premature Termination, *Journal of Information Technology*, 20(3), 170–8.

Easterby Smith, M., Thorpe, R. and Lowe, A. (1991) *Management Research: An Introduction*, Sage, London.

Etzkowitz, H. and Leydesdorff, L. (2000) The Dynamics of Innovation: From National Systems and 'Mode 2' to a Triple Helix of University-Industry-Government Relations, *Research Policy*, 29(2), 109–23.

Fitzgerald, B. (2000) System Development Methodologies, the Problem of Tenses, *Information Technology and People*, 13(3), 174–85.

Fitzgerald, B. and Howcroft, D. (1998) Competing Dichotomies in IS Research and Possible Strategies for Resolution, *Proceedings of the 19th International Conference in Information Systems*, Helsinki, December.

Flood, R. L. and Carson, E. R. (1993) *Dealing with Complexity: An Introduction to the Theory and Application of Systems Science*, Second Edition, Plenum Press, New York.

Fujigaki, Y. and Leydesdorff, L. (2000) Quality Control and Validation Boundaries in a Triple Helix of University-Industry-Government: Mode 2 and the Future of University Research, *Social Science Information*, 39(4), 635–55.

Gadamer, H. G. (1988) *Philosophical Hermeneutics*, translated and edited by David E. Linge, California University Press, Berkeley, CA.

Galliers, R. D. and Sutherland, A. R. (1991) Information Systems Management and Strategy Formulation: The 'Stages of Growth' Model Revisited, *Journal of Information Systems*, 1, 89–114.

Gane, C. and Sarson, T. (1978) *Structured Systems Analysis*, Prentice Hall, Englewood Cliffs, NJ.

Garfinkel, H. (1967) The Rational Properties of Rational and Common Sense Activities, in Garfinkel, H (ed.) *Studies in Ethnomethodology*, Prentice Hall, Englewood Cliffs, NJ.

Garg, A. X., Adhikan, N. K. J., Mcdonald, H., Rosas-Adhikan, M. P., Devereaux, P. J., Beyene, J., Sam, J. and Haynes, R. B. (2005) Effects of Computerised Clinical Decision Support

Systems on Practitioner Performance and Patient Outcomes, *Journal of the American Medical Association*, 293(10), 1223–38.

Geisler, E. (1995) When Whales are Cast Ashore: The Conversion to Relevancy of American Universities and Basic Science, *Engineering Management*, 42(1), 3–8.

Gibbons, M. (2000) Mode 2 Society and the Emergence of Context Sensitive Science, *Science and Public Policy*, 27(3) 159–63.

Gibbons, M., Limoges, L., Nowotny, H., Schwartman, S., Scott, P. and Trow, M. (1994) *The New Production of Knowledge: The Dynamics of Science and Research in Contemporary Societies*, Sage, London.

Giddens, A. (1984) *The Consitution of Society*, Polity Press, Cambridge.

Giddens, A. (1990) *The Consequences of Modernity*, Polity Press, Cambridge.

Gill, J. and Johnson, P. (1991) *Research Methods for Managers*, Paul Chapman Publishing, London.

Gill, J. and Johnson, P. (1997) *Research Methods for Managers*, Second Edition, Paul Chapman Publishing, London.

Glaser, B. G. and Strauss, A. L. (1967) *The Discovery of Grounded Theory*, Aldine, Edison, NJ.

Glass, R. (1998) *Software Runaways: Lessons Learned from Massive Software Project Failures*, Prentice Hall, NJ.

Goffman, E. (1959) *The Presentation of the Self in Everyday Life*, Penguin, Harmondsworth.

Gopinath, C. and Hoffman, R. C. (1995) The Relevance of Strategy Research: Practitioner and Academic Viewpoints, *Journal of Management Studies*, 32(5), 575–94.

Gordon, S. R. and Gordon, J. R. (2004) *Information Systems, A Management Approach*, Third Edition, Wiley, Chichester.

Gorman, R. A. (1977) *The Dual Vision: Alfred Schutz and the Myth of Phenomenological Social Science*, Routledge and Kegan Paul, London.

Gowler, D. and Legge, K. (1986) Personnel and Paradigms: Four Perspectives on Utopia, *Industrial Relations Journal*, 17, 225–35.

Guba, G. and Lincoln, Y. S. (1994) Competing Paradigms in Qualitative Research, in Denzin, N. K. and Lincoln, Y. S. (eds) *Handbook of Qualitative Research*, Sage, London.

Guport, P. J. and Sporn, B. (1999) Institutional Adaptation: Demands for Management Reform and University Administration, National Center for Postsecondary Improvement, Stanford University, in Smart, J. (ed.) *Higher Education: Handbook of Teaching and Research*, Agathon Press, New York.

Gupta, U. G. (2000) *Information Systems, Success in the 21st Century*, Prentice Hall, Upper Saddle River, NJ.

Habermas, J. (1972) *Knowledge and Human Interests*, Heinemann, London.

Habermas, J. (1974) *Theory and Practice*, Heinemann, London.

Hambrick, D. A. (1994) 1993 Presidential Address: What if the Academy Actually Mattered?, *Academy of Management Review*, 19, 11–16.

Hammersley, M. (1992) *What's Wrong with Ethnography? Methodological Explorations*, Routledge, London.

Handy, C. (1994) *The Empty Raincoat: Making Sense of the Future*, Hutchinson, London.

Harvey, J., Pettigrew, A. and Ferlie, E. (2002) The Determinants of Research Group Performance: Towards Mode 2?, *Journal of Management Studies*, 39, 747–74.

Hassard, J. (1990) An Alternative to Paradigm Incommensurability in Organization Theory in Hassard, J. and Pym, D. (eds) *The Theory and Philosophy of Organizations*, Routledge, London.

Hassard, J. (1991) Multiple Paradigms and Organizational Analysis: A Case Study, *Organizational Studies*, 12(2), 275–99.

Hassard, J. (1994) Postmodern Organizational Analysis: Toward a Conceptual Framework, *Journal of Management Studies*, 31(3), 303–23.

Hirschheim, R. (1985) Information Systems Epistemology: An Historical Perspective, in Mumford, E., Hirschheim, R, Fitzgerald, G. and Wood-Harper, A. T. (eds) *Research Methods in Information Systems*, Elsevier, Amsterdam.

Hirschheim, R. and Klein, H. (1989) Four Paradigms of Information Systems Development, *Communications of the ACM*, 27(11), 1199–216.

Hirschheim, R. and Klein, H. K. (2003) Crisis in the IS Field? A Critical Reflection of the State of the Discipline, *Journal of the Association for Information Systems*, 4, 237–93.

Hochstrasser, B. (1994) Justifying IT Investments, in Willcocks, L. (ed.) *Information Management: The Evaluation of Information Systems Investments*, Chapman & Hall, London.

Hochstrasser, B. and Griffiths, C. (1991) *Controlling IT Investment*, Chapman & Hall, London.

Hodgkinson, G. P. (2001) (ed.) Facing the Future: The Nature and Purpose of Management Research Re-Assessed, *British Journal of Management*, 12, Special Issue, S1–S80.

Hopper, T. and Powell, A. (1985) Making Sense of Reason in the Organizational and Social Aspects of Management Accounting: A Review of its Underlying Assumptions, *Journal of Management Studies*, 22(5), 429–65.

Huff, A. S. and Huff, J. O. (2001) Re-focusing the Business School Agenda, *British Journal of Management*, 12, Special Issue, December 2001, S49–S54.

Hussey, J. and Hussey, R. (1997) *Business Research: A Practical Guide for Undergraduate and Postgraduate Students*, Macmillan, Basingstoke.

Ives, B., Hamilton, S. and Davis, G. (1980) A Framework for Research in Computer Based Management Information Systems, *Management Science*, 26(9), 910–34.

Jackson, N. and Carter, P. (1991) In Defence of Paradigm Incommensurability, *Organization Studies*, 12(1), 109–27.

Jackson, N. and Carter, P. (1993) 'Paradigm Wars': A Response to Hugh Willmott, *Organization Studies*, 14(5), 721–25.

Jayaratna, N. (1994) *Understanding and Evaluating Methodologies*, McGraw-Hill, Maidenhead.

Jessup, L. and Valacich, J. (2003) *Information Systems Today*, Prentice Hall, Upper Saddle River, NJ.

Johnson, P. and Dubberley, J. (2000) *Understanding Management Research: An Introduction to Epistemology*, Sage, London.

Johnson, P. and Gill, J. (1993) *Management Control and Organizational Behaviour*, Paul Chapman Publishing, London.

Johnson, G. and Scholes, K. (1997) *Exploring Corporate Strategy*, Fourth Edition, Prentice Hall, Upper Saddle River, NJ.

Kaplan, B. and Duchon, D. (1988) Combining Qualitative and Quantitative Methods in Information Systems Research: A Case Study, *Management Information Systems Quarterly*, 12(4), 571–86.

Kawalek, J. P. (1996) Modelling Information Processes and Flows: For Specification or for Learning?, *4th Annual Conference of the CFP-BCS on IS Methodologies*, September, Cork.

Keen, P. G. W. (1980) MIS Research: Reference Disciplines and a Cumulative Tradition, in Mclean, E. and Mcfarlan, W. (eds) *Proceedings of the 1st International Conference on Information Systems*, AIS, Atlanta, GA.

Kelly, G. A. (1955) *The Psychology of Personal Constructs*, Norton, New York.

Koestler, A. (1967) *The Ghost in the Machine*, Hutchinson, London.

Kolakowski, L. (1972) *Positivist Philosophy*, Penguin, Harmondsworth.

Koppel, R., Metlay, J. P., Cohen, A., Abaluck, B., Localio, A. R., Kimmel, S. E. and Strom, B. L. (2005) Role of Computerised Physician Order Entry Systems in Facilitating Medical Errors, *Journal of the Americal Medical Association*, 293(10), 1197–203.

Kroenke, D. M. (2005) *Teaching MIS*, http://www.teachingmis.com/blog/archives/2005/10/the_missed_oppo.html, accessed 4 March 2006.

Kroenke, D. M. (2007) *Using MIS*, Pearson Education, Upper Saddle River, NJ.

Kuhn, T. S. (1962) *The Structure of Scientific Revolutions*, Chicago University Press, Chicago, IL.

Lam, W. and Chua, A. (2005) Knowledgement Management Project Abandonment: An Exploratory Examination of Root Causes, *Communications of the AIS*, 16(35), 723–43.

Lambert Review (2003) *The Lambert Review of Business-University Collaboration*, HMSO, Norwich.

Lash, S. (1994) Reflexivity and its Doubles: Structure, Aesthetics, Community, in Beck, U., Giddens, A. and Lash, S. (eds) *Reflexive Modernization*, Polity Press, Cambridge.

Laudon, K. C. and Laudon, J. P. (2006) *Management Information Systems, Managing the Digital Firm*, Ninth Edition, Pearson, Upper Saddle River, NJ.

Lee, A. S. (1991) Integrating Positivist and Interpretivist Approaches to Organizational Research, *Organization Science*, 2, 342–65.

Lee, A. S. (1999) Rigor and Relevance in MIS Research: Beyond the Approach of Positivism Alone, *MIS Quarterly*, 23, 29–34.

Lemon, W. F., Liebowitz, J., Burn, J. and Hackney, R. A. (2002) Information Systems Project Failures: A Comparison of Two Countries, *Journal of Global Information Management*, 10(2), 59–67.

Lewin, K. (1935) *A Dynamic Theory of Personality*, McGraw-Hill, New York.

Lewin, K. (1947) Frontiers in Group Dynamics I: Concepts, Method and Reality in Social Sciences: Social Equilibiria and Socail Change, *Human Relations*, 1, 5–41.

Lewin, K. (1951) *Field Theory and Social Science*, Harper & Row, New York.

Lewin, K., Lippitt, R. and White, R. K. (1939) Patterns of Aggressive Behaviour in Experimentally Created Social Climates, *Journal of Social Psychology*, 10, 271–99.

Lewis, P. J. (1992) Rich Picture Building in the Soft Systems Methodology, *European Journal of Information Systems*, 1(5), 351–60.

Lewis, P. J. (1994) *Information-Systems Development*, Pitman, London.

Liebenau, J. and Backhouse, J. (1990) *Understanding Information*, Macmillan, Basingstoke.

Lindesmith, R., Alfred, L., Anselm, S. and Denzin, N. (1975) *Social Psychology*, Dryden Press, Hinsdale, IL.

Lippitt, G. and Lippitt, R. (1978) *The Consulting Process in Action*, University Associates, La Jolla, CA.

Littlejohns, P., Wyatt, J. C. and Garvican, L. (2003) Evaluating Computerised Health Information Systems: Hard Lessons Still to be Learnt, *British Medical Journal*, 326, 860–63.

Livari, J., Hirschheim, R. and Klein, H. K. (2004) Towards a Distinctive Body of Knowledge for Information Systems Experts: Coding ISD Process Knowledge in Two IS Journals, *Information Systems Journal*, 14, 313–42.

Luckman, T. (1978) (ed.) *Phenomenology and Sociology*, Penguin, Harmondsworth.

Lyytinen, K. (1999) Emprical Research in Information Systems: on the Relevance of Practice in Thinking of IS Research, *MIS Quarterly*, 23(1), 25–8.

Maclean, D. and Macintosh, R. (2002) One Process, Two Audiences: on the Challenges of Management Research, *European Management Journal*, 20(4), 383–92.

Maclean, D., Macintosh, R. and Grant, S. (2002) Mode 2 Management Research, *British Journal of Management*, 13, 189–207.

March, J. (2000) Citigroup's John Reed and Stanford's James March on Management Research and Practice, *Academy of Management Executive*, 14, 52–64.

Marcus, M.L. (1999) Thinking the Unthinkable: What Happens if the IS Field as we Know it Goes Away?, in Currie, W. and Galliers, R. (eds) *Re-Thinking MIS*, Oxford University Press, Oxford.

Markus, M. L., Axline, S., Petrie, D. and Tanis, S. C. (2000) Learning from Adopters' Experiences with ERP: Problems Encountered and Success Achieved, *Journal of Information Technology*, 15(4), 245–65.

McFarlan, W. (1984) Information Technology Changes the Way You Compete, *Harvard Business Review*, May–June, 98–103.

McLuhan, M. (1964) *Understanding Media*, McGraw-Hill, New York.

Mead, G. H. (1934) *Mind, Self and Society*, Chicago University Press, Chicago, IL.

Mintzberg, H. and Quinn, B. (1996) *The Strategy Process: Concepts, Contexts, Cases*, Prentice Hall, London.

Morris, S. (1998) *The Handbook of Management Fads*, Thorogood, London.

Mumford, E., Hirschheim, R., Fitzgerald, G. and Wood-Harper, A. T. (eds) (1984) Research Methods in Information Systems, *Proceedings of the IFIP WG 8.2 Colloquium*, September 1984, Manchester Business School, Elsevier, Amsterdam.

Natanson, M. (1973) Phenomenology and Social Role, *Journal of the British Society for Phenomenology*, 3, 218–30.

NCC (1972) *Documenting Systems (The Users View)*, National Computing Centre, Manchester.

NCC (1978) *Student Notes on NCC Data Processing Documentation Standards*, NCC Publications, Manchester.

Nolan, R. (1979) Managing the Crises in Data Processing, *Harvard Business Review*, March–April, 115–26.

OASIG (1995) *The Performance of Information Technology and the Role of Human and Organizational Factors*, Report to the Economic and Social Research Council, ESRC, London.

O'Brien, J. (1999) *Management Information Systems, Managing Information Technology in the International Enterprise*, Fourth Edition, Irwin Scarborough, ON,

O'Shea, J. and Madigan, C. (1998) *Dangerous Company: Management Consultants and the Businesses They Save and Ruin*, Penguin, Harmondsworth.

Otley, D. T. and Berry, A. J. (1980) Control, Organization and Accounting, *Organizations and Society*, 5(2), 231–44.

Ouchi, W. G. (1977) The Relationship Between Organizational Structure and Organizational Control, *Administrative Science Quarterly*, 22, 95–112.

Ouchi, W. G. (1979) A Conceptual Framework for the Design of Organizational Control Mechanisms, *Management Science*, 25, 833–48.

Oz, E. (2004) *Management Information Systems*, Fourth Edition, Thomson, Boston, MA.

Pan, G. (2005) Information System Project Abandonment: A Stakeholder Analysis, *International Journal of Information Management*, 25(2), 173–84.

Pascale, R. (1995) The Reinventing of Roller Coaster, *Harvard Business Review*, Apr–May.

Paul, R. J. (2002) (IS)[3]: Is Information Systems An Intellectual Subject?, *European Journal of Information Systems*, 11, 174–7.

Pettit, P. (1969) *On the Idea of Phenomenology*, Scepter Books, Dublin.

Pinault, L. (2000) *Consulting Demons: Inside the Unscrupulous World of Global Corporate Consulting*, HarperBusiness, New York.

Polanyi, M. (1961 [1969]) *Knowing and Being, in Knowing and Being: Essays by Michael Polanyi*, Grene, M. (ed.) Routledge & Kegan Paul, London.

Polanyi, M. (1964 [1969]) *The Logic of Tacit Inference in Knowing and Being: Essays by Michael Polanyi*, Grene, M. (ed.) Routledge & Kegan Paul, London.

Porter, M. (1980) *Competitive Strategy*, Free Press, New York.

Porter, M. (1985) *Competitive Advantage: Creating and Sustaining Superior Performance*, Free Press, New York.

Porter, M. (2001) Strategy and the Internet, *Harvard Business Review*, March, 63–78.

Porter, M. and Millar, V. E. (1985) How Information Gives You Competitive Advantage, *Harvard Business Review*, 63(4), Jul–Aug, 149–60.

Power, R. and Laughlin, R. (1992) Critical Theory and Accounting, in Alvesson, M. and Willmott, H. (eds) *Critical Management Studies*, Sage, London.

Public Accounts Committee Report (1999) *First Report*, House of Commons, http://www.publications.parliament.uk/pa/cm199900/cmselect/cmpubacc/65/6502.htm, accessed 22 September 2006.

Radnitzky, G. (1970) *Contemporary Schools of Metascience*, Second Edition, Vol I. Anglo-Saxon Schools of Metascience, Vol. II. Continental Schools of Metascience, Scandanavian University Books, Copenhagen.

Rainer, R. K. Jr, Turban, E. and Potter, R. E. (2007) *Introduction to Information Systems, Supporting and Transforming Business*, Wiley, Chichester.

Reed, J. (2000) Citigroup's John Reed and Stanford's James March on Management Research and Practice, *Academy of Management Executive*, 14, 56–62.

248   *Bibliography*

Reed, M. (1985) *New Directions in Organizational Analysis*, Tavistock, London.
Robbins-Gioia, LLC (2001) Survey Results for Higher Implementation Success, *Business Wire*, on Lexis Nexis Database, accessed 21 January 2006.
Roche, M. (1973) *Phenomenology, Language and the Social Sciences*, Routledge & Kegan Paul, London.
Rose, A. (1962) *Human Behaviour and Social Processes*, Rouledge & Kegan Paul, London.
Saunders, M., Lewis, P. and Thornhill, A. (1997) *Research Methods for Business Students*, Pitman, London.
Scarborough, H. and Corbett, J. M. (1992) *Technology and Organization, Power, Meaning and Design*, Routledge, London.
Schein, E. H. (1969) *Process Consultation: Its Role in Organization Development*, Addison-Wesley, Reading, MA.
Schein, E. H. (1987) *Process Consultation. Vol. 2*, Addison-Wesley, Reading, MA.
Schein, E.H. (1988) *Process Consultation. Vol. 1*, Addison-Wesley, Reading, MA.
Schein, E. H. (1993a) How Can Organizations Learn Faster? The Challenge of Entering the Green Room, *Sloan Management Review*, 34, 85–92.
Schein, E. H. (1993b) On Dialogue, Culture, and Organizational Learning. *Organizational Dynamics*, Winter, 40–51.
Schön, D. (1983) *The Reflective Practitioner, How Professionals Think in Action*, Basic Books, New York.
Schutz, A. (1962, 1964, 1966) *Collected Papers Vols I, II, III*, Nijhoff, The Hague.
Schutz, A. (1972) *The Phenomenology of the Social World*, Heinemann, London.
Shannon, C. and Weaver, W. (1964) *The Mathematical Theory of Communication*, University of Illinios Press, Urbana, IL.
Shoniregun, C. A. (2004) An Investigation of Information Systems Project Failure and its Implications on Organizations, *International Journal of Services Technology and Management*, 5(1), 25–41.
Sidorova, A. and Sarker, S. (2000) Unearthing Some Causes of BPR Failure: An Actor-Network Theory Perspective, *Proceedings of the AMCIS Conference*, AMCIS, Long Beach, CA
Silverston, L. (1997) *The Data Model Resource Book: A Library of Universal Data Models for All Enterprises*, Wiley, Chichester.
Silverston, L. (2001a) *The Data Model Resource Book, Volume 1, Revised Edition. A Library of Universal Data Models by Industry Types*, Wiley, Chichester.
Silverston, L. (2001b) *The Data Model Resource Book, Volume 2, Revised Edition. A Library of Universal Data Models for All Enterprises*, Wiley, Chichester.
Simon, H. (1969) *The Sciences of the Artificial*, MIT Press, Cambridge, MA.
Singer, E. A. Jr (1959) *Experience and Reflection*, edited by Churchman, C. W., University of Pennsylvania Press, Philadelphia, PA.
Stair, R. M. and Reynolds, G. W. (2003) *Principles of Information Systems*, Sixth Edition, Thomson, Boston, MA.
Starkey, K. and Madan, P. (2001) Bridging the Relevance Gap: Aligning Stakeholders in the Future of Management Research, *British Journal of Management*, 12, S3–S26.
Strauss, A. and Corbin, J. (1990) *Basics of Qualitative Research*, Sage, London.
Tannenbaum, P. (1968) Comment: Models of the Role of Stress, in Albeson, R. P., Aronson, E., Mcguire, W., Newcombe, T., Rosenberg, M. and Tannenbaum, P. (eds) *Theories of Cognitive Consistency*, Rand-McNally, Chicago, IL.
Tapscott, D. (1998) *Blueprint to the Digital Economy: Creating Wealth in the Era of E-Business*, McGraw-Hill Professional.
Tapscott, D. (2006) *Re-Thinking in A Networked World (Or Why Michael Porter Is Wrong About the Internet)*, http://newparadigm.com/default.asp?action=category&ID=87, accessed October 2006.
Taylor, F. (1947) *Scientific Management*, Harper & Row, London.

Tim Scott, J., Rundall, T. G., Voght, T. M. and Hsu., J. (2005) Kaiser Permanente's Experience of Implementing An Electronic Medical Record: A Qualitative Study, *British Medical Journal*, 331, 1313–16.

Tranfield, D. and Starkey, K. (1998) The Nature, Social Organization and Promotion of Management Research: Towards Policy, *British Journal of Management*, 9, 341–53.

Turban, E., Mclean, E. and Wetherbe, J. (2001) *Information Technology for Management, Making Connections for Strategic Advantage*, Second Edition, Wiley, New York.

Vaihinger, H. (1911) *Die Philosophy des als Ob: System der Theoretischen, Praktischen und Religiösen Fiktionen der Menschheit auf Grund eines Idealistischen Positivismus: Mit einem Anhang über Kant und Nietsche*, Reuther und Reichard, Berlin.

Van Aken, J. E. (2001) *Mode 2 Knowledge Production in the Field of Management*, Eindhoven University of Technology, ECIS Working Papers, No. 01.13., http://fp.tm.tue.nl/ecis/working%20papers/eciswp46.pdf, accessed 18 November 2004.

Van Aken, J. E. (2005) Management Research as a Design Science: Articulating the Research Products of Mode 2 Knowledge Production in Management, *British Journal of Management*, 16(1), 19–36.

Vickers, G. (1965) *The Art of Judgement: A Study of Policy Making*, Harper & Row, London.

Vickers, G. (1983) *Human Systems Are Different*, Harper & Row, London.

Wainright M. E., Brown, C. V., Dehayes, D. W., Hoffer, J. A. and Perkins, W. C. (2005) *Managing Information Technology*, Fifth International Edition, Pearson Education International, Upper Saddle River, NJ.

Wasser, H. (1990) Changes in the European University: From Traditional to Entrepreneurial, *Higher Education Quarterly*, 44, 111–22.

Wastell, D. G. (1996) The Fetish of Technique: Methodology as a Social Defence, *Information Systems Journal*, 6, 25–40.

Watson, H. J., Taylor, K. P., Higgins, G., Kadlec, C. and Meeks, M. (1999) Leaders Assess the Current State of the IS Academic Discipline, *Communications of the Association for Information Systems*, Volume 2, Article 2, Terry College of Business, University of Georgia.

Wears, R. L. and Berg, M. (2005) Computer Technology and Clinical Work: Still Waiting for Godot, *The Journal of the American Medical Association*, 293(10), 1261–3.

Weick, K. (2001) *Making Sense of the Organization*, Blackwell, Oxford.

Willcocks, L. (1994) Managing Information Technology Evaluation, in Galliers, R. D. and Baker, B. S. H. (eds) *Strategic Information Management*, Butterworth-Heinemann, Oxford.

Willcocks, L. and Margetts, H. (1994) Risk Assessment and Information Systems, *European Journal of Information Systems*, 3(2), 127–38.

Willmott, H. (1990) Beyond Paradigmatic Closure in Organizational Enquiry, in Hassard, J. and Pym, D. (eds) *The Theory and Philosophy of Organizations*, Routledge, London.

Willmott, H. (1993a) Breaking the Paradigm Mentality, *Organization Studies*, 14(5), 681–719.

Willmott, H. (1993b) Paradigm Gridlock: A Reply, *Organization Studies*, 14(5), 727–30.

Wilson, B. (1990) *Systems Concepts, Theory, Methodologies and Applications*, Wiley, Chichester.

Wilson, B. (2001) *Soft Systems Methodology, Conceptual Model Building and Its Contributions*, Wiley, Chichester.

Wilson, D. C. (1992) *A Strategy of Change*, Routledge.

Winograd, T. and Flores, F. (1986) *Understanding Computers and Cognition*, Ablex Publishing, Norwood, NJ.

Wittington, R. (1993) *What Is Strategy and Does It Matter?* Routledge, London.

Ylijoki, O.-H. (2003) Entangled in Academic Capitalism? A Case Study on Changing Ideals and Practices of University Research, *Higher Education*, 45(3), 307–35.

Yourdon, E. (1989) *Modern Structured Analysis*, Prentice Hall, Englewood Cliffs, NJ.

Zuboff, S. (1988) *In the Age of the Smart Machine*, Basic Books.

Zuboff, S. (1994) Informate the Enterprise: An Agenda for the Twenty First Century, in Cash, J. I. Jr, Eccles, R. G., Nohria, N. and Nolan, R. (eds) *Building the Information Age Organization*, Irwin, Scarborough, ON.

Index

Printed in the United States
by Baker & Taylor Publisher Services